$\mathcal{A}$ USER'S GUIDE $\mathcal{T}_{O}$ $\mathcal{T}_{he}$ NEW EDGE

NEW ENGLAND INSTITUTE
OF TECHNOLOGY
LEARNING RESOURCES CENTER

Rudy Rucker, R.U. Sirius & Queen Mu

A USER'S

*CYBERPUNK, VIRTUAL REALITY, WETWARE,

GUIDE To

DESIGNER APHRODISIACS, ARTIFICIAL LIFE,

The NEW

TECHNO-EROTIC PAGANISM, AND MORE

EDGE*

HarperPerennial
A Division of HarperCollins*Publishers*

MONDO 2000. Copyright © 1992 by MONDO 2000. All rights reserved. Printed in the United States of America. No part of this book may be used or reproduced in any manner whatsoever without written permission except in the case of brief quotations embodied in critical articles and reviews. For information address HarperCollins Publishers, Inc., 10 East 53rd Street, New York, NY 10022.

HarperCollins books may be purchased for educational, business, or sales promotional use. For information please write: Special Markets Department, HarperCollins Publishers, Inc., 10 East 53rd Street, New York, NY 10022.

FIRST EDITION

Designed by Bart Egon Nagel

Library of Congress Cataloging-in-Publication Data

MONDO 2000 : a user's guide to the new edge / edited by Rudy Rucker, R. U. Sirius & Queen Mu.—1st ed.

   p.   cm.

ISBN 0-06-096928-8 (pbk.)

1. New Age movement. I. Rucker, Rudy v. B. (Rudy von Bitter). 1946– .

II. Sirius, R. U., 1952– . III. Mu, Queen.

BP605.N48M65   1992

001.9—dc20   91-58470

92 93 94 95 96 RRD 10 9 8 7 6 5 4 3 2 1

Edited by: *Rudy Rucker, R. U. Sirius and Queen Mu* • **Designed by:** *Bart Nagel*

Additional Design and Layout: *Heide Foley* • **MONDO Shopping Mall Editor:** *Jas. Morgan* • **With:** *Andrew Hultkrans* • **Typography:** *Peter Ivey*

Editorial Assistance: *Andrew Hultkrans, St. Jude Milhon, Adam Beyda and Gareth Branwyn* • **Special Contributors:** *Sally Rosenthal, Gary Wolf*

Contributing Artists: *Angel Studios, Larry Ashton, Marcus Badgley, Betty Bates, Stephen Beck, John Borruso, Jay Blakesberg, Khyal Braun, Tim Brock, M. Cairns, Jim Cherry, Emily Cohen, Julia Colmenares, Didier Cremieux, Colin Dodsworth, Kevin Evans, Nori Ezo, Dr. Fishmonger, Heide Foley, Pierre Fortin, David Fremont, Maria Gibert, Larry Goode, Jill Greenberg, Martha Grenon, Rob Hafernik, Sandra Hamburg, Pamela Hobbs, Sebastian Hyde, Jordin Isip, Glen Kim, James Koehnline, Mark Landman, Michael Llewelyn, Kent Marshall, Greg Nersessian, Erol Otus, Peg Pasternak, Joel Peril, Stephanie Rausser, Mary Rich, Yvette Roman, Jonathon Rosen, Ahmet Sibdialsau, Steve Spear, Kim Stringfellow, Mike Swaine, Robert Waldman, Eric White, Frank Wiedemann, Winternitz, Rose X, Catherine Yuh* • **Special Thanks to:** *John Perry Barlow, Roz Barrow, Custom Process, Gracie & Zarkov, Michael Katz, Craig Nelson, Stephan Ronan, Stafford, Top Copy Graphics, Tulip Publishing*

The MONDO 2000 Staff: *Linda Murmann, Marcy Walpert, Brett Murmann*

Plus: *Barbara Imhoff, Robyn Zeitler and Jacqueline Neuwirth, Laurenn Feldman.*

Contents

On the Edge of the Pacific

Rudy Rucker

When my family and I moved to California, one of the first things I did was to visit the City Lights bookstore on Columbus Avenue in San Francisco's North Beach, right across Jack Kerouac Alley from the funky old beatnik bar/cafe called Vesuvio. Whenever I go into City Lights, I get so excited seeing all the cool books and magazines that I can barely even breathe. One particular magazine that caught my eye on this visit was a huge pink thing with a Ben-Day dot picture that seemed to be a cross between Tim Leary and Art Linkletter. Art Linkletter was the host of a fifties candid-camera TV show called "People Are Funny," and he authored the book *Kids Say The Darndest Things*. Linkletter's daughter had a mental illness which may or may not have been compounded by the use of LSD, and she ended up committing suicide by jumping out a window, so Art Linkletter became a prominent spokesperson against psychedelia. So now here's these California weirdos putting out this big pink magazine—which is called *High Frontiers*—and they have Linkletter's face merged with Leary's, and out of the mouth is coming a shaky speech-balloon saying, "Kids do the darndest drugs!" And if that weren't enough, walking across the top of the picture is a drooling, three-eared Mickey Mouse holding out the logo of the Central Intelligence Agency. The magazine *High Frontiers* became *Reality Hackers*, which became the magazine *MONDO 2000*, and now I'm coediting the *MONDO 2000 User's Guide to the New Edge*. Software packages always come with a book that says "user's guide" on it, even though in the rest of the culture a "user" is usually using drugs. Are people who buy software the same as the people who buy drugs? People are funny!

At first California was hard to get used to. My family and I were coming from a small town in central Virginia, you understand, a place called Lynchburg, the home of that notorious God-pig Jerry Falwell, always on TV, preaching fear and asking for money. The main thing you notice first about California is how much you have to drive. At first I'd see all these little shopping centers along the highways, and I'd be thinking, "Oh, I better come back here sometime and check out those nice stores." It took me awhile to realize that the little shopping centers, the strip malls, were all the same, and that there was no point in going into one except for an instantaneous purchase. In this great American urban mega-suburb, shopping is a parallel, distributed process. Shopping for ordinary things, that is. For special things you need special, nonmall sources like the addresses in the "Mall" section at the back of this *User's Guide*.

California drivers aren't usually rude—if there is a necessity to merge, people will pause and wave each other on—but they are pushy. If you don't take advantage of a hole in traffic, someone else will squirm around you to get at the hole. Once, in Santa Cruz, when I paused flounderingly in an intersection in our big old Chevy station wagon, two separate drivers called me an asshole. I was blocking a hole and I was driving an American station wagon with Virginia plates; therefore I was an asshole. I notice a fair amount of standoffishness and impatience among Californians. It's like Californians know that there is the possibility of getting REALLY GOOD STUFF out here, and when they have to settle for something inadequate—like seeing a whale-wagon in the middle of an intersection—they get very miffed. When I first got here, I was so happy to see restaurants that weren't Red Lobsters and Pizza Huts that I was bewildered by all the "Very Best Restaurants" guides I kept seeing in the paper. "Hell," I'd say, "I don't need the VERY BEST. I'm perfectly happy with something that's REASONABLY ADE-QUATE." But now, of course, after six years here, I don't feel that way anymore. I'm a Californian, and I want the very best all the time! My guiding philosophy in making the selections for this *User's Guide* has been simply that: to get the very best things I could find in all the issues of the magazine *High Frontiers/Reality Hackers/MONDO 2000*.

Some of the first Californians I befriended were fellow science-fiction writers. There's few enough SF writers that we're always glad to see each other. The one thing that my new SF friends were most interested in telling me about was Mark Pauline of SRL (Survival Research Labs) and the cool things he did with machines. They knew, of course, that I like machines a lot—my novel *Software* is about the first intelligent robots, and *Wetware* is about the robots using bioengineering processes to build people like machines. Cyberpunk fiction is really ABOUT the fusion of humans and machines. That's why cyberpunk is a popular literature for this point in time—this is a historical time when computers are TAKING OVER many human functions, and when humans are TAKING IN much more machine-processed information. There is a massive human/computer symbiosis developing faster than we can even think about it realistically. Instead of thinking realistically, we can think science-fictionally, and that's how we end up writing cyberpunk near-future science fiction. Cyberpunk is really about the present.

YVETTE ROMAN

You would think science-fiction conventions would be very hip and forward-looking, but often they are dominated by a fannish, lowest-common-denominator, Star Trekkie, joiner kind of a mentality. At times there's even a nostalgic, BACKWARD-LOOKING streak to science-fiction gatherings, with ancient writers saying reactionary things like, "The future isn't what it used to be." When the idea of cyberpunk SF first developed, it was very unpopular at SF cons. Along with some of my fellow cyberpunk writers, I was practically booed off the stage for talking about cyberpunk at an SF con in Austin a few years back. In California, I finally went to a good and intelligent science-fiction conference. It was called Sercon (which is SF fan jargon for "serious and constructive") and was held at the huge old Claremont resort hotel in Berkeley soon after I moved here. All my new S.F. SF friends were there. The British SF writer Ian Watson was there, too, and I spent a lot of time hanging out with him and with Faustin Bray and Brian Wallace of Sound Photosynthesis. Faustin and Brian were videotaping everything everybody said, which made us feel smart and important. In the morning the grounds of the Claremont were full of beautiful flower beds and big pastel sculptures, with a warm, damp breeze off of the bay. Ian Watson and I had lobster ravioli for lunch. This, I felt, was California as I'd dreamed it would be.

Faustin brought me into contact with the editor and the owner of *MONDO 2000*, R. U. Sirius and Queen Mu. R. U. is a pale-skinned individual with very long hair and a goony, gap-toothed smile. Mu is fey, thin, attractive in a toothy Camelot-Kennedy way, also with long hair. They invited me to come and give a "Reality Hackers" speech/reading in a space called Shared Visions on San Pablo Avenue in Oakland down below Berkeley. Before the reading, they gave me and my wife Sylvia a good meal at the "MONDO house"— the huge, rambling, redwood, California-craftsman deco pile in the Berkeley hills where *MONDO 2000* is produced. I was nervous about the talk, for which I was billed as a cyberpunk—in my past experience, the public's reaction to cyberpunk had been quite negative. I kept my shades and leather jacket on and read a chapter of my novel *Wetware* in which some people have sex, and one of them turns out to be a robot meat-puppet with a steel rat living in his skull. The audience was about seventy strong, and R. U. and Mu had charged them $10 apiece. And they totally got into what I was talking about. I'd expected them to be snobby arty/literary East Coast types, but they weren't like that at all. They were reality hackers, nuts, flakes, entrepreneurs, trippers, con-men, students, artists, mad engineers—Californians with the naive belief that (a) There is a Better Way, and (b) I Can Do It Myself.

To put it in a clear gelatin capsule for you, I'd say that (a) and (b) are the two beliefs that underlie every single entry in the *MONDO 2000 User's Guide*. The way that Big Business or The Pig does things is obviously not the best way; it's intrusive, kludgy, unkind, and not at all what you really want. I mean, look at what they show on TV! Look what the government does with your taxes! How can we make things better? The old political approach is to try to "work within the system," to spend years trying to work your way up to a position of influence so you can finally set things right; only by then, you no longer even want to. But now, thanks to high-tech and the breakdown of society, you're free to turn your back on the way "they" do it, whatever it might be, and do it yourself. You can make your own literature, your own music, your own television, your own life, and—most important of all—your own reality. There is no reason to believe in or even care about the stale, self-serving lies being put out by the media day after dreary day. The world is full of information, and some of it is information YOU NEED TO KNOW, so why waste time on the Spectacle of the politicians and the media?

At my Reality Hackers talk, I finally relaxed enough to take off my mirrorshades and put on my regular glasses, and we all sat in a circle and people did show-and-tell. Someone had a mind machine with earphones playing pulsed sound to match the flickering rhythms in two rings of tiny red light bulbs mounted in goggles that went over your eyes. As soon as I put them on I saw close-ups of the Mandelbrot set, just like the ones I'd been seeing on my new computer. The Mandelbrot set is a mathematical pattern discovered by Benoit Mandelbrot of IBM, the same guy who coined the word "fractals." Fractal shapes have the property that each small part resembles the whole thing. Trees are a kind of fractal, in that the branch of a tree tends to look like a shrunken version of the whole tree, and the sub-branches look like the tree as well, on down through about seven levels. The Mandelbrot set is shaped like big, fat, warty buttocks with a knobby disk stuck on one side, and with a bumpy stinger sticking out of the disk. If you zoom in on the edges of the Mandelbrot set you find little copies of the butt, warts, disk, and stinger, some of the copies wound around into gnarly spirals, all swathed in diaphanous veils and gauzes of the loveliest imaginable colors. The really HEAVY thing is that the whole endlessly various pattern is based on nothing but repeatedly evaluating a single quadratic equation. A potentially infinite information structure can emerge from one simple equation, if the equation is iteratively coupled to a repetitive computation. And THAT could very well be how the world is made, you dig, a simple rule plus lots and lots of computation. The world's "rule" is the Secret of Life and the world's "computer" is matter; pursuing the analogy another step, the "system software" for the world's "computer" is physics.

My new California physics friend is Nick Herbert. Nick is lean, button-nosed, and over fifty, with Ben Franklin spectacles and a fringe of white hair around his bony pate. He holds to the belief that maybe there really IS some laboratory way to build a time-machine or a matter-transmitter or a telepathy-inducer. For all this, Nick is neither a charlatan nor a self-deluded nut, meaning that Nick does not LIE about being already able to build these physical devices (as a venture-capitalist-wooing charlatan would) and doesn't THINK he knows how to build them on the basis of some badly flawed or even nonsensical "symbolic proof." No, Nick isn't a nut; he's more like a gymnast who decides to spend the rest of his life walking on his hands, just to see how it is to have the world permanently upside-down.

I already knew Nick before moving here by his having written me some letters arguing about synchronicity and time-travel. When I got out here, he had me invited for a free weekend at Esalen in Big Sur. I'd read about Esalen for years, of course, and was really tripped to go there. Nick's scam was that it was a workshop having to do with fringe concepts in Mind and Physics. Esalen has workshops on all kinds of things; if you're a presenter it's free, and if you're a participant it might cost a couple of hundred dollars.

While the *MONDO/Reality Hackers* scene felt really happening, the Esalen scene did not. A lot of the other guests from the other workshops seemed very pushy, cold, and uptight. They were like unkind Swiss and German tourists into their own personal health, man, I mean like readers of *Self* magazine. Going to Esalen felt like going to visit Thomas Jefferson's house Monticello in Virginia. There used to be something there. The scenery is beautiful. But now it's run for tourists by park rangers. At least that's how it struck me that one time, but in all fairness to Esalen remember that I was then still undergoing the economic and cultural "bends" at moving from hideous Lynchburg to lovely CA.

The wealth of Californians annoyed me a lot at first, and the indifference—the hard, glossy surfaces of people's character armor. I soon realized that if I was going to make any money at all, I was going to have to retool and become high-tech. I began practicing looking at things—like the rocks and surf off Big Sur, for instance—and trying to believe that THIS TOO was a computer calculation. This was the big mental transformation I was needing to make—to think of everything as a computer—and talking about things like enlightenment or the theory of relativity struck me as a waste of time, dead-horse topics left over from the past.

One of the great scientific centers for the study of the mathematical theory of chaos is the University of California at Santa Cruz. Soon after moving here, I had my first opportunity to give a talk to Ralph Abraham's chaos seminar at UC Santa Cruz. Ralph is a ruminative man with a dark beard. He speaks softly but is somehow rather intimidating. You never feel like interrupting him. He showed me a file drawer full of computer circuit boards and said that he wanted to use computer processes to generate musical output. After my talk we went to a great Chinese restaurant in Santa Cruz on Route 1, just north of Bay Road, which leads up to the UC campus. The place is called the Oh Mei. The day's special was called "Ants on a Tree," though that's not really what it was; I think

it was zucchini with transparent rice-flour noodles. The talk had been publicly announced, so in addition to Ralph, me, and his students, a couple of random strangers showed up. The next time I saw Ralph he was mostly interested in talking about cosmic historical trends, primordial Chaos, the Mother Goddess, way-out things like that. California culture is like an organico-chemical bath with thousands of distinct kinds of macromolecules with open bonding sites. No matter what kind of triple-cis-alpha-desoxy thought probe you might be waving around, you know you'll find minds with receptor sites you can bond to.

Speaking of chemicals, after one of my talks somewhere else, a random stranger who nobody knew walked outside with me and pulled out a paper packet of white powder. "This is a new drug, Rudy. It's like ecstasy. Some people I know made it. They'd be very interested to hear how it affects you." "Wow, thanks." I saved the powder and was finally unwise and idle enough to eat it one night a month or two later. It made me grind my teeth a lot, and then I got into a phone-calling jag, getting in touch with various weird old-time computer-programming and hacker types whom I hadn't had the nerve to talk to before. Merged on the phone with them, I had the feeling of being jacked into some huge synchronistic Net. But then the full force of the drug hit me, and I sat in the living room feeling crazed and frightened. The next day I was so depressed that I wanted to die—this chemically induced clinical depression being the usual aftereffect of psychedelics on me, and the reason why I very rarely take them. I enjoy READING about people taking psychedelics, and I like to THINK ABOUT the effects they have, but I don't really like to TAKE them, nor would I wholeheartedly recommend them to others. To me the political point of being pro-psychedelic is that this means being AGAINST consensus reality, which I very strongly am. Psychedelics are a kind of objective correlative for being weird and different.

But drugs are "out" these days, or at least that's what the media would like us to believe. Can computers supplant psychedelics? As one of my fellow teachers at San Jose said to me, "Computers are to the nineties what LSD was to the sixties." With cool graphics and virtual reality, we can pursue the dream of the pure, nonphysical, software high. When I first got my computer I still knew very little about programming. The only software that I had was a free Mandelbrot set program someone had given me, and my idea of "hacking" was to reach around to the back of the monitor and randomly change the little switches I found there. One of them toggled the monitor between digital and analog mode, and when I set it the "wrong" way, it would make the Mandelbrot image look like a bunch of gray and white lines on the top of the screen with new little white pixels moving around. I liked to imagine that it was a picture of penguins on the Antarctic ice, but this wasn't exactly a great feat of hacking I could impress my family and friends with. "Look, when

I turn this little switch the picture gets different!"

No, to do neat things with my machine I needed to understand how its insides worked so I could make up my own switches. Just as you can't write a story without having something to write about, you can't program without having something to program about. But I knew right away what I wanted to program: cellular automata (CAs for short), which are parallel computations that turn your screen into self-generating computer graphics movies. In a two-dimensional CA, every pixel on your computer screen is "alive," in that each pixel looks at the colors of its neighboring pixels and adjusts its own color accordingly. This is analogous to the way in which each spot on the surface of a swimming pool is "alive" and sensitive to the neighboring spots. When you throw a piece of redwood bark into a swimming pool, the ripples spread out in perfect uniformity and mathematico-physical precision. How do they know where to go? Because each spot on the water's surface is updating itself in parallel a zillion times a second. The world is a huge parallel computation that has been running for billions of years. The folks putting on this all-encompassing show we live in—they've really got the budget!

Even within the small budget of a PC's memory and clock-rate, CAs are a rich environment for letting the computer do weird things. By blending together a succession of CA rules you can, for instance, do something like this: start with a blank rectangle, fill it in with concentric ellipses, break some of the ellipses into globs, arrange the globs into a moving face, grow a detailed skin texture, turn the skin's pores into small beetles that crawl around and chew the picture up, send connecting lines between nearby beetles, bend the lines into paisley-shaped loops, and fill the loops with growing fetuses.

I really got into the heart of California computer culture when I started going to the annual Hackers Conference held here. The first time, I was invited on the strength of my science fiction, but by then I was already trying to be a hacker, so I brought my machine to the conference to show off what I'd achieved with my cellular automata. It was the most fun I'd ever had. Everyone there seemed happy. They were happy because they could actually DO something. We stayed up all night partying, bullshitting, and hunching over one another's machines. It all began to seem so SIGNIFICANT.

The human brain gets along by grouping things into patterns and assigning meanings to them. If you have a nice, fast, chaotically changing computer graphics program, you have lots of things to try to make patterns out of. And, unlike with watching clouds or fire, with a computer you also have the meta-level to play with—meaning that you can stop the process, go in and look at the rules generating it, tweak the rules if you like, then start it up again. And then there's the meta-meta-level, the discourse about what this image in connection with this program MEANS—like do fire and clouds really work this way? Are the thought patterns in our brains like computer-generated fire and clouds?

While my new friends and I were gloating over one another's graphics, other hackers were doing entirely different kinds of crazy stuff. Someone had linked his computer to the public telephone and was talking to Russia using the blank spaces between successive TV screen images going across the satellites. That little bar between frames that you see if your TV loses its vertical hold—that was this guy's Panama Canal to everywhere. And the things in the real world these guys had done! "I wrote the software for the first Versateller machines," someone might say, or, "I wrote this arcade game your kids play," or "My program is used in the carburetor of your car." What really impressed me was that people could play around on machines in their homes and end up affecting the events in the big Industrial World. Before hackers it seemed like you needed a factory and an accountant and a bunch of workers before you could actually make something. But in the information economy, you can package it up and ship it out right from your home.

Not that all the hackers were only into information. Hacking is an elastic concept; some guy showed up at the conference without paying, and proudly told me that he'd "hacked the Hackers Conference"—hacking in the sense of finding your way through some hindering thicket. Another told me he was going to hack Death by having his head frozen. (He had a zit on his nose, and I had to wonder about freezing the zit, too.) Another guy took me out to the parking lot and showed me an electronic lock that he'd designed for his Corvette. There's a three-position toggle switch by the door, and to unlock the car, you jiggle the switch sixteen times up or down from center. The whole glove compartment was full of chips to make the system work. Someone else had robot cars that seek light—little radio-controlled-type trucks with no radio-control, having instead a chip that the guy himself had made. The cars liked the edges of shadows; they liked to find a place where they could keep wavering in and out of the light. Another guy had programmed his own flashing electronic jewelry. Someone else had a bottle of liquid nitrogen to show off a superconductor he had. When we got tired of seeing the superconductor levitating magnets, he poured a lot of liquid nitrogen into the swimming pool. The liquid nitrogen froze itself little boats of water-ice that it sat on, boiling. A lot of play, but beyond that, there was a real sense of being engaged in THE GREAT WORK—much the same sense as workers on the Notre Dame cathedral might have felt.

Once, fellow freestyle SF writer Marc Laidlaw took me and the family to a Survival Research Labs show held under a freeway in San Francisco. It was terrific, a mad swirl of politics and collaged machinery, with a giant flame-thrower that seemed continually about to explode, a pile of burning pianos, a giant metal arm poking at the pianos, and so on. After the show, my son and I found a heap of what seemed to be unexploded dynamite—a clayey substance packed into an officially printed wrapper saying "FRONT LINE DEMOLITION PURPOSES ONLY," and with a long fuse. My son and I love fireworks. We tried lighting one, but it didn't go off. We were spending the night at the Laidlaws' apartment in Haight-Ashbury. Sylvia kept saying that it was too dangerous for us to keep the dynamite, that it was unstable and might go off. After some thought I agreed. So how were we to throw it away? Laidlaw didn't exactly want it in his kitchen trash can, so he and I went outside to ditch the dynamite. The sidewalks of Haight-Ashbury are crawling with homeless stoners every hour of the night and day, and we didn't want them to get hold of the dynamite, so we couldn't just leave it on the curb. The public trash cans were out of the question, as some Haighties practically LIVE in the trash cans—you throw something in a trash can and there's a guy inside the can to catch it. Finally we found a church with a metal grating over the entrance. We pushed the dynamite through there, out of reach. A few days later I saw an article in the *San Francisco Chronicle* about a rash of "fake dynamite" being found all over the city. It had all been a mindgame that was part of the Survival Research Labs show. The show had kept going on for several days, as it were, and the Establishment's Spectacle had been (ever so slightly) taken over and co-opted by Mark Pauline.

The reality is that there is no unifying Great Work, there are just a lot of people here in the pit together, slamming and hacking. Our Great Work is to stay in the pit, to control our own destinies, and to hack what we can of the world. There are no nations in the pit, no us against them, and the Japanese are not our enemies. Recently Sylvia and I went to Japan, where I was to appear on a cyberspace panel along with hacker Jaron Lanier and some others. Queen Mu of *MONDO* was there as well, as chance would have it. The building where our panel was had some really great graphics supercomputers. One of them had a simulation of a flag which was made of a grid of points connected by imaginary springs, with two of the points attached to a flagpole. You could crank up the wind, or change the wind's direction, and see the flag start to ripple and flap. I kept thinking of the Zen story about three monks looking at a flag flapping in the wind. A: "What is moving?" B: "The flag is moving." C: "No, the wind is moving." A: "Ah no, the mind is moving." You could rotate the flag, too, and as a last touch you could cut one or both of the flag's tethers to the pole and see it blow away, a crumpling wind-carried shape.

After our talks we were invited to the Gold Disco, where a Mr. Takemura was putting on his monthly show. His show is a series of collaged videos he makes, plus lighting effects, smoke clouds and scent clouds, and fast acid-house music. The video show is a mélange consisting of a) the chaotic pattern you get by pointing a TV camera at a monitor in a feedback loop, the key thing being, as Santa Cruz chaos mathematicians discovered, to have the camera upside-down,

b) gay porno films of men kissing and dicks with studs and rings, c) dolphins and politicians in black and white d) screens from the new Sim Earth computer game, and e) SIGGRAPH style computer graphics. Standing with Mr. Takemura and Jaron by the club control panel, the Japanese kids dancing like crazy, vogueing, some of them in bathing suits, a geisha off there somewhere, the video projected on seventeen different screens, Sim Earth going by, Mr. DataGlove right next to me—I get this really heavy flash that the New Edge really IS happening, it matters to these people here, it is going to happen, and we're all hanging out at the surfin' edge. Right then Mr. T. takes my arm and leads me off to a corner of the room, past the guy in the bathing suit, past the beautiful Japanese girl in the high shorts, and there on a PC monitor is...my own program, CA Lab! The "Rug" rule, boiling away, bopping right to the beat as the casual viewer might think, my program running live here in the hippest club in Tokyo. Hallelujah; my information had made it this far on its own. I'd GOTTEN OVER, as they say.

And that thought sets off the flash that none of us hackers or writers or rappers or samplers or mappers or singers or users of the tech are in it solely for the Great Work—no, us users be here for our own good. We work for the Great Work because the work is fun. The hours are easy and the pay is good. And the product we make is viable. It travels and it gets over. And if you help make a piece of it, then that piece is part of you. You're part of the thang.

Now what exactly IS this Great Work which is taking place on the New Edge? We are not given to truly know WHAT IT IS. The Great Work is like a Mandelbrot set of which we are the pixels, or even the steps of the computation. The Great Work is like a living body in which you and I are like a cell, or even like a specific chemical process, like an enzyme which copies ten thousand rungs of DNA. The Great Work is so big that nobody alive can even put a name on it. In a few hundred years they can look back and say what it was, but here inside it, nobody can see. It has something to do with people getting more and more mixed up with machines, it has to do with do-it-yourself, it has to do with sampling and collaging, it has to do with the end of the old style of politics. A wave of revolution is sweeping all of Planet Earth. Incredible: The Soviet Union is no more. How many more years can it be until the revolution comes back here to the United States, back to where it started? To reduce it to a bumper sticker: "IF THE RUSSIANS CAN GET RID OF THE COMMUNISTS, THE AMERICANS CAN GET RID OF THE REPUBLICANS!" Pass it on. Surely the ever-escalating rape of the environment, the crazy wastage of the "drug war," the warmongering, the elitist selfishness, surely this will someday come to an end—blown away, perhaps, by the onslaught of total New Edge information? Maybe soon.

Let's follow the Great Work and see.

—Rudy Rucker, Silicon Valley, January 29, 1992

A User's Guide to Using This Guide

R.U. Sirius

UTANT YOUTH screams the cover of *Image*, San Francisco's Sunday news magazine. Hip youth stoked on technology! There's a cultural revolution sweeping the urban centers of the Western world. But unlike past cultural revolutions, it doesn't generate slogans. It doesn't even have a name.

See, this is the situation. We're living in *extremely* fast and *extremely* dense times. One day you're lucky to have a FEDEX account, the next day everybody who calls you asks, "What's your FAX number?"

"Huh?"

As you go to the phone to get a FAX line installed, the Berlin Wall comes down and your globe-trotting friends are calling you from the Wall rave: They're dancing on the detritus. With a really good portable MIDI sound system. And you're thinking you'd like to get a drink to celebrate, but now your non-globe-trotting friends won't drink alcohol, even for world peace—*dumb drug*—and anyway they gotta talk to that doctor down in Stanford who's working on the bio-chip, the first digital implant that talks to nerve cells.

So the Evil Empire fragments, and the Western economic system teeters, and as the losers of World War #2.0 win control of the new economic order, and media-hip, surgically-enhanced neo-nazis run for president; as IBM announces a chip the size of a few atoms that can flip and flop with the best of them, and the Human Genome Project maps the genetic structure of the species...you pause for a moment and wonder at your identity.

"HUH?!?"

Technology escalates on your very block: Knives turn to pistols, pistols become Uzis. Cocaine turns to crack, crack to nuke. Charles Atlas turns to Arnold Schwarzenegger, 48DD turns to *64GG*, Mick Jagger sings "Sympathy for the Devil" on the easy-listening station, and after an evening of techno hard-core sounds, the first Sex Pistols album sounds mellow and quaint.

I could go on forever. And, as we shall see later, I will. But my purpose here is to introduce you to this book you're holding in your hand. *It's a book! How comforting! But what in hell is the* New Edge?

When you come to an edge, that generally means if you go any farther you'll fall off. People thought Christopher Columbus would sail off the edge of the world, and he did: He entered a new territory, off the map. The New Edge is unmapped, and we've only begun the exploration.

We *can* say some things about the territory. It involves the collection of human experience—mediated by the mind—on tiny slabs of silicon. It involves humans living not only in their bodies, but in images and data permutated and projected across planetary distances with extraplanetary—satellite-assisted—technologies. It involves the Frankenstein Myth, and Prometheus and Faustus: (hu)man at play with the creation of life, at war with the limitations of biology and time. And it involves *so much more.*

Back when I was going for a master's in fiction, my faculty advisor, Stan Rubin, said I was trying to pack the entirety of human experience into a paragraph. Sounds reasonable to me. That kind of speed and complexity is all the New Edge folks want. That speed and complexity is what our technology is starting to deliver at last...and that speed and complexity could never be captured in a mere book.

So, what we've provided here is a multilayered look at the *data.* We went through past issues of *MONDO 2000* and picked out some gems—mind-jiggering quotes from the various explorers and pranksters therein. On top of these we've layered explanations and explications—historical data, funny tie-ins, personal commentary...even a little gossip—to bring it all back home.

We listed the themes that emerged, from *A* to *Z*—Aphrodisiacs to Zines. Then we asked ourselves if we'd covered all the categories that obsess the denizens of the New Edge—that is to say, our hip friends. Where we found something missing, we wrote a few paragraphs that would *nail* the concept.

And, at the back of the book, we added the "MONDO Shopping Mall." This is an access guide to *products*—yes, things you can *buy.* Educational toys, you could call them—to advance your understanding or just seduce you into joining this cultural New Thing. *Shopping Mall?!!!!* We could have called it something less crass: maybe "Tools for Access," like our respectable older cousins in the *Whole Earth Catalog.* But why be pretentious about it? We are present at the apotheosis of commercial culture. Commerce is the ocean that information swims in. And as we shall see in the *Guide,* the means of exchange in commercial culture is now *pure information.*

HOW TO READ THE GUIDE

So here's how you read the book. On the left side of the page, you'll find quotes from existing issues of *MONDO 2000* dealing with New Edge obsessions. On the right side of *some* of the pages, you'll find *more stuff*—background data on the writer, canny definitions, related ideas, and whatever else might illuminate the text. The supporting materials are color-coded. Whenever you hit a "colored" word or phrase, I strongly suggest that you finish the sentence and look at the supplementary data.

The first time people are quoted they are introduced with biographical and historical—and perhaps mythological—supporting material. When they reappear in the book, their name simply precedes the quote. The symbol ▲ indicates that this is a product listed in the MONDO Shopping Mall. Products indicated are listed in the Mall alphabetically under the same subject head as in the *Guide*. The Mall also tells you how to access lots of other stuff, so you'll want to check it out before going on a major consumer spree.

That's all there is to it. It's *very* simple. Once you start reading it, you'll see. Less to fear than your electronic appliances, heh heh.

Welcome to MONDO 101. And remember. This may seem really *out there* to you now, but by the time you finish reading this book it'll seem quaint to all of us.

—R. U. Sirius

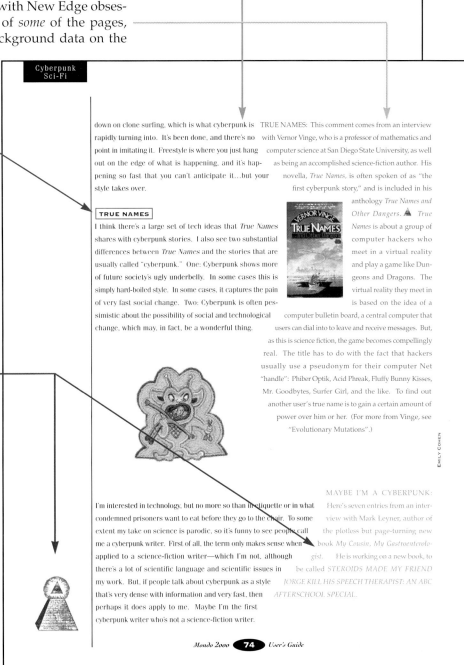

Cyberpunk Sci-Fi

down on clone surfing, which is what cyberpunk is rapidly turning into. It's been done, and there's no point in imitating it. Freestyle is where you just hang out on the edge of what is happening, and it's happening so fast that you can't anticipate it...but your style takes over.

TRUE NAMES

I think there's a large set of tech ideas that *True Names* shares with cyberpunk stories. I also see two substantial differences between *True Names* and the stories that are usually called "cyberpunk." One: Cyberpunk shows more of future society's ugly underbelly. In some cases this is simply hard-boiled style. In some cases, it captures the pain of very fast social change. Two: Cyberpunk is often pessimistic about the possibility of social and technological change, which may, in fact, be a wonderful thing.

I'm interested in technology, but no more so than in etiquette or in what condemned prisoners want to eat before they go to the chair. To some extent my take on science is parodic, so it's funny to see people call me a cyberpunk writer. First of all, the term only makes sense when applied to a science-fiction writer—which I'm not, although there's a lot of scientific language and scientific issues in my work. But, if people talk about cyberpunk as a style that's very dense with information and very fast, then perhaps it does apply to me. Maybe I'm the first cyberpunk writer who's not a science-fiction writer.

TRUE NAMES: This comment comes from an interview with Vernor Vinge, who is a professor of mathematics and computer science at San Diego State University, as well as being an accomplished science-fiction author. His novella, *True Names*, is often spoken of as "the first cyberpunk story," and is included in his anthology *True Names and Other Dangers*. ▲ *True Names* is about a group of computer hackers who meet in a virtual reality and play a game like Dungeons and Dragons. The virtual reality they meet in is based on the idea of a computer bulletin board, a central computer that users can dial into to leave and receive messages. But, as this is science fiction, the game becomes compellingly real. The title has to do with the fact that hackers usually use a pseudonym for their computer Net "handle": Phiber Optik, Acid Phreak, Fluffy Bunny Kisses, Mr. Goodbytes, Surfer Girl, and the like. To find out another user's true name is to gain a certain amount of power over him or her. (For more from Vinge, see "Evolutionary Mutations".)

EMILY COHEN

MAYBE I'M A CYBERPUNK: Here's seven entries from an interview with Mark Leyner, author of the plotless but page-turning new book *My Cousin, My Gastroenterologist*. He is working on a new book, to be called *STEROIDS MADE MY FRIEND JORGE KILL HIS SPEECH THERAPIST: AN ABC AFTERSCHOOL SPECIAL.*

Mondo 2000 **74** *User's Guide*

aphrodisiacs

St. Jude: Historically, aphrodisia has been a subset of poisoning: You slip a substance into someone's drink, they go toxic—delirious, manic, or itchy—and you take advantage of their altered state. Misjudging the dose—as in *Dream of the Red Chamber*, an eighteenth century Chinese classic—can alter the state unto death. Or you slip it into your own drink in hopes of impressing your partner with your anything-that-moves frenzy.

Interest in aphrodisia for chemically assisted rape may have damped down, but the desire to experience *more desire* burns on. Effective and nonlethal chemical assistance is still elusive. Hot eyes are looking into brain chemistry—the brain is the primary sexual organ—particularly at drugs that amplify effects of the neurotransmitter dopamine. Of course: Let's find those buttons and learn how to push them…

ST. JUDE is the patron saint of the hopeless, the hapless, and children's aspirin. Testimonials to the quality of her work can be found in the Notices column of major newspapers everywhere. In real life she is Jude Milhon, deteriorated hebephrenic and senior editor of *MONDO 2000.* Ex-nerd, ex-medic, ex-Maoist, she is blonde and polymathically perverse.

L-DOPA

L-dopa is an amino acid that the brain readily converts to dopamine. Dopamine is a neurotransmitter that is involved in emotion, aggression, and sexual turn-ons. For most people, there's a simple equation: more dopamine equals more libido.

In one L-dopa study, an eighty-year-old man began having nocturnal emissions and erotic dreams, an eighty-three-year-old woman began making suggestive remarks to hospital staff members, and most of the men in the study (mean age: fifty-nine) increased their sexual activity. Whew!

I take 325 mg of L-dopa every day, but then I'm my own research animal. I take it because I want to be more aggressive and horny, and it makes animals live longer than their litter mates…so what's not to

L-DOPA: These next three entries were researched by L. Mellow-Whipkit, a man who garnered this info by logging onto Knowledge Index (an inexpensive and easy-to-use on-line information service offered on certain computer networks) and querying a medical data base for scientific research papers containing the descriptors "Sex Behavior" and "Drug Effects."

KHYAL BRAUN

like? Durk Pearson and Sandy Shaw told me to take antioxidants, including Vitamin E, with L-dopa or else it will auto-oxidize into something nasty.

DEPRENYL

Deprenyl increases brain dopamine levels by the indirect process of inhibiting the enzyme which removes old dopamine from the synapses. Deprenyl (also sold under the name Eldepryl) was originally developed for the treatment of Parkinson's disease, with the aphrodisiac effects being noted as a side effect. One particular caveat: Combining Deprenyl with an average dose of amphetamine or MDMA (ecstasy) can kill you.

BROMOCRIPTINE

Bromocriptine (sold as Parlodel) stimulates dopamine release. Judging by the references I found, bromocriptine makes rats and people hornier. Caveat: In *Life Extension: A Practical, Scientific Approach*, Pearson and Shaw warn postmenopausal women that bromocriptine may reset their biological clocks, making pregnancy a possibility.

L-DOPA AND BROMOCRIPTINE

An L-dopa/Parlodel combination works on females as well as males. It stimulates the dopamine track in the brain. In a bunch of old-folks' homes in Europe, where they were working on a combination L-dopa/Parlodel for Parkinson's patients in their seventies and eighties, they found out it had a 100 percent aphrodisiac side effect. The old ladies and little old men started fucking like fiends.

TRY ALL THREE

L. Mellow-Whipkit: A few friends and I have experimented with combining small doses of all the above dopaminergics, with interesting effects. Two friends, both women, started finding all the guys they saw "really cute," although neither of them have acted

DURK PEARSON and SANDY SHAW run a company called Designer Foods, a mail-order source of all manner of neurotransmitter-enhancing substances. They are also the authors of *Life Extension: A Practical, Scientific Approach*, and can often be seen at new age events dressed in their Star Trek-like black leather costumes and smiling broadly.

L-DOPA AND BROMOCRIPTINE: This entry is from Durk Pearson.

TRY ALL THREE: Note that L-dopa, Deprenyl, and bromocriptine are only available by prescription in this country. But, due to a new FDA ruling which allows the importation of a three-month personal supply of drugs regarded as safe in other countries, one can get these drugs without prescription by mail order from InHome Health Services and Interlab in, respectively, Switzerland and England. (See page 290 for new information.)

upon any subsequent urges to date. I noticed an increased interest in and a concomitant enrichment of actual sex. Way cool!

Be forewarned that jacking up the levels of dopamine in your brain can initially cause nausea. If you start with small doses and gradually increase the dose, you will probably avoid this problem.

MDA

MDA can make you feel erotic. The neurophysical side effects are similar to the neurophysical side effects of sexual arousal. For instance, it causes, particularly in women, water retention, particularly in the breasts and buttocks. At the same time, it makes everything, especially other people, appear much more beautiful. So if you're in a sexual setting, like a sex party, the results can be amazing. The first time I witnessed the mass consumption of MDA at a sex party, a usually shy woman stood up and said, "There are six horny, hopped-up women in the hot tub, and we hope there are some men who want to fuck us!" to lead the party off. That sort of behavior in the right setting is not atypical with MDA.

NAUSEA: If people experiment, they should be extremely careful to adjust their dosages to avoid too much dopamine release. For information on symptoms of too much dopamine, check the Eldepryl entry in *Physicians' Desk Reference* (Elvis Presley was never without his copy!).

MDA: This contribution is from Zarkov, part of the *MONDO 2000* writing team Gracie & Zarkov. Investment bankers by day, they are notorious in the psychedelic underground for their interest in sex magick, hardcore political libertarianism, and general expertise on most any subject you might ask them about. Their self-published book, *Notes From Underground,* chronicles their hallucinatory experiences drug-by-drug.

MDA is a psychedelic drug, grandparent to the popular MDMA, otherwise known as ecstasy. It's molecularly related to mescaline, dopamine and amphetamine. MDA went through a brief period of popularity in the late sixties as "the love drug." It's more visionary than ecstasy.

DATURA

Something of the aphrodisiac character of datura is suggested by Chimon Mana, the jimsonweed maiden of the Hopi. She is conceived of as preying on males, eventually driving them insane.

DATURA: This is from our very own domineditrix/publisher, Queen Mu. Aside from her fame with *MONDO 2000*, Mu is a widely respected, if somewhat gonzo, ethno-pharmacologist. She is the one who uncovered the hallucinogenic properties of toad venom, for instance.

Datura contains such witchy deliriants as atropine, hyoscyamine, and scopolamine. Mu's article cites Hindu mythology, German folklore, Navaho lore, and ethnographic literature from Peru, Egypt, China, and India to make a case for Datura's aphrodisiac qualities. Leaving nothing to chance, Mu also reports a favorable response to self-experimentation. "Initial experimentation by the author indicated that a mixture of two to four dried leaves of datura with female cannabis bud is reasonably psychoactive and a stimulating and effective aphrodisiac." Datura is smoked for these effects. Eating it is most definitely *poisonous*.

SEX PACKETS

Dr. Cook, when I met him, he was trying to put Sex Packets into large distribution. He was trying to get with some underground laboratory and do somethin' with it, so I came through and told him it would be a dope concept for an album—you can get the idea out that way, and then we can further pursue the distribution later. This is what he was saving his money to do when I met him. This is how deep this moth-afucka is, you know what I'm sayin'?

One of the concepts to the Sex Packets was, "Wouldn't this be a great safe-sex device?" An anti-AIDS type thang. If this was really happening, this would be the drug of the nineties, because if you meet someone, you know, you don't actually have

SEX PACKETS: This wouldn't-this-be-fun fairy tale is selected from an interview with Shock G of the hip-hop recording group, Digital Underground. Digital Underground sold a million copies of a rap send-up of dance music called "The Humpty Dance" the first time out, and more recently shipped two million copies of an album called *Sex Packets*. The Dr. Cook referred to by Shock G is a fictional music character like Sergeant Pepper.

A Sex Packet is a science-fictional concept invented for the *Sex Packets* album. It comes in foil like a condom (or "jim hat," as Shock would say), even though it's something like a pill. On

to go home with the person, you just say, "May I exchange packets with you?" If she said "Okay," you can go home and check it out—you know what I'm sayin'? If you drop the person's packet, you can say, "Yeah, it's cool, I wanna get with you," or, "No, I don't wanna get with you." You just exchange packets and you go through the experience with them, and being that it has the power, having that particular person's essence in each particular packet, it's the only thing safer than using your hand.

When I met Dr. Cook, he was making unknown-people packets, he was making "Young Black Teenager" packets, I think, because they had the most sexual essence to them. The street packets of unknowns, they just satisfy a category of race or sex or size or height, whatever somebody might want, like, "I just want a fat white bitch"—blam, there you are. But in the case of a celebrity, where there's just the one, it costs more.

If you was to have your own packet made, that would be real expensive, you see what I'm sayin', because you would have to get your essence drained and all that, to have your supply of your own packets. It would be much cheaper to just go to the average packet dealer on the street and say, "Hmm, let me try this big-titty bitch right here, 'cause she reminds me of Tina Turner—I always wanted to do her." **4**

each Sex Packet is the name of the person, or type of person, represented by the Packet. Using the Sex Packet provides a simulated sexual experience with the person, or type of person, on the label. As DU explains, "Now let me tell you how to take it/you either sit or lie down/and you really should be naked/otherwise you're gonna mess up your clothes/know what I mean/this is more than just a dream/these are very realistic and they're gonna blow your mind/so be careful, only take one at a time."

The recent DU release, *Sons of the P* is selling even better than the *Sex Packets* album. As of this writing, it never leaves R. U. Sirius's tape player.

APPROPRIATION

R. U. Sirius: One could trace the history of appropriation back to the first piece of artwork that was based on photography. But most art historians refer back to Marcel Duchamp's "ready-mades." Duchamp, for instance, took a urinal and turned it upside-down, calling it art. "Art" would never be the same.

Andy Warhol can probably be credited with first bringing the appropriationist sensibility to pop culture. In his pop art, Warhol started off by copying logos and painting exact replicas, the most famous being his exact-same-sized copies of Brillo boxes and Campbell's soup cans. He very quickly escalated to direct appropriation by taking *actual* news photos and silk-screening them into multiples.

In the eighties, the digital sampler became an important instrument in pop music. Bands started taking bits of sounds from previously recorded music and incorporating it into their own. By the nineties, a "modern rock" song was as likely as not to contain sampled bits, and record companies had developed procedures for crediting and paying for the appropriated materials. Appropriation is now completely mainstreamed.

DIGITAL SAMPLER: The media has emphasized virtual reality as the central technology of the New Edge, but I say that the central technology is the digital sampler. The sampler is a device used in electronic music synthesis that digitizes and stores a musical tone or phrase. The sampled signal may be the sound of an instrument played at a particular pitch or it may be composed of previously recorded materials. It can then be subjected to various digital signal processing techniques to change duration, pitch, timbre, etc. This modular sound source can be controlled either by external MIDI (see "Electronic Music") devices (such as keyboards and drum pads) or from software sequencers (see "Industrial/Postindustrial Music & Art"). Samplers are central to the creation of much of today's "modern rock" sound; particularly hip-hop, house, and industrial. Musicians combine the various sounds already stored within the sampler with "found sounds" appropriated from existing recorded material to collage together an original.

THIS IS NOT PLAGIARISM

My publishers took *The Adult Life of Toulouse-Lautrec* off the market because they were afraid Harold Robbins might sue me. I had told them that I *use* other people's material—I *appropriate*—and this was not plagiarism. Plagiarism is using somebody else's material and representing it as your own.

THIS IS NOT PLAGIARISM: This is from Kathy Acker, the postmodernist feminist author of such books as *Empire of the Senseless* and *In Memoriam to Identity*. Heavily tattooed and into bodybuilding, Acker helped establish her work using the force of her strong punk image. Her books are partly collaged out of text from other books. She currently teaches at the Art Institute in San Francisco.

DIDIER CREMIEUX

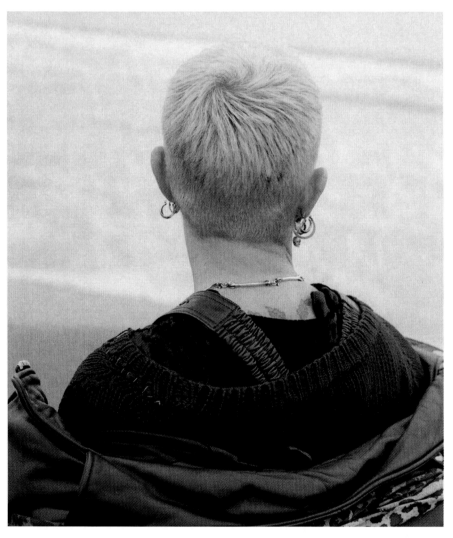

APPROPRIATION IS THE HALLMARK OF POSTMODERNISM: The next two entries are from Stephan Ronan, taken from his interview with Negativland. Ronan was an editor at City Lights Books and has served as a consultant on various media projects on the Beats, most recently the reissue of Jack Kerouac's recordings by Rhino Records. He also self-publishes an anarcho-surrealist zine, "Ammunition."

POSTMODERNISM is the defining sensibility of the late twentieth century. The postmodern sensibility is one in which hard reality and belief systems are up for grabs. Without absolutes, people put together tentative gestalts by connecting together pieces of existing data into new patterns. Thus postmodern art essentially appropriates ideas, material, and data from the existing "data base" of information and experience to create an "original"—generally, the original comments on the situation of postmodernity. Postmodernism is fraught with irony and is infinitely self-reflective and self-conscious.

Kathy Acker

APPROPRIATION IS THE HALLMARK OF POSTMODERNISM

As art theory evolved in the eighties, the hallmark of postmodernism has turned out to be appropriation. Somehow it seems more important to use recombined images supplied to you through the media—through whatever source you got them from—than manufacturing or drawing something wholly new. On an audio level, this is what Cabaret Voltaire and Throbbing Gristle did. And it's what Negativland is doing.

LEGAL QUESTIONS

There were always legal questions—going back to Andy Warhol with his exact-same-sized copies of Brillo boxes and so forth—which came to nothing.

CABARET VOLTAIRE AND THROBBING GRISTLE were two of the founding bands in Industrial Music in the late seventies (see "Industrial/Postindustrial Music & Art"). Throbbing Gristle was fronted by Genesis P-Orridge, who went on to front Psychic TV, the founders of the acid-house movement (see "House Music").

NEGATIVLAND is without a doubt the most peculiar presence on college radio's alternative music playlists. They might be described as an industrial/media/humor band, but then again some of their stuff is so peculiar that even that description sounds too self-consciously arty. Their most controversial albums have been *Escape from Noise*, *Helter Stupid* and *U2*. They are media pranksters more famous for getting in trouble than for their records. (See "Media Pranks" for much more.)

EXCITING SOUNDS: The next four entries are from an interview with John Oswald, a Toronto-based experimental composer and creator of *Plunderphonics,* which was a self-produced, not-for-sale, selectively-mailed-out-for-free CD with eighteen tracks of music, entirely filched, scrambled, and reinterpreted through electronic means. Elvis, Dolly Parton, Paul McCartney, Captain Beefheart, Verdi, Bix Beiderbecke and the 101 Strings, Michael Jackson, and others are tossed into the electronic blender. Oswald was forced to take *Plunderphonics* out of circulation by Michael Jackson's lawyers. However, a mutual friend of M2 and Jackson's assures us that Michael thought the collage on the cover of the CD (Michael's head on a young female body), which we reprinted in *MONDO* #2, was very funny.

EDGARD VARÈSE was an experimental composer early in the century. He is Frank Zappa's favorite composer.

EXCITING SOUNDS

Edgard Varèse was excited by the sounds of airplanes and things like that. He had been around for long enough to have experienced the time before these things existed. He wanted to incorporate them into his music in some way, either by imitation or sometimes by actually recording things like that. I have the same feeling about a lot of media. Media has changed a lot during our lives, but it is very much a part of our lives, and I think we both somehow want to incorporate that in how we work with things. And it's more interesting to us as musical material than melodies. In private, I make up melodies. I like to use the current technology to create pieces where I write melodies into computers and the computers can play them for me…play variations. I like dealing with that sort of stuff. And some of the melodies I like very much, but I have little inclination to put them out in this world along with billions of other tunes. I find it more worthwhile to do things like *Plunderphonics,* where I'm taking a big risk and maybe getting in trouble for quoting people.

IMPROVING MICHAEL JACKSON

I hear somebody coming up the street with some windows open in their van, and I can hear Michael Jackson playing "Bad." Okay, that's Michael Jackson. That sounds pretty good, but there's something missing. I wonder what it is. I wonder what I can do to make that sound the way I want it to sound.

I wrote a paper about Michael Jackson's process in making "Bad," and presented it at

a conference for a bunch of serious music tape composers. Jimmy Smith—
the famous Hammond organ jazz musician—was brought in to play two or four
bars of the Jimmy Smith sound, and the lead-off from that sounds really hot,
really live. You hear it and say, "This is great." So they're trying to put together
this mosaic of something that sounds live by very repetitive mechanical means. And
they'll spend probably weeks putting the whole thing together, mixing it, and making
something where the end result is
something they're hoping will feel
live to their audience. These couple
of bars by Jimmy Smith help give
the illusion of a live performance by
a band. So I started getting into this
thing, and it doesn't sound live enough
to me. There's something quite
boring and dead about the track,
particularly compared to earlier
efforts by Michael Jackson. I really
admire his voice, actually, and how
he uses it. So I fiddled with it in an
even more mechanical way, sometimes using computers to approxi-
mate aspects of a group feel, in order
to make something that made me feel more alive as a listener. And I helped it
sound like it had some sort of verve to it. So I think we are aiming at similar goals
but just with different aesthetics or different concerns.

**Pictured at right:
Mark Hosler and
Don Joyce of
Negativland**

MY METALLICA

I knew nothing about Metallica. I knew they existed, but I hadn't heard them at all. However, I'm
very fond of heavy-metal sounds. So I went into this store and the clerk said, "Well, try these guys out."
And I thought it was the most satisfying recording I'd heard of a heavy-metal band. I don't really care
what they're playing, but I just like the sound of the instruments, and I very much like the sound of
the bass drum. I quickly noticed that I didn't like what the drummer was playing at all, and I think
my major compositional focus was on making the drummer sound good, having him play certain
patterns…things that I felt were much more conducive to what the guitar guys are doing. So,
in a way, I made a drum concerto out of it, and everybody else gets to tag along as a result.

WHY I PLUNDER

I'm not afraid to fiddle with music that I like but doesn't quite satisfy me.
There's a possibility that I can make something better of it. So I'm really trying
to plug the holes in my own meager record collection.

PAYING FOR THE SAMPLES

The "authors" of every sampled squeal, cymbal crash, rhythm, or recognizable sound effect feel entitled to remuneration.

Most established producers today have to take their finished product and play it for the original artist or publisher and agree to either a flat fee or a statutory royalty, in which the original artist may receive a penny or so per sale for a few seconds of his or her sound. This was originally considered chump-change. If, however, a record sells a million copies, one cent adds up to ten thousand dollars, which is getting expensive. Jimi Dright Jr., "Chopmaster J" of the innovative group Digital Underground, says it's all a game of cat and mouse. "This is how you can work it. You can call them, or you can wait, and they can call you."

Rick Ross, managing director of Delicious Vinyl, one of the most successful hip-hop labels, said, "Record companies are building in costs for samples, because most publishers are asking for a cut nowadays…We thought we made the Tone Loc album for ten thousand dollars, but with the royalties it's cost us between a hundred eighty and two hundred thousand."

HIP-HOP AS CYBERPUNKING

So who has the right to manipulate electronic images and sounds? When is art theft? When is theft art?

Sampling is the auditory form of hacking through a data base. A certain functional anarchy is involved which one might argue is good for the soul. For hip-hop, a sampler is not a toy, it's an important instrument in the function of the rap song statement.

FOUND SOUNDS

When Negativland started, I was buying a lot of independent music, and was starting to find out that there was this whole other world out there. I liked a lot of what I heard, but there was definitely something missing that I wanted to hear. So I started mixing in all of this stuff from my world—you know, my dog barking, the sprinklers on outside, and the TV set was always on. It was a totally naive thing really. ◢

PAYING FOR THE SAMPLES: This item is sampled from an article by Rickey Vincent, who is the Uhuru Maggot, host of "The Funk Feast" on KALX radio in Berkeley.

Samples are bits of sound taken from existing recordings using digital technology.

FOUND SOUNDS: This is from Mark Hosler, founding member of Negativland, described above.

ARTIFICIAL LIFE Rudy Rucker: "Alife" studies ways of building systems that act as if they are alive. This broad area of study encompasses chemical attempts to synthesize self-replicating molecules, the linguistic analysis of self-perpetuating belief systems, robotics, and the design of computer programs capable of evolving into new forms.

Most current work is in the area of computer programs. The idea here is to set up a computer world—a virtual reality—and to populate it with a bunch of small, autonomous programs. The little programs are your Alife critters.

In a typical Alife world, the critters will look like small colored patterns that move about on the two-dimensional grid of the screen or in a three-dimensional virtual world that is projected onto the screen. Each critter has a "chromosome" which consists of, say, a thousand bytes of raw zeroes-and-ones information. The appearance of a critter's body is determined by the bits and bytes of the critter's chromosome. That is, the chromosome acts as program information that the host computer uses to calculate a critter's body-image.

The critters are normally endowed with sensory input—each of them might, for instance, be able to see the location of the two or three critters closest to it in their virtual world. The critters react to their sensory input by moving this way and that, possibly chasing after each other. A critter's responses to inputs are also determined by the individual critter's chromosome.

Two critters can mate by breaking their chromosomes at a mutually agreed-upon random point and then piecing together two new chromosomes, each of which is partly from the "Mom" and partly from the "Dad." The two new chromosomes can be used to grow two new critters. Once the reproductive process is in full swing, evolution can be brought about by instituting survival of the fittest. The programmer defines some "fitness function" that measures how well the critters are doing, and periodically removes the low-scoring critters and replaces them by the "children" of high-scoring critters. All kinds of fitness functions are possible. One might, for instance, give the highest scores to the critters who move the greatest distance, to the critters who manage to bump into the most of their fellows, or to the critters whose trails exhibit the highest degree of unpredictability (mathematically definable as information-theoretic entropy). Alternately, one can hover over the world like a jealous God and use a mouse to reward and punish

"ARTIFICIAL LIFE studies man-made systems which exhibit behaviors characteristic of natural living systems," wrote Christopher Langton in his introduction to *Artificial Life I*,  which is the proceedings of a conference held in 1987. The second U.S. Artificial Life Conference was held in 1990, and the third was in 1992. Several Alife conferences in other countries are now scheduled as well. Another popular Alife reference is Przemyslaw Prusinkiewicz and Aristid Lindenmayer's *The Algorithmic Beauty of Plants.*

individual critters according to wholly subjective criteria. It takes a surprisingly short amount of time for the critters to evolve and get better and better scores.

Present day applications of Alife programs include computer graphics that draw themselves, methods of finding solutions to intractably difficult problems, and, of course, robotics. In the future we can expect to see large numbers of Alife organisms wandering around in cyberspace—this will keep virtual reality from being sterile and boring.

BIG IDEAS

Some of the Big Ideas about Alife: Life might be a phase transition, a sharp, thin line between periodic or static routines (solids) and nonperiodic chaos (liquids). Like a phase transition, life tends to bloom "on the border between boredom and chaos."

Human-designed genes are no match for natural-evolved genes.

Punctuated equilibrium can be demonstrated in artificial evolution.

There is a nested hierarchy of control in lifelike systems.

WHY GET ALIFE?

Alife gives a picture of nature as a whole. We need to study Alife because it is inevitably going to be with us (computer viruses are a form of Alife that is already here).

Alife provides a better way to engineer complex software—if you can't build it, you can evolve it.

Alife is a means to study biological life in a simulated form and therefore is easier and safer than actually messing with the biology of life itself.

FORMULA FOR INVENTING SEX

Suppose that you have to find some way of making an optimal choice for, say, a hundred different program

BIG IDEAS: These next three entries are by Kevin Kelly, formerly editor of the *Whole Earth Review* ▲ Kevin also edited the excellent book *SIGNAL* ▲, which covered some of the same ground as this *User's Guide.*

A PHASE TRANSITION is what happens when matter changes its state, as when a liquid freezes or comes to a boil. On the social scale, when a malcontent population rises up and throws off its government, a phase transition takes place. The mathematics of phase transitions are exceedingly complex.

PUNCTUATED EQUILIBRIUM is a modern idea about how the evolution of plants and animals takes place. Traditional Darwinian evolutionary theory holds that changes accumulate at a slow, steady rate. Punctuated equilibrium holds that there might be a kind of plateau of ten million years when the species don't change much, followed by a very "happening" hundred thousand years in which lots of old species die out and new species get started. Stephen Jay Gould's book *Wonderful Life* ▲ touches on some of these ideas.

parameters. You can use the "genetic algorithm" approach, which is a simulation of sexual reproduction:

Make a random start.

Score fitness.

Select survivors.

Choose mates.

Combine genes.

Mutate next time around.

HOW CELLULAR AUTOMATA TURN PEARLS INTO SWINE

The most remarkable thing that I guess I discovered is that you can have very simple underlying rules and generate from those very complicated behavior. Cellular automata, of course, are the best example of that phenomenon. But the phenomenon really changes one's intuition about what the philosophical theories of biology and other areas should be, because often we've been looking at very complex behavior and assumed that the theory that underlies what's going on must itself be very complex. Cellular automata show us that's not true.

TODAY'S ASSIGNMENT

Here's the problem that I really want to solve right now. I want to find a quantum mechanical analog of cellular automata. Cellular automata are kind of a caricature of classical physics. I want to find the quantum analog of that.

GENETIC ALGORITHMS are a technique for producing a good program when you don't know how. Say, for instance, that you want to visit a hundred cities, and you want to know what order to visit them in so as to minimize your travel expense. There's so many possible routes that even a computer can't exhaustively look at them all. So instead you might start with one randomly chosen route, and then spawn off like ten mutated "children" of the original route, each of the "children" with the order, say, of one pair of cities changed. You compare the total cost of each of the child routes, pick the best one, then look at ten "grandchildren" spawned by that "child." Pick the best "grandchild" and continue. As time goes by you are likely to converge on a better solution. This is a simple example of genetic programming. To make it a bit funkier, one also chooses the best TWO solutions and finds a way of "sexually" combining them. Like breed programs "Mom" and "Dad" onto a Child by having the first half of Child's code be the same as Mom's and the second half be the same as Dad's.

Here the "genes" of the programs are those hundred numerical parameters, and combining two programs' genes means making a new hundred-parameter program which has fifty of its parameters set to Mother's values, and the other fifty of its parameters set to Father's values.

HOW CELLULAR AUTOMATA TURN PEARLS INTO SWINE: The next two heavy thoughts are from Stephen Wolfram, who received his Ph.D. from Cal Tech at age eighteen and won the MacArthur "millionaire" prize the year after that. He proceeded to open up the field of computer chaos by his studies of cellular automata, and then settled down by creating the best computer-mathematics program ever, Mathematica. ▲

The best-known cellular automaton rule is known as "the game of Life." Here the plane is divided into a grid of blank cells, and each cell regards the eight cells which touch it (at a side or at a corner) as its neighbors. To start the game of Life, marks are put in some of the cells. From then on all the cells are updated in parallel, according to the rule: A blank cell becomes a marked cell if it has exactly three marked neighbors, a marked cell remains marked if it has exactly two or three marked neighbors, and in all other cases the cell is made blank. Over the course of many generations, very simple starting patterns can produce enormously complicated amounts of cell-markings.

CELLULAR AUTOMATA

In a way, your body is a cellular automaton. It's made of cells, and each cell obeys more or less the same rule, and each cell is influenced at any given time only by its immediate neighbors. An aspect of society is like that. This is a computer model of parallel computation where, for example, each pixel on the screen is acting like an independent computer, and each pixel is looking at the pixels that touch it and might take the sum of the colors of the neighbors, average them, add one, and make that its new color. *A*

CELLULAR AUTOMATA: This quote is from Rudy Rucker, who has published sixteen books: eight novels, four popular-science expositions, two anthologies of stories, one autobiographical memoir, and one book of poetry. His two best-known science books are *Mind Tools* ▲ and *The Fourth Dimension*, ▲ and his two best-known novels are *Software* ▲ and *Wetware*, ▲ each of which won the Philip K. Dick Memorial Award. In the words of Faustin Bray's intro to the original version of this interview: "This Davy Crockett pioneer superman Einstein/Gödel adventurer computer nerd demigod of the Matrix wears corduroys, horn-rimmed glasses, and drives a station wagon."

Cellular automata are self-generating computer graphics movies of hallucinatory diversity. In 1989, Rucker coauthored CA Lab, ▲ a cellular automata package for IBM PC-compatible computers. Rucker also worked on another Autodesk Science Series product: James Gleick's Chaos: The Software. ▲

GRAHAM CHAFFEE

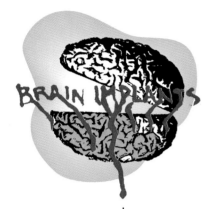

BRAIN IMPLANTS

St. Jude: This is the technology of our dreams. We long to be drilled for our skull plugs, a longing implanted in us just a few years ago by William Gibson's *Neuromancer*, George Alec Effinger's *When Gravity Fails*, and a whole sick crew of follow-up cyberpunks. The dream involves microchips that you clip into snug contact with your central nervous system for instant fluency in a language you've never heard, for expert-systems knowledge of new tech, for a new personality. The wickedness of it adds to the lure: We were warned against this sort of thing when we were growing up—YOU MISSED YOUR PRACTICE AGAIN; YOU THINK YOU'LL JUST WAKE UP ONE MORNING AND KNOW HOW TO PLAY THE PIANO? OF COURSE NOT, DAD, I'M SAVING UP FOR THE CHILDMOZART CHIP.

WIREHEADS

We're dealing with electrical stimulation of the brain, and all the different uses that can be put to. What goes on is—you drill a hole in the skull, insert the electrode into whatever part of the brain you want, and then you can either fix the connecting plug directly over it, or loop it under the skin to another place. Once that's done, you can repeat it—some humans have been implanted with up to a hundred, in various deep brain structures. Depending on where you put this electrode, you get different effects.

These implants can be left in for years without any real damage. They can be implanted completely under the skin—put the receiver on top of the skull and suture up the skin over it, then

WIREHEADS: These first three entries are based on an anonymous article that *MONDO* sampled from *RE/SEARCH Magazine*. The interviewee claimed to be privy to secret knowledge of advance work in this field. In reality, this is probably creative science faction (mix of fact and fiction). After publishing this, *MONDO* received a not unpleasant note from the anonymous party claiming that he had since then become a dedicated fascist. This was stated in the sort of matter-of-fact tone you'd expect if someone were telling you that he'd recently got married and gotten a job selling real estate.

Many science-fiction writers have dealt with the idea of "wireheads," these being people who get a wire implanted in their brain's pleasure center and spend all their time pushing the button for more pleasure. One of the most thorough massmarket treatments of this theme is in Spider Robinson's *Mindkiller*. One of the earlier wirehead sections can be found on page 24 of William S. Burroughs's novel *Naked Lunch*: "Squatting on old bones and excrement and rusty iron, in a white blaze of heat, a panorama of naked idiots stretches to the horizon. Complete silence—their speech centers are destroyed—except for the crackle of sparks and the popping of singed flesh as they apply electrodes up and down the spine."

ERIC WHITE

let it heal so there's no break in the skin, no route for infection. They've mapped out areas they call Type 1, Type 2, and Type 3. Type 1 is just mild joy, relaxation. Type 2 is a little more intense, and type 3 is orgasmic rushes.

SIGHT FOR THE BLIND

In one experiment, a patient had each implant tuned to a different receptive frequency. So by beaming radio energy at this implant, the person could see different pictures. By stimulating certain electrodes in the right patterns and combinations, the guy could see letters and patterns. Eventually they hope this can allow blind people to experience vision.

A recent implant by Dr. Dabelle of the University of Utah featured sixty-four electrodes, with a connecting plug which emerges right above the subject's ear. The guy just lifts his hair up like a flap. So this guy with the flap got hooked up to a computer which automatically stimulated him with sentences. He was blind and he knew how to read braille This guy got so he could read about eight times faster than he could read braille with his fingers.

They also hooked up a camera in direct link so that the camera image was being fed to the brain directly. They put the guy with the flap in a room, gave him control of the camera, and he could make out the difference between horizontal and vertical lines. It's a crude beginning.

HEAR LIKE A DOG

They're working on cameras small enough to fit into the ocular cavity and on hooking up the muscles themselves to the camera. This opens up whole new worlds of perceptual experience, because we have cameras sensitive to regions of the electromagnetic spectrum that our natural eyes aren't sensitive to—infrared or ultraviolet, for example.

TYPE 1, TYPE 2, AND TYPE 3: In Philip K. Dick's classic SF novel *Do Androids Dream of Electric Sheep?* ▲ (which was made into the movie *Blade Runner* ▲), the main character, Rick Deckard, and his wife each have a "Penfield mood organ," named after the Dr. Penfield who did some of the first direct brain-stimulation research. When Deckard's wife tells him that she is going to dial for "a six-hour self-accusatory depression," he protests, even though she says she plans to follow it by "a 481. Awareness of the manifold possibilities open to me in the future." Deckard turns on the TV and suggests that instead she "Dial 888. The desire to watch TV, no matter what's on."

CAMERAS: In William Gibson's trilogy of cyberpunk novels, *Neuromancer, Count Zero,* ▲ and *Mona Lisa Overdrive,* ▲ there are characters who are a cross between news anchorpeople and soap-opera actors. These folks have cameras implanted in their eye sockets, so that their ongoing lives can be broadcast as entertainment. In one gross scene, an actress is slain by terrorists, and a producer rushes to her corpse to pry the very expensive cameras out of her head.

GREG NERSESSIAN

You could hook up your eyeball to telescopes, microscopes. Not only that, you could do the same types of things with all your senses. You could hear high noises like a dog. You could feel minute irregularities in a flat mirror. You could heft things like an ocean tanker.

CONSUMER RESISTANCE

I think brain implants are going to be about as popular as trepanning. I just don't think that people are that interested in having something which may effect a permanent change. Surgical solutions have rarely been among the more attractive. You don't want to keep opening your cranium every time somebody comes out with a new model.

I'D LIKE A NEURAL INTERFACE, PLEASE

"I don't know if the future is necessarily going to be cyberpunk or cyberprep, but it's going to be cyber-something. And as soon as they announce that skull implants are available, I'm gonna line up for mine.

"I'd like to add a few languages, be able to go without sleep, and obviously, I'd like to get a direct neural interface with my computer. That would be great."

BETTER THAN DRUGS

I think that what will help us become more intelligent, better evolved, and more loving and trusting individuals, with a greater capacity for self-control—in other words, have autonomy over our emotions—will not be chemicals. It will be a lot of nonchemical, electronic implants. The chemical base of life is a very primitive thing. As we evolve into more complex organisms—trans-universal and immortal beings—we will have to transcend our chemical past. *B*

CONSUMER RESISTANCE: This note is from an interview with a video artist who calls himself Stefan. He has worked with Bowie, Flo and Eddie, and Jello Biafra.

TREPANNING: To trepan someone is to remove a small circular section of his or her skull. In earlier times this was a popular remedy for conditions as diverse as stroke, senility, and madness. The point being made here is that the idea of wires into your brain really IS just science fiction at this point in history. Nobody has nearly enough knowledge of the brain's microarchitecture to dream of doing a wire/brain interface. The next best thing to this kind of interface seems to be the promise held out by the computer-graphical techniques called cyberspace or virtual reality.

I'D LIKE A NEURAL INTERFACE, PLEASE: This comment is from Steve Jackson, of Steve Jackson Games, publisher of role-playing games, including GURPS (Generic Universal Role Playing System) Cyberpunk. More on Jackson in "Electronic Freedom."

BETTER THAN DRUGS: This quote is from F. M. Esfandiary. Esfandiary is a futurist who has published several books including *Upwingers* and *Are You a Transhuman?* He teaches a course on the future at the UCLA Extension.

KHYAL BRAUN

Rudy Rucker: There is a spectrum of orderliness that runs from something like a crystal at one end to something like a fluid at the other. At the crystalline end we have stasis and constancy. One step up from that is periodicity, like the cycling of the seasons. At the fluid end of the spectrum is full randomness. In the middle, where order melts into disorder, is the domain of chaos. One can move into chaos from either direction.

As an example of moving from order to chaos, think of the breaking of a rack of pool-balls on a frictionless billiard table. One starts with a precise triangle of balls in a precise rectangular enclosure. The balls move (at least in an idea thought-experiment) totally deterministically and according to Newton's three laws of motion. Yet the longer the balls bounce around, the more disordered their pattern becomes. The table is in effect acting as a computer which calculates more and more steps of a deterministic evolution. The fact is that many calculations become, as time goes by, wildly unpredictable. Another point to note here is that no matter how slightly you change the way in which you break the rack of balls, if you let the balls bounce long enough, their positions will become radically different according to the slight change in the starting condition.

The world is full of very complicated structures. People used to think that this meant there must be some very complicated laws of nature. But the notion of chaos shows us that a very simple process can in fact produce complex outputs provided that the process RUNS LONG ENOUGH. Our universe might be thought of as a very simple program which has run for a very long time, with successive outputs overlapping onto each other and building up a hyperdimensional moiré.

As an example of moving from disorder to chaos, think of the way that an impatiently applauding crowd ("Start the show!") is likely to fall into a resonant rhythm frequency and end up clapping in unison. Many completely random and scuzzy processes tend to be attracted towards certain kinds of approximately repeating cycles. Rather than being perfectly repetitive, these strange attractors embody chaotic behaviors whose rhythms slowly drift.

Far from being a bad or a negative thing, chaos is a positive aspect of the world, expressing the beautiful diversity of phenomena as well as the underlying cosmic rhythms. The fact that the world is an incompressibly complex chaotic computation means that there is no way to predict the future other than physically living through the time it takes to get there. Surprise is always possible, and a state of chaos is a state of health.

L. Ashton 1992

CHAOS, GAIA, AND EROS

Gaia points to the planet as an organism, and the plain as its surface. Gaia is very chaotic. If you reject chaos, you reject Gaia. The Orphic trinity is Chaos, Gaia, and Eros.

That's what I suggest you think about. Gaia as the Earth, the love of the planet, the integrity of life-forms; Chaos as the essence of life—more chaos is healthier; Eros as human behavior in resonance with Chaos and Gaia.

THE EVOLUTION OF SOCIETY

Human society is an evolving system—including its psyche, its mythology, its cultural structure. This evolution is punctuated by bifurcations, mutations caused by the planetary equivalent of lightning—comets. Comets were probably very important in the history of consciousness—they still are. There are some mutations where changes are made in the memes, the cultural genetic structure. Then there's a kind of natural selection that goes on when two societies are in conflict over a common goal, and in this conflict one would be selected not just by military strength but also through the stability of its social structure.

ARE ACID VISIONS FRACTALS?

There's an interesting theory of the geometric forms in psychedelic hallucinations based on mathematics by Jack Cowen and Bard Ermentrout. These two mathematicians see psychedelic hallucinations as mathematical forms inherent in the structure of the physical brain.

What I think about psychedelic visuals is not so different, except that I wouldn't locate them in the physical brain. I think that we perceive, through some kind of resonance phenomenon, patterns from another sphere of existence that is also governed by a certain mathematical structure which gives it the form that we see. I can't speak for

CHAOS, GAIA, AND EROS: These excerpts are from an interview with Ralph Abraham, a professor of mathematics at the University of California, Santa Cruz. With Chris Shaw, he has authored and published a wonderful series of four picture books about chaos called *Dynamics—The Geometry of Behavior*. Thomas Bass's book *The Eudaemonic Pie* tells the fascinating story of how some of Ralph's best chaos students got together and built a computer that fit into a shoe to try to break the bank at roulette in Las Vegas. A good popular book on chaos is James Gleick's *Chaos*. See also the excellent software product (cowritten by Rudy), James Gleick's Chaos: The Software.

GAIA: The use of the old word "Gaia" for Earth was popularized by James Lovelock's *Gaia Hypothesis*, which proposes that our planet is in effect a single large organism, and that things like global climate fluctuations are the self-regulating metabolic activities of Gaia.

ORPHIC: Orpheus played such lovely music on his lyre that animals, trees, and stones followed him. He tried to bring his dead wife Eurydice back from Hades, but she was snatched back when he looked at her too soon. Later some of Orpheus's female fans tore him into pieces and floated the pieces down the river to Hades. Axl Rose, look out!

BIFURCATIONS: A bifurcation is a splitting in two—as when a tree branch forks in two. There are certain kinds of mathematical forms which depend on a control parameter P. For low values of P the form might have one piece, but beyond some critical value Pc of P the form will be made up of several distinct pieces. Here we would say that Pc is a bifurcation point.

everyone, but in my experience, this form moves. And the mathematicians of fractal geometry have made movies and—to me—they don't move right. So I think that the resemblance between fractals and psychedelic visuals is very superficial.

LIFE IS A BIFURCATING CHAOTIC ATTRACTOR. AND THEN YOU DIE.

The idea of the exponential divergence, the so-called sensitive dependence on initial conditions, is very much misunderstood. When a process follows a trajectory on a chaotic attractor, and you start two processes from fairly close initial conditions, they do indeed diverge for a while. But—in point of fact—what is happening is that both of the trajectories go 'round and 'round. You can think of yarn being wound on a skein. They diverge for a while, but pretty soon they reach the edge of the skein and they fold into the middle again. They have a certain maximum separation—it might be four inches or something, and that's it. They do not diverge indefinitely and go off into infinity. That's exactly what doesn't happen with chaotic attractors.

So chaotic attractors ought to be very reassuring to people who would otherwise have anxiety about chaos, because the chaos in a chaotic attractor is very bounded, and the degree to which things go haywire is extremely limited. So that's the good news. Chaos is very much the same as the steady state. It's not that scary at all.

Now if our evolutionary path were modeled by a chaotic attractor, then we could answer the question of where we'd be in the twenty-first century. We'd be pretty much in the same mess as now. But it's not.

A better kind of mathematical object for modeling evolutionary processes is a bifurcation diagram. In this context, a chaotic attractor is changing in time. There may be bifurcations—for example, a catastrophe, a comet or something. Who knows? And it may be that some bifurcations can occur

A FRACTAL is a shape whose details resemble the whole thing. A mountain range is a kind of fractal, since if you look at an outcropping of rock on a mountain, it looks like a small mountain itself, and if you lean closer to the rock outcropping, you find bumps on the boulders which themselves look like mountains, and so on. Here the parts are only APPROXIMATELY like the whole thing. One can also define mathematical fractals in which each part looks EXACTLY like the whole thing—some examples of this kind of fractal are the so-called Julia Sets and the Sierpinski Gasket. Somewhere in between are the mathematical fractals, such as the Mandelbrot set, whose parts look sort of, but not exactly, like the whole thing. Some good books on fractals are Benoit Mandelbrot's *The Fractal Geometry of Nature* ▲ (difficult, but fun to skim) and Heinz-Otto Peitgen and Peter Richter's gorgeous color-illustrated *The Beauty of Fractals.* ▲

CHAOTIC ATTRACTOR: Imagine that every morning on waking you assigned a number between 1 and 10 to your level of dread and a number between 1 and 10 to your current level of sexual desire. Each day's pair of numbers could be represented as a point on a little graph, with one axis for dread and one axis for sex desire. As time went by, you might discover that the points tended to cluster in some—not necessarily smooth or linear—shape. This shape would be an example of a chaotic attractor, a ghostly locus in an arbitrary "phase" space created by trying to relate two measurements of some complexly evolving system (you). As a point moves about on a chaotic attractor, one typically DOES NOT know which point will come next, but one DOES know that the next point will be SOMEWHERE on the attractor. Ralph's idea of a "bifurcation diagram" suggests that over time the shape of an underlying chaotic attractor may change.

under the action of parameters that are controlled by us…how much energy we use, how much waste we make, etc. That's why bifurcation diagrams are more interesting than chaotic attractors for modeling our own process. Under this more general kind of model, we cannot say where we will be in the twenty-first century. Or *if* we'll be.

A RANDOMNESS ANTENNA

Stephen Wolfram: An interesting question is, "Can we produce true randomness with quantum mechanics?" Like, I'd really find it interesting to have a randomness chip that I could plug into my computer and clock some lines on the chip and out of it you get this completely random sequence. Physical, perfect randomness, no pseudo- random stuff. The question is: "Can you build such a chip?"

One of the things one learns about these chips is there's a limit to the speed at which you can get randomness out. Where is the randomness coming from in the first place? It's coming from thermodynamic effects: from heat, essentially. And in order to have a lot of randomness, what you have to end up with is a "randomness antenna" that comes out of your computer and is sensitive to all the cues in your environment, and picks up all these fluctuations in the environment. The finite speed at which heat diffuses into the region in which you're doing amplification-making measurements is going to limit the speed at which you generate your random bits. **C**

ROSE X

RANDOM: Any computer computation (not using a "randomness chip") is completely determinisitic and repeatable. Thus, whenever a program includes the ability to generate a so-called "random" number, the number you get is in fact really the result of some complicated computation, and was in some sense predictable, or "pseudo-random." So that each run of a game is not the same, most programs jolt their randomizers by putting in a "seed number" when the program is started. Where does a computer find a random seed number? It checks the time! When many programs start up, they seed their randomizer with the number of seconds that have elapsed since 00:00:00 Greenwich Mean Time, January 1, 1970. Kind of like the switch from B.C. to A.D.

SANDRA HAMBURG

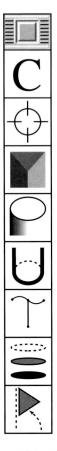

COMPUTER

Graphics

Sally Rosenthal: An example of the art of science and the science of art, computer graphics is the field of electronic images. This includes analog imaging techniques (those that involve visual representation of numerical qualities by means of physical variables like, for example, voltage) and digital (those that involve discrete numerical values, all processes of which are based upon a dual-state condition, such as on-off, open-closed, and true-false). All computer graphics use one of two techniques to electronically "draw" images: vector graphics are those in which lines and curves are drawn point-to-point; raster graphics are those in which each individual pixel (dots that compose the image, short for picture element) is illuminated or colored individually. The number of pixels in an image determines its resolution, sometimes referred to as "dpi," or dots per inch.

Images can be mathematically generated, scanned-in with an electronic camera, or hand-drawn with an electronic kind of pen and paper. They can be changed—edited or animated—interactively (instantly, in "realtime," like in video games, with peripherals such as mice, joysticks, and trackballs), programmatically, manually, electronically, photographically, or by means of any phenomenon that can be converted to a digital or analog signal (like if you want the intensity of light to control something, it can be measured, and that measurement used to effect change).

Computer graphics is a relatively new field. In 1961, Ivan Sutherland (the "father of computer graphics") created the first computer graphics program, **Sketchpad,** which enabled a person to electronically draw lines and circles by using an electronic pen. Extremely sophisticated techniques are now possible and are used in special effects for motion pictures, commercial advertising, scientific visualization, video production, photographic retouching, art, design (CAD), and

SALLY N. ROSENTHAL is a cofounder of big Research, a company devoted to the holistic planning and implementation of technically superb presentations. With cofounder Johnie Hugh Horn, she produces and directs events which involve art and technology, specifically ones that require the research and development of eccentric or elaborate new technologies to optimize the display of computer graphics.

Sally recently joined Magic Box, based in Los Angeles, to produce movies, theme park attractions, and video games. She's a member of the World Arts Council, which will create a "world arts village," to attain the same significance in the arts as the Olympiad in international sports. Among the other nominees for the 300-person council are Pierre Cardin, Quincy Jones, Nicholas Negroponte, David Bowie, David Hockney, Paul McCartney, Ieoh Pei, Lord Rothschild, Isaac Stern, and Stevie Wonder.

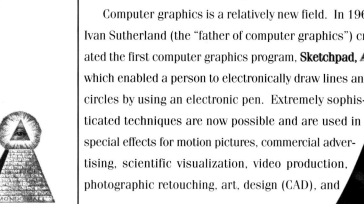

manufacturing (CAM). Virtual reality, artificial intelligence, multimedia, artificial life, and hypermedia all share a dependency on computer graphics.

Some popular developments include the following: morphing, used in Michael Jackson's video "Black Or White" to visually change people of different ethnicities into each other; fractals, a class of mathematical equations used to describe natural phenomena; and texture-mapping, with which surfaces can be painted by textures.

The annual SIGGRAPH conference ▲ is the place to feel the pulse of the field. Artists, scientists, engineers, bureaucrats, and the lunatic fringe from around the world congregate to share the newest computer graphics hardware, software, theory, and application, from personal systems and clip art (little computerized drawings that you can buy) to supercomputers and physically-based phenomena (like black holes).

COMPUTER GRAPHICS AT INDUSTRIAL LIGHT AND MAGIC

The computer graphics section used to be a dinky place: a very tiny, ill-thought-of corner. It's been growing for a couple of years, starting with *The Abyss*, but it really mushroomed for *Terminator 2*.

COMPOSITING

Compositing has become a major factor in filmmaking. Take pieces of film, put 'em together. Often we generate pieces of film with computer graphics, or computer animation, and we combine them with live action.

In *The Abyss* there were several amazing optical composites combining many elements: flying birds, the Golden Gate Bridge, ocean waves, a car…but they were very difficult. The digital element doesn't make an impossibility possible, it just makes it more fluid and plastic. You can work with it more freely, experiment constantly. Another advantage is that you can go back and just touch up one frame. Before this was possible, you'd just be stuck with your negative.

THE BIG COOKIE

3D modeling, that's the big cookie. That's the Holy Grail. It's really a new aesthetic, a more direct extension. You can create things that are impossible to create with models, sets, stages, or actors. You can create creatures that are made of water like the pseudopod in *The Abyss*. Water is so peculiar in its action that how it really looks is very recognizable. So to make a creature out of plastic or glycerin bags just wasn't going to work. One guy had the idea of spraying water hoses, shooting end-

COMPUTER GRAPHICS AT INDUSTRIAL LIGHT AND MAGIC: These next three entries come from Mark Dippe, the first special effects supervisor at George Lucas's Industrial Light and Magic (ILM) to come from a computer graphics background. He had a lot to do with creating that evil scary creature that chases Arnie Schwarzenegger around in *Terminator 2*, the guy who transforms himself into just about anything or virtually nothing, only to reemerge in "human" form. THAT'S computer graphics. Dippe's personal tastes lean toward the surrealistic, grotesque, and horrific, and he's currently collaborating with R. U. Sirius on a music/performance project called MONDO Vanilli.

less footage of spraying water, trying to manipulate the arcs and then picking the ones that matched the action. That's an example of what people were thinking. But it's a natural for computer animation, because if you simulate water you can control how it behaves.

ONLY WITH
COMPUTER GRAPHICS

I like to do things that you can only do on a computer. Computer models that mutate off of outside photographs. A lot of my stuff can best be described as looking like Jamaican space stations.

I do a lot of texture mapping, so I use a lot of photographs. And then I always find uses that weren't intended, generally to interesting effect. That's really the key, I think. Most computer graphics seem really similar...like obvious ways to respond to the capabilities of the machine. But there are plenty of people doing interesting things. The worthwhile stuff usually goes beyond the intentions of the programmer who wrote the software they're using. I'm kind of limited because I can't program, but I seem to have a better imagination than most people I've met who are programmers. It's a shame I didn't learn programming, but I don't know...maybe I lost a few too many brain cells! **C**

ONLY WITH COMPUTER GRAPHICS: This thought comes from Gibby Haynes, who's part of a rock band called the Butthole Surfers. They put out crazed dadaist thrash-rock albums with titles like *Locust Abortion Technician* and *Rembrandt Pussyhorse.*

MARK LANDMAN

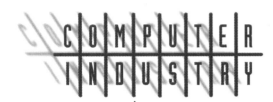

Opposite page:

The Homunculus

LEAVING LOTUS

In a nutshell, I started this little company called Lotus and made this software product that several million people wound up buying. The little company turned into this enormous thing with thousands of employees making hundreds of millions of dollars a year. And it felt awful to me. So I left. I just walked away one day.

Large businesses are collective organisms. We have this assumption that because something exists and acts, it has some central controller, some little homunculus inside it that makes the thing go. But physics is dead as a model for organizations. Biology is in the ascendant. And if you study biology, things are very decentralized, very distributed. You get emergent behaviors coming out of the workings of a whole bunch of little pieces. Each piece is pretty dumb. Organizations are like that. Still and all, I agonized over my responsibilities toward Lotus before I left.

APPLE

I think Apple's a lot WORSE than GM, because Apple is still clinging to a mythology that just gets in the way. I mean, if Apple could just kind of settle in and *be* GM, everybody there would be a lot happier.

Apple is like the Chinese Cultural Revolution conducted by people in three-piece suits. Any corporation has a totalitarian quality, but people work for them because it's supposed to be safe, right? You give up your mind but get the benefit of the collective immune system that will protect you against the slings and arrows of individual fortune. So IBM takes care of their employees. They rarely fire anybody. They've got a nice retirement plan...

Apple exercises much the same kind of totalitarian control over its employees and offers them *none* of the benefits. **C**

LEAVING LOTUS: This is from an interview with Mitch Kapor. Mitch Kapor founded Lotus, the company which makes 1-2-3, the most popular spreadsheet, or electronic ledger.

A HOMUNCULUS is a "little person." In the Middle Ages, some people thought that each sperm cell had a complete homunculus inside it waiting to grow to full size in the egg and womb of a woman. Others, called "ovists," thought that the complete homunculus resided in the woman's ovum, and that the sperm only served to irritate and awaken this homunculus into growth. In another context, people sometimes imagine the human brain as being like a control room with little TV screens and speakers and consoles and a little person—a homunculus, the "real you"—sitting inside the brain and making the decisions. The fallacy of the homunculus-in-the-brain idea is that it leads to an infinite regress, for what is inside the brain of the homunculus? A yet smaller homunculus? The same fallacy applies to the sperm or egg homunculi as well, with homunculi inside the homunculi's sperm or egg cells, and so on forever. Homunculi are a way of "begging the question," a way of avoiding the real issues of how specks of biological matter can grow into people or of how a glob of gray matter can form the concept, "I am." The personality seems to arise as a kind of external, polished-off, average result of all the brain's tiny processes, and, in the same way, a large business's (or country's) policies are more the result of very many parallel processes rather than being the result of the actions of any one individual.

APPLE: This is from John Barlow, a charismatic hippie who divides his time between the family ranch in Wyoming and a pied-á-terre on Potrero Hill in San Francisco. He writes lyrics for the Grateful Dead, is a contributing editor at *MONDO 2000,* and is currently working on a book called *Everything We Know Is Wrong* for Viking Penguin. It's about cyber-everything.

Apple took personal computing to the world under the auspices of a pair of acid-headed computer hackers, Steven Jobs and Steve Wozniak. The company long had a reputation for an eccentric and creative work environment and California-hippie undertones. This quote comments on the current state of affairs.

JOHN BORRUSO

CRACKERS

R. U. Sirius: Once there were computer hackers. These early pioneers of computing were fanatically dedicated to inventing and exploring how things worked. As part of the sixties generation, they were also prone toward being anti-establishment and somewhat disrespectful toward property rights. The early hackers were fond of breaking bureaucratic laws and regulations, particularly if they got in the way of learning something or doing something useful. Eventually a pair of these early hackers, Steve Wozniak and Steven Jobs, hacked together the first commercially successful personal computer, the Apple, and the computer industry was off to the races. The sixties-generation hackers flooded into the new industry and many quickly attained positions of wealth and authority. Most of them maintained a semblance of their early antibureaucratic attitudes but generally settled down to the task of creating the information/communications ecology that now dominates Western life.

Meanwhile two things happened. 1) A new generation of hackers emerged who were not yet part of the establishment. Like their predecessors, they were inventive, curious, and too smart to buy into dumb laws and bureaucratic regulations. As the earlier hackers were influenced by the idealism of the hippie and new-left movements, the new-generation hackers were influenced by the nihilism and alienation of the punk movement. 2) The world economic and social order went completely digital. And so CRIME went digital too.

It is somewhere at the interstices of the new generation of alienated young hackers (they sometimes refer to themselves as "cyberpunks") and the world of sometimes-organized crime that we locate the concept of the cracker. The term is, to some degree, an attempt by the now-established older-generation hackers to separate themselves from computer crime. The debate still rages as to what constitutes the difference between hacking and cracking. Some say that cracking represents any and all forms of rule-breaking and illegal activity using a computer. Others would define cracking only as particularly DESTRUCTIVE criminal acts. Still others would claim that the early hackers were EXPLICITLY anarchistic and that acts of willful destruction against "the system" have a place in the hacker ethos, and that therefore the term cracker is unnecessary and insulting.

ON THEFT OF INFORMATION

Information can't be stolen. Unless they've come up with something new, phenomenologically speaking. If I tell someone a fact, I still know the fact. Property laws were set up to handle tangible objects. We're dealing with raw data, information, the stuff of dreams. The whole system to handle "ownership" is obsolete. In a world where you can copy information, leaving the original intact, and wind up with the perfect copy, the debate over ownership is over.

ON THEFT OF INFORMATION: The following four entries are from Michael Synergy, a *MONDO 2000* associate editor. Aside from being a legendary ex(?)-cracker, Synergy holds down serious work in the computer industry. He's currently part of the team working on making IBM and Apple compatible.

ON BROWSING

I'm an information addict. When I crack into computers, I browse and read people's mail, papers, notes, programs, etc. I'm an inquiring mind and I want to know. This is a *real* issue. I want to learn and *they* want to impose "need to know" on everything.

ON THE DEBATE OVER THE TERMS "HACKER" OR "CRACKER"

The only difference is that one is employed. Or runs the company.

ON MONEY & COMPUTER CRIME

You know who was the most important president? Richard Nixon. You know why? Because he took us off the gold standard. Once upon a time, money in the bank had to be related to a real-world object. But suddenly the governor was removed. Money was just a bunch of bits and bytes in computers. Money became the first exploration into cyberspace (see "Cyberspace"). This is why the economy is messed up. This is why banks are messed up. This is why computer crime is growing exponentially. This is why the damage that can be caused electronically is so great. We stopped using reality as the "acid test" for what was represented in our machines.

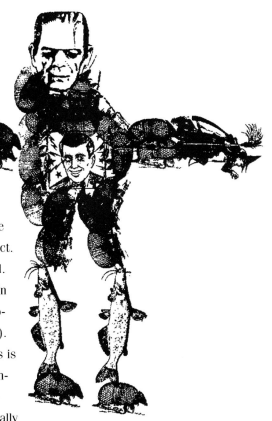

NO FINGERPRINTS

The more digital the society gets, the more we'll be able to completely change money. We'll be able to change a date on a document. We'll be able to add a figure to a bank balance. We'll be able to change a "no" to a "yes." How do you trace things like that? If you're a good programmer, there are no fingerprints.

THE MORE DIGITAL SOCIETY GETS: This comment is from a hacker/cracker who calls himself Emmanual Goldstein. Emmanual Goldstein of Orwell's *1984* was a legendary author whose forbidden book fueled the fires of discontent among the thought-criminals of Oceania. The real-life Goldstein edits *2600*,  the premier North American hacker journal.

THE ATM CRACK: TERMINAL DISORDERS

The banking industry has acted with almost criminal negligence when it comes to the security of their customers' ATM (Automatic Teller Machine) accounts. This is in the face of almost daily media coverage on the antics and depredations of cyberpunks. The industry's apparent nonchalance betrays a level of stupidity, at the highest levels of bank security, undreamt of by the average patron.

The banks have set themselves up for a wave of incredible losses. This is particularly true of the way data is handled at remote ATM terminals at the grocery stores and gas stations. If you use an ATM card, your bank account is particularly vulnerable at such terminals, as we shall soon see. And all ATMs are sitting ducks for the dedicated cybercracker.

Let's track the procedure for drawing money out of an ATM to observe the fatal flaw. First, the customer inserts his ATM card and is instructed to enter his "secret code," which is usually four to six characters long. This information is modulated by a modem and sent to the bank's computer, which checks the nineteen-digit card number and the four-to-six-digit PIN (Personal Identification Number) code. If a match is made, the machine asks how much cash is desired (or authorizes the purchase) and sends the central computer the details of the transaction. All this takes place through standard modem protocol with no attempt, at present, to encrypt the important details. Banks, while using more secure dedicated phone lines for their own ATM machines, have allowed many "convenience" locations for twenty-four-hour fast cash to spring up without making even a perfunctory bow toward security. The many gas stations and grocery stores with ATM card services are easy marks for tapping. If you have an ATM card which you use at any of these locations, your account information is out there for the asking.

THE ATM CRACK: TERMINAL DISORDERS: This is from a piece by Morgan Russell, a former *MONDO* editor who moved to Europe and has since sponsored various conferences on virtual reality (see "Virtual Reality" and like subjects). He lives in Transylvania, a fact which fits his general comportment perfectly. The piece originally came with a diagram that purportedly would have shown technically savvy people how to withdraw money from other people's ATM accounts. The editors decided not to publish it.

GLENN KIM

Silicon Valley Surplus in Oakland, California, advertised "Voice Response Terminals" in its Summer 1988 catalogue. Its ad copy states, "We got these from Crocker Bank as excess inventory when Wells Fargo bought them out. Brand new units still in the factory box!" "Only $9.99" (originally over $400) to own the same type of credit-card reader used by the banking industry for credit verification. Any enterprising cyberpunk can modify these devices into card-writers which produce credit cards with whatever numbers are desired. Simply put, Wells Fargo (or Crocker) released its supply of extra card-readers to Silicon Valley Surplus for approximately $5 apiece rather than have them collect dust—a somewhat less-than-brilliant move.

Security Pacific National Bank—a misnomer if ever there was one—lost nearly $350,000 over the Veterans Day weekend last year to someone using a special bank card. She only went to ATMs without surveillance cameras. She was never found.

ATM-cracking has even become a family activity. On February 4, 1989, the FBI arrested Mark Allan Koenig and a group of his friends and relatives for planning a large ATM job involving the Bank of America. One might imagine a close-knit, convivial group—a financial-affinity group—gathered around their IBM PC and a borrowed encoding machine. They must have looked like a bunch of kids working on a class project—with poster board, paper cutter, glue, and a roll of magnetic tape at the ready. And what a class project—a projected $7 to $14 million heist! Yet trouble came when a friend, asked to participate in the ATM outing, went to the Secret Service to inform them of her friends' plans. She then recorded a meeting of the group in order to set it up for a bust.

Both the $350,000 Veterans Day heist and the Koenig Plan relied on information and materials that aren't accessible to the ordinary individual without special connections. And the ATM companies appear

to be taking protective measures: "Plus Systems (a network linking 25,000 ATMs) plans new steps to ensure that contractors comply with procedures to protect secret account information," states the *Los Angeles Times* reassuringly. Yet while these financial groups are protecting data from people on the inside, any enterprising cyberpunk on the outside can knock off ATMs at any of 72,000 convenient locations twenty-four hours a day. Sleep well, citizens...

The average person doesn't bear the brunt of the loss. "Customers do not lose money from this type of fraud because they are reimbursed for any changes to their accounts," states Douglas Frantz of the *L.A. Times* in its account of the Koenig affair. Banks, eager to allay customer paranoia about the safety of accounts, have let it be known that they'll absorb any loss. This, of course, is the final detail which will send the wavering cyberpunk to the nearest salvage store—people have about as much sympathy for banks as they do for sharks. Poor babies!

Prosecution of the cyberpunks will do little to stem the tide. The information will become more widely known through newspaper accounts and court transcripts. As the banks scramble to change their security

MARK LANDMAN

measures, the cyberpunks' repertoire expands; it's like fighting a guerrilla army on its own terrain. Cyberpunks are precisely the ones best able to adapt to rugged field conditions and shifting game rules. They thrive on complexity. And there's nothing the average Joe can do but become a Luddite or refill his Valium prescription.

ACCESSING CREDIT INFO

There's this panic about hackers being able to access TRW…credit records. Everybody who subscribes to TRW can get your credit record. Everybody! *Every* employee at every company that wants to sell you things, people who want to sell you loans—they can *all* get your credit ratings.

ACCESSING CREDIT INFO: This one's from Rop Gonggrijp, Amsterdam's equivalent to Emmanual Goldstein and publisher of *Hack-Tic*  Rop and his compatriots in Amsterdam sponsor the Galactic Hackers Party and love to spook the media, as they did recently with a bogus entry into "Classified" NASA documents, shown live on *Geraldo*.

DIGITAL SKATEBOARDERS

John Barlow: I had been part of an on-line *Harper's Magazine* forum on computer hackers. In the course of this, I'd met these cracker kids from New York and elsewhere. They were young and brash, and there had been a kind of nasty symmetry that set itself up over the course of the conference between the old techno-hippies and these young sort of digital skateboarders. It culminated in one of them downloading my TRW file with my credit history—with the implication that he could change it if he wanted to.

OPERATION SUN DEVIL

The Internet Worm

November 1988: The Internet Worm runs wild across many of the nation's computer networks, shutting down an estimated 6,600 computers tied to Internet and causing an estimated loss of $40 to $90 million. The code, written by Robert Morris Jr., was intended to go around to every node on the net and report back in, so as to provide a map of the net. But, due to faulty code, it winds up reproducing itself at a phenomenal clip, eating up all the cyberspace in its path and closing many systems.

OPERATION SUN DEVIL: This timeline was compiled by R. U. Sirius and George Gleason.

Operation Sun Devil was the Secret Service name for a series of warrants and raids carried out over three days, most of them without any results. The agency had a big press conference over it, though, and tried to stir fear of hacker chaos into the hearts and minds of America. Over time, Operation Sun Devil has come to represent a series of vaguely interconnected busts, confiscations, and legal harassments that took place throughout 1990. The government action had an impact on crackers, hackers, and innocents, resulting in the formation of the Electronic Frontier Foundation (see "Electronic Freedom").

CRACKING 911

December 1988: Legion of Doom member "The Prophet" downloads a Bell South document on the administration of E-911 systems, and then posts it around bulletin board systems (BBSs) such as Jolnet. It reaches Knight Lightening, aka Craig Neidorf. Knight republishes it in his electronic magazine, *Phrack.*

CRACKING APPLE

June 1989: A group calling itself NuPrometheus League releases bits and pieces of Apple source code: the software equivalent of Macintosh DNA NuPrometheus promises more to come. Apple has the proverbial cow.

STRUTTING IN HARPER'S

December 1989: *Harper's Magazine* hosts a virtual hackers' conference on The WELL, a BBS whose members include a number of computer and communications industry pioneers. Hackers and cyberpunks of all stripes attend. The result is published as a cover story.

THE PHONE SYSTEM CRASHES

January 15, 1990: AT&T has a spontaneous near-death experience in the form of a nationwide system crash. Somehow a rumor circulates that a coven of hackers had cast the deadly spell, though AT&T denies it.

THE LEGION OF DOOM is a loose alliance of young computer hackers. The Legion's most eloquent spokesman calls himself The Mentor, and he published this manifesto in *Phrack:*

"This is our world now—the world of the electron and the switch, the beauty of the baud. We make use of a service already existing without paying for what could be dirt-cheap if it weren't run by profiteering gluttons, and you call us criminals. We explore—and you call us criminals. We seek after knowledge—and you call us criminals. We exist without skin color, without nationality, without religious bias—and you call us criminals. You build atomic bombs, you wage wars, you murder, cheat, and lie to us and try to make us believe it's for our own good, yet we're the criminals.

Yes, I am a criminal. My crime is that of curiosity. My crime is that of judging people by what they say and think, not what they look like. My crime is that of outsmarting you, something that you will never forgive me for. I am a hacker, and this is my manifesto. You may stop this individual, but you can't stop us all."

After the shock wave of Operation Sun Devil, several members of the Legion of Doom reemerged as a computer-security consulting team. Their ultraslick promotional photos show them looking like the Magnificent Seven—guns for hire.

PHRACK was an electronic magazine for people interested in computers and telecommunications. Most of the articles dealt with "system vulnerabilities," meaning ways in which one could hack into various computer installations or telephone systems. The name "Phrack" is a combination of the words "phone," "freak," and "hack."

MACINTOSH DNA: What makes the Apple Macintosh special is the fact that built into each machine is the special Apple software that controls the mouse, the screen-writing, and all the nice windows. Rather than putting this special software on a disk—which might be copied and used on potential Macintosh clones—Apple put its special software on a chip. This chip is called a ROM, for "read-only memory." You can read from it, but you can't write to it. IBM PCs and clones also have some special operating system software on a built-in ROM chip, but it is not so highly evolved, which is why IBM has clones and Apple doesn't. There is a sense in which the MAIN thing that Apple sells is the code on its ROM chips, and the thought of losing control of this code is enough to panic the company's managers. Some have compared them to dull, spoiled rich kids who panic over any threat to their inheritance.

THE WELL ▲ is the Whole Earth 'Lectronic Link, a computer network run by the *Whole Earth Review.* ▲ *Whole Earth Review* emerged out of Stewart Brand's *Whole Earth Catalog* ▲ but is not nearly as hippie-dippie as it sounds. It often deals with many of the same issues as *MONDO 2000*, albeit in a far different style. The WELL is the most intellectually stimulating computer network in the world. AND it holds a *MONDO 2000* conference.

to the **61** *New Edge*

THE BUSTS

January 24, 1990: Secret Service agents raid [Acid Phreak] and [Phiber Optik] (two of the more controversial participants in the above-mentioned *Harper's Magazine* conference), holding a gun to the head of Acid Phreak's twelve-year-old sister and confiscating all his electronic equipment, including CDs and a telephone answering machine. Though no charges are filed, Phreak and Phiber are interrogated on suspicion of having caused the AT&T crash and of being key members of the Legion of Doom.

February 2, 1990: Secret Service agents raid Len Rose, aka Terminus. Rose, his wife, and their child are terrorized at gunpoint, denied food and use of the bathroom. Calls to lawyers are denied, computers and other property are confiscated.

February 7, 1990: In the by-now-familiar gestapo style, the SS raids Robert Riggs ("The Prophet"), Franklin Darden ("The Leftist"), and Adam Grant ("Necron 99"). This time, an indictment charges various federal felonies—including fraud and conspiracy, involving taking copies of proprietary software and unauthorized entry into the Bell South computer systems—and specifically mentions the Legion of Doom.

February 15, 1990: Craig Neidorf, editor of the on-line magazine *Phrack* is raided, charged (among other things) with publishing the Bell South E-9ll document. His computers—in essence the electronic printing presses for his magazine—are confiscated, putting *Phrack* out of business. Bell South claims that the E-9ll document is worth over $79,000.

Late February 1990: Rich Andrews, operator of Jolnet, is visited by the Secret Service. Andrews's crime? Just to be on the safe side, he'd informed AT&T officials about the E-911 document that had appeared on his network. As a reward for his good citizenry, his computer equipment is confiscated. No charges are filed. Significantly, the computer also contains the electronic mail of uninvolved Jolnet subscribers, raising substantial privacy issues.

March 1, 1990: The SS raids [Steve Jackson Games] and its employees. Jackson is the second-largest game publisher (after Milton Bradley), has published numerous fantasy-role-playing games, and was about to launch one called GURPS Cyberpunk. ▲ The [SS confiscates computers] at Jackson's offices and employees' homes.

MORRIS GETS WHAT'S COMING TO HIM

May 4, 1990: Robert Morris Jr. is sentenced to a $10,000 fine and four-hundred hours of community service for unleashing the Internet virus.

ACID PHREAK AND PHIBER OPTIK: Crackers' love of the "ph" letter combination stems from their fascination with the telephone system. People who hack around with telecommunications often call themselves "phone phreaks."

STEVE JACKSON GAMES: In Steve Jackson's words: "The basic idea behind the Generic Universal Roleplaying System (GURPS) is that any role-playing game, regardless of genre, has a system for making decisions about how the characters behave in the game. There's a system for creating the characters and resolving various kinds of tasks—things like was the character successful at jumping across the ditch or whatever. Now each game system comes up with a different way of dealing with all this. I found this totally obnoxious. I realized that most games, regardless of the genre (fantasy, sci-fi, horror, etc.), need pretty much the same rules, so you could get that out of the way easily and start playing. So why not make one generic system of rules and a series of worldbooks that tailor those rules to specific genres?"

SS CONFISCATES COMPUTERS: The Electronic Frontier Foundation has entered a civil suit against the United States Secret Service, Secret Service agents Timothy Foley and Barbara Golden, Assistant United States Attorney William Cook, and Henry Kluepfel, on Jackson's behalf. As of this writing, the case is still pending.

OPERATION SUN DEVIL

May 9, 1990: The Secret Service and prosecutors in Phoenix, Arizona, announce twenty-eight new raids under Operation Sun Devil. In three days, twenty-eight search warrants are executed in fourteen cities; forty-two computers and twenty-three thousand disks are confiscated. Only four arrests are made. Most of the raids are targeted against credit code abusers and similar minor players. **C**

MICHAEL SWAINE

Cyberpunk

R. U. Sirius: Cyberpunk escaped from being a literary genre (see "Cyberpunk Science Fiction") into cultural reality. People started calling themselves cyberpunks, or the media started calling people cyberpunks. In fact, in the last six months, I've been labeled a cyberpunk on *CBS Night Watch* and *The Ron Reagan Show*, although I've never actually called myself a cyberpunk. The first people to identify themselves as cyberpunks were adolescent computer hackers who related to the street-hardened characters and the worlds created in the books of William Gibson, Bruce Sterling, John Shirley, and others. As we were going to press with our first issue of *MONDO 2000*, cyberpunk hit the front page of the *New York Times* when some young computer kids were arrested for cracking a government computer file. The *Times* called the kids "cyberpunks." From there, the performers involved in the high-tech-oriented radical art movement generally known as "Industrial" (see "Industrial/Postindustrial Music & Art") started to call themselves—or be called—cyberpunks, largely thanks to an article in *Electronic Musician* by Mark Dery. Turned out that most of the people involved in that artistic sensibility did, in fact, feel a rapport with the worlds created by Gibson & Co. Finally, cyberpunk has come to be seen as a generic name for a much larger trend more or less describing anyone who relates to the cyberpunk vision. This, in turn, has created a purist reaction among the hard-core cyberpunks, who feel they got there first.

Gareth Branwyn posted the following description of the cyberpunk worldview to general approval at a *MONDO 2000* conference on the WELL:

A) The future has imploded onto the present. There was no nuclear Armageddon. There's too much real estate to lose. The new battlefield is people's minds.
B) The megacorps *are* the new governments.
C) The U.S. is a big bully with lackluster economic power.
D) The world is splintering into a trillion subcultures and designer cults with their own languages, codes, and lifestyles.

MARK DERY is the hot new writer on the cyber scene. His writing appears regularly in the *New York Times* and *Rolling Stone*. He is currently at work on a book called *Cyberculture: Road Warriors, Console Cowboys and the Silicon Underground*. His regular column for *MONDO 2000* is called "Guerrilla Semiotics."

GARETH BRANWYN is the street tech editor for *MONDO 2000* (see "Street Tech") and the main editor of a HyperCard Stack (see "Hypertext") called "Beyond Cyberpunk."

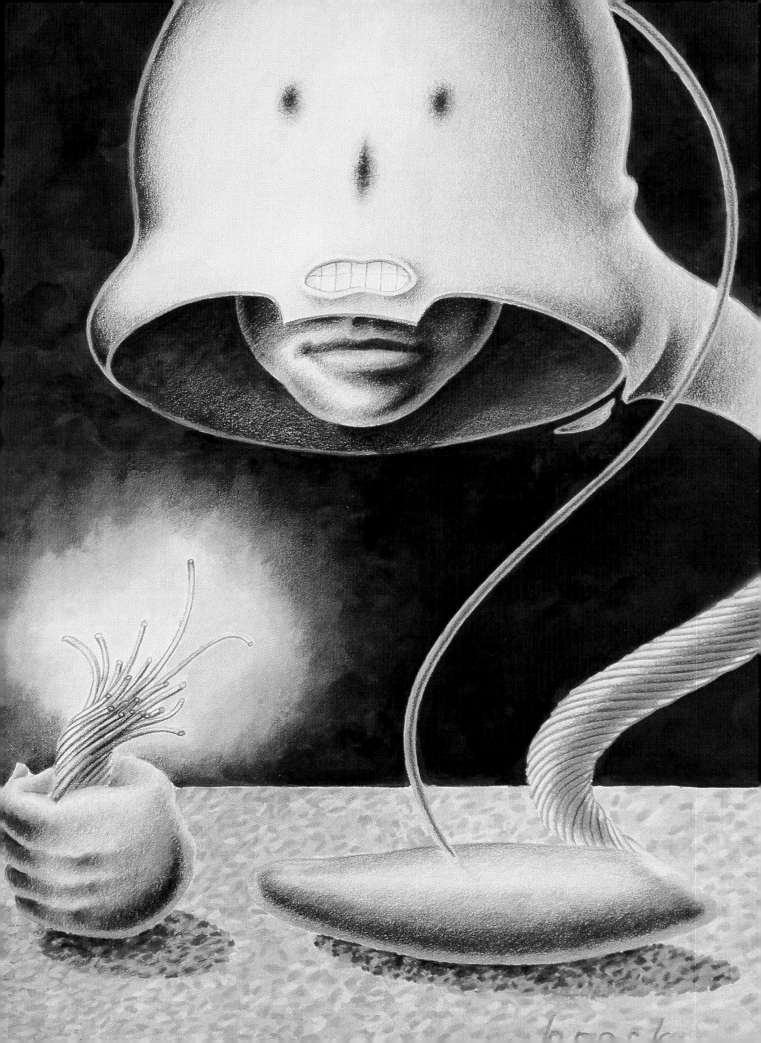

E) Computer-generated info-domains are the next frontiers.

F) There *is* better living through chemistry.

G) Small groups or individual "console cowboys" can wield tremendous power over governments, corporations, etc.

H) The coalescence of a computer "culture" is expressed in self-aware computer music, art, virtual communities, and a hacker/street tech subculture (see "Hackers" and "Street Tech"). The computer nerd image is passé, and people are not ashamed anymore about the role the computer has in this subculture. The computer is a cool tool, a friend, important human augmentation.

I) We're becoming cyborgs. Our tech is getting smaller, closer to us, and it will soon merge with us.

"CYBORG" is a science-fictional shorting of "cybernetic organism." The idea is that, in the future, we may have more and more artificial body parts—arms, legs, hearts, eyes, and so on. The logical conclusion of this process is that one might become a brain in a wholly artificial body. And the step after that is to replace your meat brain by a computer brain.

J) Some attitudes that seem to be related:
* Information wants to be free.
* Access to computers and anything which may teach you something about how the world works should be unlimited and total.
* Always yield to the hands-on imperative.
* Mistrust Authority.
* Promote Decentralization.
* Do It Yourself.
* Fight the Power.
* Feed the noise back into the system.
* Surf the Edges.

RELATED ATTITUDES: A few of these "attitudes" have time-traveled directly from the 1960s hacker's ethic as defined by Stephen Levy in his 1984 book *Hackers* (see "Hackers").

MICHAEL SYNERGY, CYBERPUNK

R. U. Sirius: Michael Synergy may be the first person I ever met who actually described himself as a cyberpunk. While the people around the Electronic Frontier Foundation are trying to gently reassure the body politic that the onslaught of information technology is *not* a threat to the stability of the system, Synergy will tell us that it *is* indeed an assault on all fronts. His message is simple: "Surrender!"

CYBPERUNK ANARCHY

In a recent computer-crime scandal, credit for the idea was given to John Brunner's Shockwave Rider. 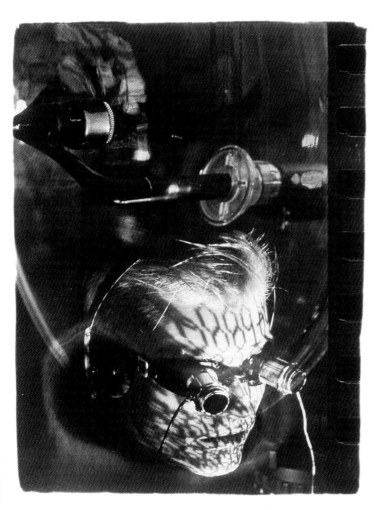 That's very encouraging to me. You could say that cyberpunk is intrinsically anarchistic. It's endlessly anti-authoritarian, and it can be employed like a weapon, like a computer virus, injecting new information by means of the existing mechanisms. The pop image of anarchism has always been a bomb—yeah, well, this is an ideological bomb that has been planted in the culture. I just saw a New York Times headline that used the term cyberpunk to describe a computer virus hacker—as if it were already part of the language. **C**

CYBERPUNK ANARCHY: This comment is from John Shirley, cyberpunk science-fiction writer. John was lead singer for a Portland punk band called Sado-Nation and cut his own album in France: Obsession by John Shirley, Celluloid Records, Alpha Presse. The word which best sums up Shirley's personality is "labile," as used by Samuel R. Delany in his classic ur-cyberpunk story "The Edge of Space." In biology, a labile cell structure is one which changes or breaks down very quickly when being examined. Delany uses it to mean rapid mood shifts sensitively attuned to the situational input. In person John Shirley initially comes on as wise, kind, and sweet—but he can break into wild ranting as easily as Axl Rose slips into falsetto. He has been known to lean into strangers' car windows and scream, "Have y'all ever ate any LIVE BRAIN?" Shirley's amazing early cyberpunk novel City Come a-Walkin' appeared in 1980. Another not-to-be missed Shirley book is A Splendid Chaos. (More from Shirley in "Cyberpunk Science Fiction," just below.)

SHOCKWAVE RIDER is the tale of a superbright young man who is able to plug into the Net and create himself new computer identities, credit records, etc. Though it has the cyber element, Shockwave Rider is not very punk, due to the fact that the main character has been brought up in a special school for cream-of-the-crop kids.

NEW YORK TIMES: John Markoff of the New York Times recently wrote a book with his wife about computer crime called Cyberpunk.

FRANK WIEDEMANN

WE MEANT IT

Read my introduction to **Mirrorshades.** I think it stands as the central public relations document for cyberpunk. Look, some people think we did this just to be cute. You know? They're wrong, very severely wrong. We meant it.

CYBERPUNK THEN AND NOW

When we first started cyberpunk, we really wanted to come in under the radar—out of this little science-fiction subculture—just knock people flat on their backs. And we really did it. Nobody could have foreseen the futures we imagined. Things have changed since the early days of cyberpunk and I, for one, am a lot more interested in the deep theoretical issues. Sure, I do stuff that's like MTV video, flash imagery—but with a sting in the tail. I want to get behind people's eyes. I want to get to the stage of knowledge as power.

TRANSCENDENCE IS JUST PART OF THE GIG

The element of transcendence is just a feature of the SF genre, like feedback in rock music. It's a move. Like I wrote a book—Schismatrix—that ends with a character attaining cosmic transcendence. He's eaten by an alien and becomes this pure spirit who gets to go around the universe and observe. It's just a riff. People who take that stuff seriously end up turning into trolls. H. P. Lovecraft was a big fan of that cosmic-type stuff. That may be okay for him, but from the outside what you see is this pasty-faced guy eating canned hash in the dim corner of a restaurant, hands trembly and a gray film over his eyes. Lovecraft was a sick old man who died young. A troll. You've got to remain equipped to deal with this world.

NEUROMANCER

What's most important to me is that *Neuromancer* is about the present. It's not really about an imagined future. It's a way of trying to come to terms with the awe and terror inspired in me by the world in which we live. I'm anxious to know what they'll make of it in Japan.

When you read *Neuromancer* the impression is very complicated, but it's all actually one molecule thick. Some of it is still pretty much of a mystery to me. You know, the United States is never mentioned in the book. And there's

MIRRORSHADES: from an interview with Bruce Sterling. Along with William Gibson, Bruce Sterling is the author most mentioned as one of science fiction's cyberpunks. Sterling's sporadically published magazine *Cheap Truth* had a lot to do with the birth of cyberpunk. As well as *Schismatrix,* other important Sterling books are his story anthology *Crystal Express* and his global epic *Islands in the Net.* Sterling also edited *Mirrorshades,* a big-selling anthology of cyberpunk science-fiction stories, available as a Bantam paperback. Writing about cyberpunk in the introduction to *Mirrorshades,* Sterling says, "An unholy alliance of the technical world and the world of organized dissent—the underground world of pop culture, visionary fluidity, and street-level anarchy, this integration has become our decade's crucial source of cultural energy. The work of the cyberpunks is paralleled throughout eighties pop culture: in rock video; in the hacker underground; in the jarring street tech of hip-hop and scratch music…"

NEUROMANCER: These next four comments are taken from an interview with William Gibson. The charming, wise, willowy William Gibson grew up near Roanoke, Virginia. In the sixties he moved to Toronto to dodge the draft. His wife supported him through the seventies as he learned to write the

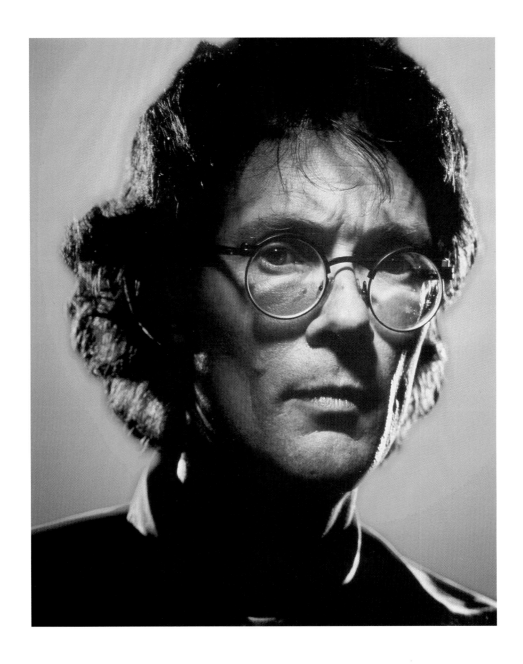

some question as to whether the United States exists as a political entity or if, in fact, it's been Balkanized in some weird way. That's kind of a favorite idea of mine, that the world should be chopped up into smaller pieces.

If there's a movie of *Neuromancer*, what I really want the special-effects guys to do is to make you see, from Case's point of view, the little acid giggies. I've never seen that in a movie. It'd be very easy to do with animation and so forth: the little lines and trails coming off of things.

hottest new science fiction on the scene, perhaps most notably the story which gives the title to Gibson's short story collection, *Burning Chrome*. 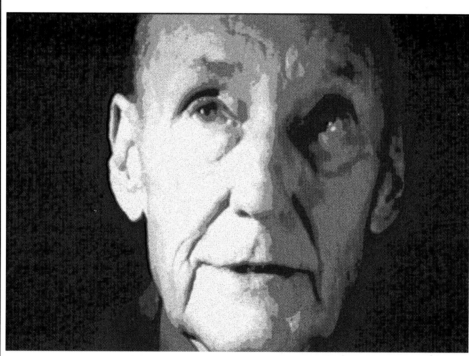 *Neuromancer* 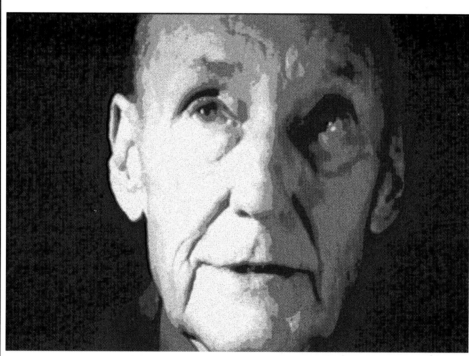 is *the* cyberpunk novel. When it came out in 1984, it won science fiction's equivalent of the Triple Crown: the Nebula Award, the Hugo Award, and the Philip K. Dick Award. Hollywood has been grinding away on plans for a film version for several years now.

BURROUGHS

I'm deeply influenced by Burroughs. I didn't think I'd be able to put that over on the American science-fiction people, because they either don't know who Burroughs is, or they're immediately hostile…he found fifties science fiction and used it like a rusty can opener on society's jugular. They never understood. But I was like fifteen when I read *Naked Lunch*, and it sorta splattered my head all over the walls. I have my megalomaniac fantasy of some little kid in Indiana picking up *Neuromancer* and POW! I had to teach myself not to write too much like Burroughs. He was that kind of influence. I had to weed some of that Burroughsian stuff out of it. In an interview in London, in one of my rare lucid moments, I told this guy that the difference between what Burroughs did and what I did is that Burroughs would just glue the stuff down on the page, but I airbrushed it all.

COUNT ZERO

At the end of *Neuromancer*, the entire Matrix is sentient. It has, in some ways, one will. And, as it tells Case, kind of matter-of-factly, it's found another of its kind on Alpha Centauri or somewhere, so it's got something to talk to. *Count Zero* starts seven years later, and like Yeats's poem about how the center wouldn't hold, this sort of God-consciousness is now fragmented. It hasn't been able to keep it together. So the voodoo cultists in the Sprawl, who believe that they have contacted the voodoo pantheon through the Matrix, are in fact dealing with these fragmented elements of this God thing. And the fragments are much more demonic and more human, reflecting cultural expectations.

COUNT ZERO: *Neuromancer* (1984), *Count Zero* (1986), and *Mona Lisa Overdrive* (1988) make up Gibson's "Sprawl trilogy." Each of them is loaded with cool things, though by the end of the third volume, some readers began to tire of Gibson's relentless bleakness. His recent *The Difference Engine* (with Bruce Sterling) is a sunnier look into an alternate past where steam-driven computers come to Victorian England.

KHYAL BRAUN

STERLING

Bruce Sterling is my favorite science-fiction writer. *Schismatrix* is the most visionary science-fiction novel of the last twenty years or so. Humanity evolves, mutates through different forms very quickly, using genetic engineering and biochemistry. It's a real mindfucker. When he first got it out and was getting the reviews back, he told me, "There are so many moving parts, people are scared to stick their heads in it." People will be mining that, ripping off ideas, for the next thirty years.

MARTHA GRENON

KHYAL BRAUN

THE ECLIPSE TRILOGY

John Shirley: I've been concerned for a while with the question of rebuilding ethical systems in a cultural vacuum. The *Eclipse* trilogy deals with a question that obsesses me: What makes a human being decide to stand up against some enormous, invincible political engine that most people quite sensibly shrink before? Try to define it, it becomes corny—but there's an endless passion built into some people, the necessity to act according to conscience. That keeps me from getting cynical.

Cyberpunk for me is both a protest and a celebration. Gibson and Sterling were already doing the celebration—although they showed the seedier sides of these things, they were also delighting in the surface textures of the hypercontemporary world. I went the next step and looked at the dark side more. I examined the political ramifications of the high-intensity manipulations of the media, subliminals, visual mind control, devices that can strip information from the brain or implant it into the brain. These have both wonderful and diabolical applications. I chose to write a warning in *Eclipse, Eclipse Penumbra, Eclipse Corona*, but I'm a great believer in the delights of technology.

ELECTRONIC TELEPATHY

In "Wolves of the Plateau" technology is a tool for the oppressed, a tool of subversion—electronic telepathy brings together the ultimate political cadre. The plateau actually is just a special frequency for people with brain-implanted chips—like an underground computer bulletin board, but on a quasi-telepathic level. I was one of the wolves, a long time ago; a much lower-tech version of criminal.

REVOLUTIONARY PARASITISM

We're seeing major alterations in the collective mind of our view of ourselves. The culture will be redefining itself constantly over the next thirty years, and cyberpunk deals actively with that redefinition. Mass culture. Ideally, we're trying to tap into its brain, live off the body, and redirect it a bit too. Call it "revolutionary parasitism." Of course, it's dangerous. People may sneer and say, you think you're redirecting it, but it's eating you, buddy. Maybe—we'll see. Of course we all want to soften the existential agony, have the money for a trained crew to roll the boulder up the hill for us, you know—we

THE ECLIPSE TRILOGY  is a detailed epic describing what would happen if the religious right took over the world. The scene where the tanks drive into Greenwich Village's Washington Square is not to be missed.

EMILY COHEN

"WOLVES OF THE PLATEAU" first appeared in *Semiotext(e) SF*. It can also be found in Shirley's short story anthology, *Heatseeker*. This volume features an admiring introduction by William Gibson that includes this cool quote: "Sometimes, reading Shirley, I can HEAR THE GUITARS, like there's some monstrous subliminal wall-o'-sound chewing at the edges of the text."

do have families to support—but some people can't help rebelling, can't acquiesce.

WHAT IS CYBERPUNK?

Rudy Rucker: What's really good about punk is that it's fast and dense. It has a lot of information. If you value information the most, then you don't care about convention. It's not "Who do you know?"; it's "How fast are you? How dense?" It's not, "Do you talk like my old friends?"; it's "Is this interesting?" So what I'm talking about with cyberpunk is something like this: literate SF that's easy to read, has a lot of information, and talks about the new thoughtforms that are coming out of the computer revolution.

Cyberpunk suggests that SF really can be about the world, and not just about the author's mind. For me, the best thing about cyberpunk is that it taught me how to enjoy shopping malls, which used to terrify me. Now I just pretend that the whole thing is two miles below the moon's surface, and that half the people's right-brains have been eaten by roboticized steel rats. And suddenly it's interesting again.

WHAT IS CYBERPUNK?: *MONDO* reprinted this Rudy rap from an issue of the academic literary magazine *Mississippi Review* 47/48, which can be found in university libraries. It's a good source for articles about and examples of cyberpunk. Some of it was reprinted, along with some new stuff, in *Storming the Reality Studio*, a book put together by the issue's editor, Larry McCaffery. *Storming the Reality Studio* is an excellent sourcebook on cyberpunk science fiction.

FREESTYLE

I'm friends with a lot of new science-fiction writers in San Francisco, like the Camper Van Beethoven of science fiction, Marc Laidlaw, who wrote a wonderful novel called *Dad's Nuke* and a beautiful new book about a science-fiction Tibet, *Neon Lotus.* There's Pat Murphy's *The Falling Woman*, Richard Kadrey's heavy, surreal *Metrophage*, and Michael Blumlein's dynamite bizzarro book, *The Movement of Mountains.* Not to mention Ferret's *Alligator Alley.* Laidlaw and I have been getting together and jamming on the idea of surfing. It's about facing the edge in the arena of the Pacific Ocean, and the only way to face the weird challenges is to freestyle. Surfers look

Here's a FREESTYLE quote from an ad in *Surfing* magazine: "Life on the edge measures seekers, performers, and adventurists." And here's Marc Laidlaw's freestyle rap off that: "There it is, Rude Dude. The Freestyle antifesto. No need to break down the metaphors—an adventurist knows what the Ocean really is. No need to feature matte-black mirrorshades or other emblems of our freestyle culture—hey, dude, we know who we are. No need to either glorify or castrate technology. Nature is the Ultimate. We're skimming the cell-sea, cresting the waves that leap out over the black abyss."

down on clone surfing, which is what cyberpunk is rapidly turning into. It's been done, and there's no point in imitating it. Freestyle is where you just hang out on the edge of what is happening, and it's happening so fast that you can't anticipate it...but your style takes over.

TRUE NAMES

I think there's a large set of tech ideas that *True Names* shares with cyberpunk stories. I also see two substantial differences between *True Names* and the stories that are usually called "cyberpunk." One: Cyberpunk shows more of future society's ugly underbelly. In some cases this is simply hard-boiled style. In some cases, it captures the pain of very fast social change. Two: Cyberpunk is often pessimistic about the possibility of social and technological change, which may, in fact, be a wonderful thing.

TRUE NAMES: This comment comes from an interview with Vernor Vinge, who is a professor of mathematics and computer science at San Diego State University, as well as being an accomplished science-fiction author. His novella, *True Names*, is often spoken of as "the first cyberpunk story," and is included in his anthology *True Names and Other Dangers*. ▲ *True Names* is about a group of computer hackers who meet in a virtual reality and play a game like Dungeons and Dragons. The virtual reality they meet in is based on the idea of a computer bulletin board, a central computer that users can dial into to leave and receive messages. But, as this is science fiction, the game becomes compellingly real. The title has to do with the fact that hackers usually use a pseudonym for their computer Net "handle": Phiber Optik, Acid Phreak, Fluffy Bunny Kisses, Mr. Goodbytes, Surfer Girl, and the like. To find out another user's true name is to gain a certain amount of power over him or her. (For more from Vinge, see "Evolutionary Mutations".)

EMILY COHEN

MAYBE I'M A CYBERPUNK

I'm interested in technology, but no more so than in etiquette or in what condemned prisoners want to eat before they go to the chair. To some extent my take on science is parodic, so it's funny to see people call me a cyberpunk writer. First of all, the term only makes sense when applied to a science-fiction writer—which I'm not, although there's a lot of scientific language and scientific issues in my work. But, if people talk about cyberpunk as a style that's very dense with information and very fast, then perhaps it does apply to me. Maybe I'm the first cyberpunk writer who's not a science-fiction writer.

MAYBE I'M A CYBERPUNK: Here's seven entries from an interview with Mark Leyner, author of the plotless but page-turning new book *My Cousin, My Gastroenterologist*. ▲ He is working on a new book, to be called *STEROIDS MADE MY FRIEND JORGE KILL HIS SPEECH THERAPIST: AN ABC AFTERSCHOOL SPECIAL.*

THE JABBERWOCKY OF SCIENCE

Using that elevated, exotic jargon creates an opportunity to use rhetoric in a way you don't usually encounter. When I say this hunk swaggers into the bar, and he's got a dick made out of corrosion-resistant nickel-based alloy that can ejaculate herbicides, sulfuric acid, tar, glue, and so on—I mean, just the sound of that lets you know this guy is one mean motherfucker!

It's this collision of different kinds of rhetoric—phallic rhetoric and the rhetoric of technology—that produces this bogus sense of power and authority. Their effect isn't much different—this hard-boiled, tough-guy lingo and scientific prose that's all no-nonsense and knows exactly what it's talking about. And when you have these things intersecting so you see them together, it's very funny.

THE FAST BURST THAT NEVER STOPS

There's a guitar solo Keith Richards did that I use as a model of what my work should be like. It's the guitar solo in "Sympathy for the Devil," where he creates this sharp, shiny, incredibly nasty violent burst. There's no lead-up to it—it's just suddenly there, like a rain of razors.

POETRY WASTES PAGE SPACE

I'd say that there isn't much of a difference between my work and poetry. The main differences are probably those of attitude. I avoid the smug, precious quality that poetry can have. Poets so often end up isolating their lines in the middle of the page without having any justification for sticking them there—except that they're writing "poetry."

I figured that if I had an 8 1/2 x 11" page, I should fill up the whole page. I want each page I write to be like a page of blotter acid my readers are ingesting. No white spaces. An overload of impressions that will do something to the readers after they're a couple of pages into it.

I won't settle for anything less than maximum, flat-out drug overkill.

THE JOY OF GASTROENTEROLOGY

Have you ever had a colonoscopic examination? They snake this fiber optic tube up through your intestines. It doesn't hurt—they give you Demerol and Valium in an IV—and they have a video camera on the end of this snake so you can watch the whole thing. It's a weird experience, lying there, high on Demerol and Valium, watching this TV screen with your intestines—probably the most introspective view of yourself you'll ever have. No kidding, you should have one done, even if you don't need it.

EMILY COHEN

THE TANG DYNASTY

The other day I was reading some Tang poets, Li Po and Tu
Fu, and I thought to myself, "I'm in the Tang dynasty," as in
people who have grown up drinking Tang, this simulated,
completely artificial orange-juice product. Pop culture is as much
a part of me as the color of my eyes. It's not like I'm making a choice
about whether or not to acknowledge it or comment on it. I'm literally
made of it. It is me.

I WANT TO BE MARCEL DUCHAMP

Duchamp would have this piece he was working on that he'd let dust collect on for several months—and then he'd let the dust formation become
part of the piece. Duchamp was personally elegant. He was very hand-
some and smoked his cigars in a
beautiful manner. He played and
wrote about chess. Mean-
while, he was making these
radically audacious ob-
jects—and making them
so well. The beauty and
precision of the way the
screws were set into his
constructions…

MARCEL DUCHAMP was a leading light of the Dadaist movement in modern art, which was
born in 1916 (see "Appropriation").

KYHAL BRAUN

So even though his works were formally daring and funny
and bizarre, they were unassailable because he had done them
so well. His work was profoundly troubling, even to people who hated
what he was doing, because its beauty and elegance couldn't be denied.

MAX HEADROOM IS A CYBERPUNK ROCKER

Cyberpunk has more to do with a way of thinking than with following a particular bible. It was only after writing the first three or four episodes of *Max
Headroom* that I actually read William Gibson's *Neuromancer*. And absolutely
erupted: "Great God! This is amazing! I'd give my right arm to be able to
write the stuff this man Gibson has written." I didn't know at the time who
he was. I didn't have a clue that it could wind up that he and John Shirley
and I were furiously writing in exactly the same style. It was in no
way derivative. It just seemed appropriate to the subject—all
of us by some kind of osmosis.

If there was a movement happening, this movement
appeared to be on autopilot. There was no organizing body

MAX HEADROOM: These words are from
Steve Roberts, who wrote the screen-
play for the original British version
of *Max Headroom*, and the
main body of the American
episodes.

Max Headroom was the
most amazingly cyber-
punk thing that's ever been
on network TV. Max started
out as an animated VJ for a
British music-video channel. In
order to introduce him, a short movie
of his creation was made. This is still
available in video stores and was also used
as the basis for the first episode of the U.S. TV
series *Max Headroom*.

promoting the concept of cyberpunk.
In terms of *Max Headroom*, it
seemed to be a way of addressing
social problems through entertainment.

It is, in fact, entertainment which
dares to be more than that. Entertainment
with all the corners filled in. I think that's
what a lot of cyberpunk writing is. And I just
hope to God that people will grasp this and
realize that this is what can be done for television. Television is the greatest cyberpunk invention of all time.

LET'S CALL IT QUANTUM SCIENCE
INSTEAD OF SCIENCE FICTION

The literature-art of any culture performs (popularizes) the science/philosophy of that epoch. Today's Science-Lit is the Word Processing of the Postindustrial Age. Quantum Linguistics. Einstein, Heisenberg, Planck, Bohr, and Fredkin faxed us the scary news. Who, among us, could handle it? It seems that the universe, from galaxy to atom, is made up of bits of very highly miniaturized units of data. These singular bit-izens of the galaxy are called Quarks. This fifteen-billion-year-old information array is literally an electronic telecommunication show. The universe is a bunch of digital programs running, running, running. There are no "laws." And no "orders." Evolution is programmed by algorithms which use the adjacent geometry of cellular automata recursion. The universe is evolving every second with or without you or me. There goes the von Neumann neighborhood! *C*

LET'S CALL IT QUANTUM SCIENCE: Who else could write the next three excerpts but Tim Leary? Tim Leary is still high and still together. He's written so many great books—some favorites are the multiplexed *High Priest*, ▲ the prison-break autobiography *Flashbacks*, ▲ and the heavy trip-guide *The Psychedelic Experience*. ▲ Tim recently published a well-received software package, Mind Mirror. ▲ His latest book is *Timothy Leary's Greatest Hits*. ▲

EDWARD FREDKIN did a lot of work with cellular automata in the sixties and seventies and eventually came to believe that the universe itself is a huge CA. A cellular automaton is a type of parallel, distributed computation—the image is of a multidimensional grid with a tiny computer at each node of the grid. Each little CA computer looks at the colors of its neighbor computers and adjusts its own color accordingly. Washes of color sweep this way and that...and it's a world. An interesting profile of Fredkin can be found in Robert Wright's book *Three Scientists and Their Gods*. ▲

VON NEUMANN: In the 1940s, John von Neumann helped build the Bomb and the Computer. Perhaps fearing that the human race might become extinct, he got interested in machine self-reproduction: the creation of robots which can build copies of themselves. At the time it was not clear if this was even theoretically possible. Working with mathematician and H-bomb guru Stan Ulam, von Neumann developed the idea of cellular automata as a model for a "toy universe" in which computations could live and reproduce. This led to a proof that robots really can build robot factories that make new robots, meaning that robot self-reproduction is possible. If you really want to find out about CAs, get hold of the CA Lab ▲ software.

CYBERSPACE

William Gibson: Cyberspace is a consensual hallucination that these people have created. It's like, with this equipment, you can agree to share the same hallucinations. In effect, they're creating a world. It's not really a place, it's not really space. It's notional space.

CYBERSPACE: Gibson invented the word cyberspace in *Neuromancer*, describing it with these phrases: "A consensual hallucination experienced daily by billions of legitimate operators, in every nation… A graphic representation of data abstracted from the banks of every computer in the human system. Unthinkable complexity. Lines of light ranged in the nonspace of the mind, clusters and constellations of data. Like city lights, receding." The dream of literally "plugging in" to a computer via a jack that goes into the back of your head is still science fiction. The trend in the nineties is to try to get a "plugged-in" feeling simply by using very advanced sound and graphics displays. Thus Gibson's "cyberspace" has permutated into today's "virtual reality," and in today's computer graphics circles the two words are used interchangeably. (For much more, see "Virtual Reality.")

IN THE WIRES

John Barlow: Cyberspace is where you are when you're talking on the telephone.

TALKING ON THE TELEPHONE: Cyberspace might be construed as all digitally mediated space. As Michael Synergy says in our section on crackers, money was the first thing to move into cyberspace. It has no material reality, existing as information, as bits and bytes in a data base. Although "virtual reality" is used interchangeably with the term "cyberspace," it's really only mimicking the notion of cyberspace.

MARK LANDMAN

DECONSTRUCTION

DECONSTRUCTION: These bon mots are from an interview with deconstructionist cultural critic Avital Ronell. What is deconstructionism? Deconstruction is the program of taking texts or cultural phenomena and trying to see what they are really saying in a social, political, and sexual context. In practice, deconstruction is performing art, a process of systematically breaking set and setting to violate people's expectations, a bit like Dada, a bit like stand-up comedy. Avital Ronell is the author of *The Telephone Book*,  a textual hip-hop mix. Her parents migrated from Germany to Israel to the United States, which brought Avital here in time for her formative school years.

I SEEM TO BE A MACHINE

The question of how to bracket "life" is considerably complicated by the itinerary of the computer virus. The degree to which we borrow traits or features of computing machines is more impressive than the opposite kind of argument that is frequently made—will machines imitate us? The very notion of having a breakdown, of a nervous sort, is borrowed from early technology—a machine that breaks down. What interests me is our immense capacity for borrowing structures, for taking them out on lease, on loan. I notice that students "click in" to things, or "delete." They're perfectly capable of reproducing the mechanisms of the machines with which they are intimate.

SCIENCE FICTION

The promise of science fiction is that it does try to invent the future in a way that very few other modes of articulation are capable of doing. And, even though it might not be able to create the conditions for certain projected futures, it dramatizes the effort to break from a servile relation to the past.

THE TELEPHONE

The telephone is exemplary, first because it's just there to operate as a part of the technological will-to-power, but also because it won't permit you to unfold a simple history around it. It

Avital Ronell

BART NAGEL

resists any kind of smooth unfolding, interrupting as it does, screaming for immediate responses.

Is the telephone an object? Is it an artwork? Is it a replicant or some sort of celestial monstrosity that has connectivity to a voice that's absent, a disembodied voice, a godlike intrusion?

The fear or alarm that attends each call is always a return to the knowledge of our finitude. That's the telephone's alarm: It is like a death knell. But, the telephone also participates in a certain dialectic that [Jacques Lacan] associated with love. You are always expecting love and yet when it comes, it's always a surprise attack. Sudden, shocking, it was meant to be, yet it is a chance encounter. I also noticed that the telephone has re-oedipalized us. One is always calling home, one is always attached to this umbilicus. Contact with the other may be disrupted, but the break is never clean.

JACQUES LACAN is a deconstructionist psychiatrist. One of his most remarkable inventions was "the short session," in which a person shows up for the hour of psychotherapy he or she has paid for and only gets five minutes—a brilliant con which gave Dr. Lacan more time to deconstruct.

STATIC

There was always static, but there are certain ways in which it has been thematized. In terms of a kind of scientific history, static is a place around which all great discoveries of the twentieth century are organized. Static is the whole other side to organized sound.

Static has this wonderful semantic range of meaning. I'm sure that's where [Public Enemy and L.L. Cool J] and others come in. There's an interference with a master discourse. They're jamming the codes. That kind of parasitic noise or random eruption has always been a constituent part of language, but a part that's been kind of obliterated. I remember when I was a teenager, "don't give me any static" meant "just comply" in a kind of smooth obedience. Always, as you know, bad neighborhoods were linked with noise, and they still are.

When I came to this country I lived in bad neighborhoods, and the telephone was a way of being off the streets and of bypassing street dialectics. **D**

PUBLIC ENEMY AND L.L. COOL J: PE has been making heavy-duty intelligent rap for several years now. Recently they were in trouble for an MTV video showing their leader, Chuck D, car-bombing the governor of Arizona, the only state unwilling to honor Martin Luther King Day. Video is getting so decentralized that people like radical musicians can actually have some influence over it, which is great. L.L. Cool J is a rapper who's been around even longer than Public Enemy. His name stands for Ladies Love Cool James.

THE MUSIC OF DNA

In the past few years, molecular biologists have discovered that a major fraction of DNA is composed of repeating sequences. Dr. David Deamer, a molecular cell biologist at UC Davis, and Riley McLaughlin, a synthesist, have developed a system for translating these sequences into music. By assigning musical notes to each of the four bases, they have found that various DNA templates resound with the cosmic boogie of the human biocomputer.

What is the sound of the genetic code? It depends on the source of the DNA. Cow DNA has a repeat of twenty-three bases and gives a lilting feeling when played. A bacterial clone features a clear melodic riff derived from its simple five-base repeat. And a three-hundred-base sequence found in human DNA produces a beautiful melody in a distinctive waltz signature. *D*

THE MUSIC OF DNA: *DNA Suite* ▲ is a collaboration between Deamer and McLaughlin. *DNA Music* ▲ is a solo work by McLaughlin.

DNA stands for deoxyribonucleic acid. As is well-known, a DNA molecule has the shape of a double helix, which looks like a long, twisted ladder or zipper. The nucleus of each of our body cells contains forty-six chromosomes, and each chromosome is thought to contain a single DNA molecule that is about SIXTEEN INCHES long! (They're VERY thin and VERY wadded up.)

The Human Genome Project, currently under way, hopes to get a complete map of the billions of chemical parts to be found in a strand of DNA.

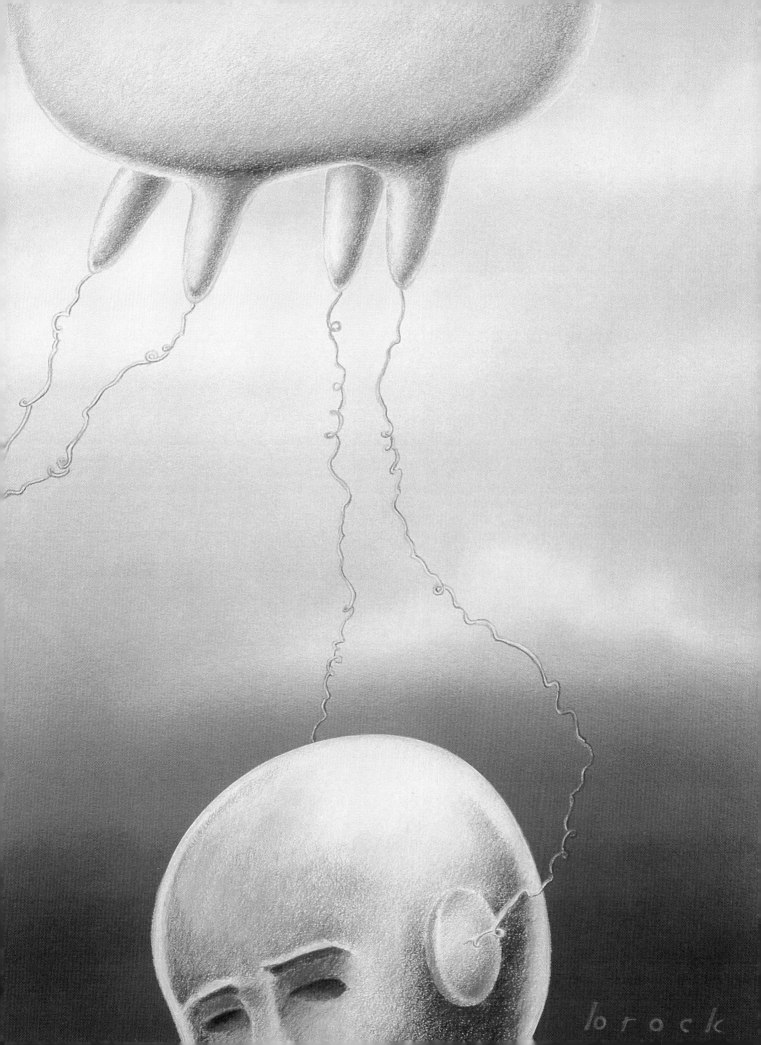

LEARNING TO LOVE COMPUTERS AND DRUGS

Timothy Leary: It's one of the great ironies of history that I was invited to Harvard in 1960 because they wanted someone to institute some innovative changes. At that time I was a very straight-arrow, narrow-minded person. I was very much against computers because, at that time, computers were mainframes that cost millions of dollars and were owned by Bell Telephone Company, IBM, CIA, Department of Motor Vehicles…no friends of mine! So I had this prejudice that computers were things that stapled you and punched you and there were these monks, the few experts, who controlled it. I was also very much against drugs at the time. This was just the period that tranquilizers were coming in, we vaguely knew that the CIA had spent twenty-five million dollars doing research on LSD, and you know how, in WWII, they used sodium amytol to get people to confess things. So I thought of drugs as another invasion of privacy and personal integrity by the system. I was totally wrong, of course, on both aspects. Personal computers and recreational computers, personal drugs and recreational drugs, are simply two ways in which individuals have learned to take power back from the state. I've learned so much about drugs and the brain from working with a personal computer. I see that to get the computer to give you a certain reality, you have to know how to activate it. There is a code. In this sense, I find it useful right now to think of drugs as access codes to open up dimensions of the brain that you want to use, either as furniture or to create your new reality.

BRAIN BITS

I don't see how you can use psychedelic drugs and not want to talk in electrons. Anyone who's had profound LSD experiences knows that the brain operates in clusters of flash on/offs, the so-called vapor trails. The clarity of atomic vision you get when you're very high on LSD or peyote or psilocybin is a sheer tuning in to the way the brain actually operates…holograms of clusters of individual bleeps and on/offs.

CARNIVAL BLAST OR EXCESS?

I believe that the human biocomputer occasionally wants a big kind of carnival blast. And I think that precisely controlled excess is absolutely necessary for sanity. On the other hand, excess which leads to too much grossness, loss of dignity, or, certainly, offense to anyone else, is to be deplored…but to be forgiven.

PISS WARS

George Bush volunteered to be one of the first Americans to take a urine test for drugs. During the Iran-Contra investigations, however, Bush refused to take a lie detector test. As Paul Krassner astutely commented, it appears Bush doesn't want us to know whether he's telling the truth or lying, but he wants us to be sure he's not stoned while doing it.

HOW GREEN WAS MY VALLEY

A friend in Silicon Valley recently told me there is a ton of grass smoked every day in that area. I couldn't believe it at first, but he worked it out on his computer and showed me. The population is four million. Assuming only half of them smoke grass and they smoke only one joint a day, one comes out with a ton of

PISS WARS: These next two excerpts are from Robert Anton Wilson, best known for his conspiracy-theory *The Illuminatus Trilogy*. Why is there an eye on the pyramid on the dollar bill? Is it true that all U.S. presidents save Jack Kennedy have been Masons? His books, stories and essays are invariably a freewheeling ride of hip, worldly chuckles, with the odd blinding blast of ultimate transcendental revelation. With Rudy Rucker and Peter Lamborn Wilson (no relation), Robert Anton Wilson edited the most outrageous science fiction anthology ever: *Semiotext(e) SF.*

PAUL KRASSNER achieved notoriety for his sixties pulp-paper magazine *The Realist*, which featured such still-unsurpassed outrages as a description of Lyndon Johnson copulating with the wound in JFK's neck and, best of all, a centerfold poster of all the Disney creatures indulging in drugs and sex. Huey, Dewey, and Louie sniggeringly point at the exposed genitalia on Daisy Duck's proud rear curve. And Daisy's unprintably obscene genitalia are: A SINGLE BLACK DOT. Krassner is still around, and he still has a bad complexion and a bad attitude, and he recently began publishing *The Realist* again.

weed, and a heavy fog of cannabis vapor circulating "in the belly of the beast." Most of the companies in Silicon Valley are unwilling to institute Piss Wars. They know if they did, they'd lose their most talented, diligent, and inspired software experts immediately. The modern "barbarians"—the cyberpunks —are not only within the gates, but have penetrated the Citadel itself.

CYBERPUNK is an elastic word, with many meanings. Here, Wilson is using it to express the idea of a computer programmer who is NOT the stereotypical "nerd" or "geek" but is rather a culturally aware and totally happening individual. New programmer: "Do I have to pee in a cup to work here?" Manager (laughing): "What for? If you're clean we don't want you."

DRUG WARS

Avital Ronell: I am interested in the links between the electronic and drug cultures, in part because drugs constitute a place of nonknowledge. As such, it has always attracted the crudest interventions. It occurs to me that we may need superior forms of drugs, superior hallucinogenres.

In a society that is cracking down on all these hallucinogenres, isn't this society going to show hostility and aggression toward all inventions of fiction and hallucination? The drug war is part of our whole puritan history of a war against artifice. It is very complicated and needs to be thought out, because at the same time we are addicted to oil, which is another type of substance, linked to our equipmental drive.

ALCOHOL

Baudelaire said that alcohol was a way to work your phantoms, to make them vanish or emerge, and you have to ask yourself: Whom are you drowning in your alcohol? Whom are you preserving in alcohol? So for Baudelaire, intoxication was hard work, and it was linked to the mnemonic apparatus. Intoxication has something to do with thinking in the mode of memory banks. **D**

ELECTRONIC FREEDOM

ELECTRONIC FRONTIER FOUNDATION

The Electronic Frontier Foundation's John Perry Barlow

The advent of personal computers and modems, coupled with the immense penetration of the telephone network, threatens the hegemony of the government/corporate paradigm by empowering millions of individuals. In the nineties, thanks to desktop communication, it is no longer necessary to "publish" "revolutionary" documents in the old sense of the word. Information can be propagated across thousands of miles in all directions in a matter of moments, and it can't be stopped, short of dismantling the entire telephone system. This genie can never be put back in the bottle. But that hasn't discouraged the Enforcement Community from doing its saurian best to try.

Acting on requests from certain corporations, the FBI and the Secret Service— armed with vaguely worded warrants—have raided businesses and homes of private citizens and seized tremendous numbers of computers and related items, with very few corresponding arrests. The language on the warrants was vague, because even in the rare case when the government knows what it's looking for, on the electronic frontier, it probably has no idea what it's looking *at*.

Enter the Electronic Frontier Foundation, formed by Mitch Kapor and John Barlow. Their alliance began with an arguably pointless act: Someone, probably an employee of Apple computer, "liberated" a relatively minor piece of Macintosh operating code and sent it, over the signature of "NuPrometheus League," to a number of industry figures. Mitch Kapor, founder of Lotus Development Corporation, was one of the lucky recipients. Kapor immediately inferred that the mysterious floppy was nothing more politically significant than an attempt to infect his computer with a virus and sent it back.

ELECTRONIC FRONTIER FOUNDATION: This fine piece of work is from David Gans, author of the recent book *Conversations with the Dead*, ▲ about the Grateful Dead, as well as a book about the Talking Heads. His celebrated "Deadhead Hour" radio program is syndicated all across the U.S.

The EFF's "Mission Statement": A new world is arising in the vast web of digital, electronic media which connect us. Computer-based communication media like electronic mail and computer conferencing are becoming the basis of new forms of community. These communities without a single, fixed geographical location comprise the first settlements on an electronic frontier.

While well-established legal principles and cultural norms give structure and coherence to uses of conventional media like newspapers, books, and telephones, the new digital media do not so easily fit into existing frameworks. Conflicts come about as the law struggles to define its application in a context where fundamental notions of speech, property, and place take profoundly new forms. People sense both the promise and the threat inherent in new computer and communications technologies, even as they struggle to master or simply cope with them in the workplace and the home.

The Electronic Frontier Foundation has been established to help civilize the electronic frontier; to make it truly useful and beneficial not just to a technical elite, but to everyone, and to do this in a way which is in keeping with our society's highest traditions of the free and open flow of information and communication.

John Barlow didn't receive a floppy disk from NuPrometheus, but because he attended the fifth Hackers Conference in October 1989, he *did* receive a visit from an FBI agent regarding NuPrometheus. Investigating Agent Baxter evinced a woefully inadequate grasp of the matter he was investigating.

"He referred to them as the New Prosthesis League," Barlow told the first EFF assembly, who howled with laughter. "He was looking for something called ‘the ROM Code.’ He didn't know what a ROM chip was, he didn't know what code was, he didn't know whether it had been stolen or what exactly had happened to whatever it was.

"And I realized that what we were looking at was a microcosm of a whole set of things that could begin to happen with government and society and computers. And it was just a little pinpoint of future shock that was going to blow up into something big and ugly if we weren't very careful about how it got managed.

"A few days later, I found out that this process was well under way in the Secret Service," Barlow continued. "They had come up with something called Operation Sun Devil, and they were breaking into the homes of teenage kids, rousting them up in the middle of the night, coming in with guns, sledgehammers and, I assume, no more knowledge of the situation

To that end, the Electronic Frontier Foundation will:

1. Engage in and support educational activities which increase popular understanding of the opportunities and challenges posed by developments in computing and telecommunications.

2. Develop among policy-makers a better understanding of the issues underlying free and open telecommunications, and support the creation of legal and structural approaches which will ease the assimilation of these new technologies by society.

3. Raise public awareness about civil liberties issues arising from the rapid advancement in the area of new computer-based communications media. Support litigation in the public interest to preserve, protect, and extend First Amendment rights within the realm of computing and telecommunications technology.

4. Encourage and support the development of new tools which will endow nontechnical users with full and easy access to computer-based telecommunications.

The Electronic Frontier Foundation
One Cambridge Center
Cambridge, MA 02142
(617) 577-1385

THE ROM CODE: Once again, what makes the Apple Macintosh special is the fact that built into each machine is the special Apple software that controls its many functions. Apple put its special software on a chip.

JULIA COLMENARES

than Agent Baxter had when he showed up at my home in Pinedale, Wyoming."

The Electronic Frontier Foundation began when Kapor, after reading an article Barlow had written (on the WELL computer network) about his visit from Agent Baxter, visited him in Wyoming one afternoon. "We realized that this wasn't so much a planned and concerted effort to subvert the Constitution," said Barlow, "as the natural process that takes place whenever there are people who are afraid and ignorant, and when there are issues that are ambiguous regarding constitutional rights.

"Whenever there's a new medium, there's always a struggle to find out whether the Constitution is going to apply to that medium, whether or not the First Amendment will apply. There's now a struggle under way to find out whether free speech can be expressed in bytes and bits. And that's basically what the Electronic Frontier Foundation is about.

"We're looking at a whole range of things dealing with future shock, the anxiety of society at large toward computers, the particular anxiety of society at large toward hackers, and what I like to call the learning curve of Sisyphus—which is what happens when you've got a technology that develops faster than anybody's ability to learn it."

THE FBI: LOST IN CYBERSPACE

Mitch Kapor: When you have a powerful force like the FBI with a charter and a history and they're fundamentally lost—they don't understand the territory they're in at all—it's a recipe for disaster.

BEYOND UNIX WEENIES

We think it's really important to do something about improving people's access to the public network. Electronic mail and conferencing has substantially expanded the scope and reach of our contacts and our community. There's one catch. You kind of have to be a Unix weenie to be able to use those particular tools to full capacity. We need to lower the barriers to entry and let ordinary folks participate in this worldwide discussion. **E**

ELECTRONIC MAIL, called "email" for short, is one of the most popular new methods of communication. To use email, you need a modem, and then you need access to the Net. Some ways in which people get the Net are by (1) working for a company which maintains a computer network of its own or (2) being a subscribing member of some commercial computer network like the WELL or CompuServe, or (3) using a local bulletin board that has access to the other Nets. A modem is a separate box or (cheaper and just as good) a card that you put inside your computer. Your modem will have two phone jack sockets. You unplug your phone and run a wire from the modem to the phone's wall jack, and (so that you can still use it) you plug your phone into the modem's other jack. Then you use some communication software to make your computer dial up the number of the business, computer network, or bulletin board that you use to access the Net. Once someone—call him "jack"—is on the Net, he can "send" a message to somebody simply by typing in her email address (typically something simple like jill@hill.com) and the message. The Net then moves this message over to a place where jill can find it, and when she logs on she will see something like "Mail for you from jack@well.sf.ca.us."

She can then read jack's message and send him a message back. It usually takes some time (a few minutes to a day or so) for the messages to get through, so jack doesn't sit there waiting for his response. He logs off email, does something else, then later checks back. An important thing to grasp about email is that it is NOT usually instantaneous, it is just a way of getting and sending messages without having to use paper or stamps. One of the big dangers with email is the dreaded "flame." This happens when you type in some furious message and send it to someone (or to twenty people, which is just as easy) and then calm down and realize you shouldn't have said all that. Sometimes this provokes a further flame in response, and a flame war occurs. The problem is sharpened by the fact that as soon as you have finished typing the message it is (unless you are cautious) already automatically sent. Unless you have good impulse control, there is no such thing as printing it out and looking at it in the morning. Knowing all this, hackers apply a lowered standard of what is acceptably polite conversation. "The way to deal with flames is to grow thick scales," as the saying goes.

UNIX WEENIES: Unix is the language which you use to talk to most large computers. Those not enamored of the somewhat prissy and fiddling language call it Weenix, and by extension Unix hackers become Unix weenies.

R. U. Sirius: In the LITERAL sense, most people who now play music play ELECTRONIC music. But the term "Electronic Music" harks back to a time when the use of electronics to create music was novel and avant-garde. The first electronic musical instrument was invented by an American associate of telephone inventor Alexander Graham Bell, Elisha Gray. In 1874, Gray invented a keyboard with enough single-tone transmitters to play an octave.

Modern electronic music is generally regarded as having emerged out of the advent of early computer-based sound synthesizers. The attitude of electronic musicians evolved out of the experimental attitudes of John Cage. The goal is not necessarily to produce a pleasant or emotionally moving piece. Electronic musicians experiment with sound as a concept using the technology of the times.

JOHN CAGE is the dean of American avant-garde music. His major contributions were in suggesting that we listen to *everything* as music and the idea of chance operations—creating music by games of chance.

VALIS

The Pompidou Center asked me to work on a project combining image and sound. I decided to do an opera. I wanted technology to be a major element in making the opera—from the scenery to the staging to the music. I also wanted the opera to be about technology. I'd read some Philip K. Dick, but I'd never read *Valis*. I decided to look through some of his books for ideas. I happened upon *Valis* in a Parisian bookstore. I read the liner notes and the first few pages, and it not only resonated, but it was just what I wanted to work on.

VALIS: The following three entries come from an interview with Tod Machover, who is a professor of music and media at M.I.T. Machover is best known for his opera version of Philip K. Dick's book *Valis*,  which featured a new instrument called the "hypercello."

Inside the remarkable POMPIDOU CENTER for Art in Paris is IRCAM (Institut de Recherche et Coordination Acoustique/Musique), run by the French composer and conductor Pierre Boulez.

REACTING TO INFORMATION

One of my obsessions has always been of living in a world which is becoming increasingly more complex and fragmented—where we have access to more and more information. There are three different levels of reacting to this.

The consumer level is to buy loads of CDs, change channels, and so on. You don't have to do any work on your own. It's easy to understand all this information just by letting it into your house. That's a frightening way of facing the situation, because it's superficial and dishonest. We'll find ourselves more isolated. The aspects of virtual reality

Opposite page: Astrophysicist Fiorella Terenzi in space, by Bart Nagel

which free individuals from trying to understand or communicate with one another scare me quite a bit. I think that every system we build and every art form we create should allow us to reach out to other individuals.

The second level of reacting to all this complexity is to wake up and say, "Oh my God, this is so fragmented and complex I don't know what to do!" This entails being initially overwhelmed by the totality of the information but mistakenly believing that it can all be absorbed and understood in a quasi-mystical sense. Someone in this situation can write thousands of pages of text trying to theorize how bits of information theory, psychological and religious theories could somehow fit together into a coherent theory of the universe. A maddening and fruitless pursuit!

The third reaction to the world's fragmentary complexity is to try to dig deeper, to find principles of similarity that begin to reveal the profound connections between things. This, I believe, is the great ethical task of our times and is the question—and quest—posed by *Valis*.

HYPERINSTRUMENTS

My most recent project is a piece called *Being Again Again...* for hypercello. I composed this for Yo-Yo Ma, and he premiered the piece at the Tanglewood Festival this summer. Part of the excitement of this project was extending hyperinstrument technology. For example, we had many sensing devices especially built to measure the refined and sophisticated technique of cello performance.

MUSIC FROM THE GALAXIES

Music From the Galaxies is the first experiment in transforming radiation from celestial objects into sound. Radio waves coming from a celestial object are very similar to musical notes. Both have an intensity that gives you loud or soft sound. They also both have a frequency that gives you high or low pitch. Instead of looking at photos of stars, I wanted to try to play the universe—the sound of radiation coming from a celestial object. I chose UGC6697.

HYPERINSTRUMENTS: "Gesture" is what musicians call the nuances of performance that are unique and subtly interpretive—that come from plucking a string or stroking a bow. Gesture is what most electronic music lacks utterly.

Tod Machover's "hyperinstruments" are designed to augment sound with such idiosyncratic nuances as to give it human expressiveness and a rich, live sound. To make a hyperinstrument, take a traditional instrument, say a grand piano, and hook it up through a light-sensor monitor to send digital data about the key-motions to a computer. Now equip the piano with a set of solenoids under the keys. When the digital data is played back, the keys duplicate the original performance, right down to the accentuation. So far you've got the ultimate player piano.

But it doesn't just replicate timbre, tone, rhythm, and phrasing—it memorizes these data and allows them to trigger other musical events. Extrapolate from this and you've got an instrument that can be its own smart accompanist.

MUSIC FROM THE GALAXIES: The next three entries are from an interview with Fiorella Terenzi, who studies music composition and operatic singing at Milan's Conservatorio di Musica Giuseppe Verdi. She is also a professor of mathematics and physics at Licio Scientifico in Milan. Her first album, *Music From the Galaxies*, on Island Records, combines her twin passions for music and astrophysics.

UGC6697

UGC6697 is very complex. It's a spiral galaxy. It's really powerful. It has a strong emission, and it's really far away—one hundred eighty million light years. There's a small satellite companion galaxy spinning around it. The two galaxies collided, and that
created the complexity you hear in its sound. I chose it for this complexity. Also because the data was available. At the beginning I was
thinking of using a pulsar. A pulsar is a star that pulses every second
or maybe every millisecond. It sends a precise signal in time. Next time
I'll use a pulsar because I want a cosmic drummer for my composition.

OR USE YOUR FM

When you're tuning your FM radio, you get a wah-wah sound. You're shifting between electromagnetic waves, so it's very similar to the sound
of the galaxy.

MUSIC COMES FROM A CULTURE'S MACHINERY

About twenty-five years ago, some friends of mine in the Village were kicking around a notion about the correlation
between sounds and music styles—like country music, it's
horseback music. It has the kind of feel you get on a horse.
Bluegrass is cylinder piston engine music. That's why it
works so well in the *Bonnie and Clyde* chase scene—you can
hear the motors running. The sounds of Frank Sinatra and
the crooners of the forties are the sounds of a big TWA Super
Constellation with the motors going. And then the Beatles came
out. It was like jet sounds, like a jet engine revving up.

DESKTOP MUSIC PUBLISHING

The dance communities really embraced the new technology first,
because it's become cheap enough for a kid to go out and buy enough
stuff to be able to produce a record in his living room.

It isn't the college community that started on this. It came from
the streets. Kids had to keep up with the new sound, techno, so
they just took over the technology. The majority of dance
music is being written in people's living rooms, like our
whole album was.

We have a Casio SV-1 sampler. And it has
eight tracks so you can like mix them right out
if you have a mixer and a computer. We use a

UGC6697: Galaxies are assigned numer-
ical names according to their listing in the
Universal Galactic Catalog. Thus,
UGC6697 is the 6697th galaxy listed.

MUSIC COMES FROM A CUL-
TURE'S MACHINERY: This
observation comes from musician Roger McGuinn. In 1965,
Roger McGuinn and the Byrds
exploded onto the pop scene with one
of the most harmonically rich and instantly
identifiable ensemble sounds of twentieth-
century music. This year's comeback album,
Back From Rio, is Roger's first recording in a
decade and his strongest work since the original
configuration of the Byrds.

DESKTOP MUSIC PUBLISHING: This comment is blenderized from an interview with
the three members of the group Deee-
Lite: Dmitri, Towa-Towa, and Lady
Miss Kier. Their record *World
Clique* is the most popular commerical example of house music.
House music, also known as "acid
house," is a style of 120-beats-per-
minute music mixed together by a
live DJ using samplers, MIDI decks,
and records. Many adherents make their
own house-music tapes, endlessly trading and
resampling them back and forth. House music
forms the aural focus for a social activity wherein location, lighting, and pharmaceuticals may be equally important (see "House Music").

**Biomuse
Musicians
D'Cückoo
by Bart Nagel**

Macintosh with Vision and Alchemy software. You can just change the sound.

We hope that the ethics can keep up with the technology, 'cause it's so exciting what's happening with technology. That's why we write all our hooks, and our samples are like less than two seconds—we just look at it as a tool to gather our sound library. It's like taking a great moment from the past and putting it together with the present to create the future. Time traveling.

BIOMUSE

The Biomuse is a portable digital signal processing system codeveloped by audio-physiologist Hugh Lusted and electronics engineer Benjamin Knapp, both of Stanford University. It's designed to provide a realtime interface between the electrical signals of the human body and any computer or MIDI instrument. This means the transformation of biological phenomena into musical sound. The bioelectric interface consists of Velcro-fastened elastic arm and leg bands, which read muscle extremity activity (EMG), as well as a headband that picks up eye-movement signals in addition to several brainwave channels (EOG & EEG).

The ultimate aim of the Biomuse is to provide a general-purpose nervous system-to-computer interface. "Our ideal techno-

BIOMUSE: This observation comes from Jas. Morgan, *MONDO's* music editor and the person responsible for putting together the MONDO Shopping Mall at the back of this book.

MIDI is short for Musical Instrument Digital Interface and represents a kind of "language" for digitally describing music. A computer music-authoring program, or for that matter a computer video game like King's Quest, sends out a stream of MIDI

bytes which say things like "set track 2 to the sound of the trumpet; now have track 2 start playing the note high C; now turn off the high C…" To interpret these MIDI signals, the computer may have a sound card—in the same sense that it has a video card for creating computer graphics. Some well-known artistic fantasy was to have a machine that would produce music directly from the brain— that is, you think or feel something, and it's immediately translated into music."

MIDI DRECK

All MIDI has done, in my estimation, is empower a whole new generation of Dreckmeisters, you know? When I heard new releases by the Beatles it was an opportunity to learn, to be exposed to some new thing. It was not just changing my wallpaper. It was knocking out the wall and putting an addition onto the mental house. **E**

LO-TECH MUSIC

As a musician and a mathematician, I ask everybody that I see playing hi-tech music, "Why don't you do mathematics, and then play music like I do. I play music. I drain my emotional system with a parallel mathematics that may well be of interest to analyze but is not analyzable in that language. It's analyzable in the language of relational data base maybe, cellular automata, cellular-processed systems. Matter of fact, it very well is analyzable under those conditions. Learn what that means, if you're so interested. If what you're trying to do is expand your depth and human emotion, be a human and play an instrument! Now that doesn't mean you can't play an electronic instrument. That doesn't mean that you can't use sampling techniques and all of that. But don't attribute any of the powers to that thing. You play that. Give me a rock, man. I'll sit over here and bang with the rock and sing—I'll hit a rock and sing and you play synthesizer— and I betcha I can get a bigger crowd. **E**

sound cards are the Soundblaster and the Roland card. The sound cards take MIDI instructions and synthesize the waveforms of the requested sounds. To actually HEAR the sound, you run a wire from two jacks in the back of the sound card into the CD jacks on the back of the receiver of your stereo system—or you can get self-powered speakers that hook directly to the card. An external keyboard can be used to provide fast input to the computer's music-authoring program; you can play through the computer in realtime.

MIDI DRECK: This acerbic thought comes from Todd Rundgren, whose musical career has spanned thirty years. In recent times, he's become a computer hacker as well. He's authored a couple of programs for the Mac, including the psychedelic Flowfazer. Most recently, Todd got hold of the new desktop video-authoring machine called the Video Toaster and used it to produce his own music video of his new song, "Change Myself." In partnership with John Sanborn, former producer of the hip PBS art program "Alive From Off Center," he has started a new video production company called Nutopia.

LO-TECH MUSIC: This is from Phil Alvin. Phil Alvin was songwriter and singer for the Blasters, the great L.A. rockabilly band from the early eighties. His solo album, *Un"sung" Stories*, mixes traditional twenties-style jazz with blues and avant-garde elements. One side is performed with *MONDO* favorite Sun Ra and the other side with the Dirty Dozen Brass Band.

Phil is also involved in the weird and wonderful world of mathematics and, when he's not touring, helps teach math at Long Beach State College in Long Beach, California. In person he exudes a strange combination of Dylanesque protopunk swagger, didacticism, and eccentricity.

BIGGER CROWD: For more positive appraisals of electronic composition, see "Hip-Hop," "House Music," and "Industrial/Postindustrial Music & Art."

EVOLUTIONARY Mutations

R. U. Sirius: Ultimately, the New Edge is an attempt to evolve a new species of human being through a marriage of humans and technology. We are ALREADY cyborgs. My mother, for instance, leads a relatively normal life thanks to a pace-maker. As a species, we are moving toward replaceable parts. Beyond that, genetic engineering and nanotechnol-ogy (see "Nanotechnology") offer us the possibility of literally being able to change our bodies into new and different forms. As we increase our understanding of matter as information patterns, it may become possible to download the information patterns and consciousness of a human being into solid state. It may also become possible to make copies of that information pattern, just as we now make copies of information stored on computer disks. Hans Moravek, director of the Mobile Robot Lab at Carnegie-Mellon University in Pittsburgh, has investigated these possibilities, and he believes that a form of postbiological humanity can be achieved within the next fifty years.

Think about it. The entire thrust of modern technology has been to move us away from solid objects and into information space (or cyberspace). Man the farmer and man the industrial worker are quickly being replaced by man the knowledge worker. (In *fact*, cybernetics is largely about self-regulating machines, so work ITSELF should soon be an outmoded concept.) As the twentieth cen-tury draws to a close, the essence of our social, political, and eco-nomic activities takes place in nonphysical, mediated space. We are less and less creatures of flesh, bone, and blood pushing boulders uphill; we are more and more creatures of mind-zapping bits and bytes moving around at the speed of light.

Billions and billions of bits of information, of media, have been strafing us pan-globally since the digital age. We are now monsters of such sophistication and complexity that we can't begin to know ourselves until we morph the human body, expand the bandwidth of our sensoria, permutate our brains, and strap on the add-ons!

MAN: I acknowledge that the use of the term "man" for the concept of human-ity is sexist. I use it here as a matter of convenience.

MORPHOLOGY is the branch of biology that deals with the evolving form and struc-ture of plants and animals.

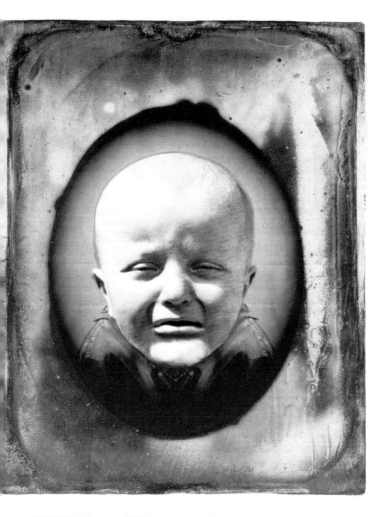

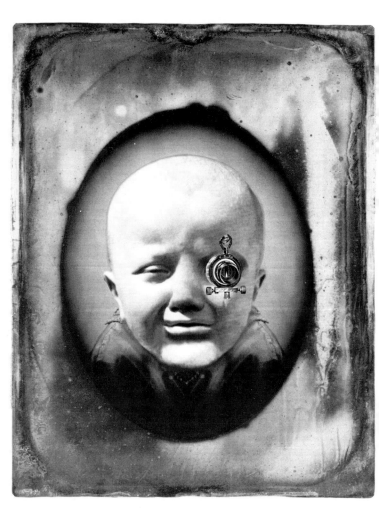

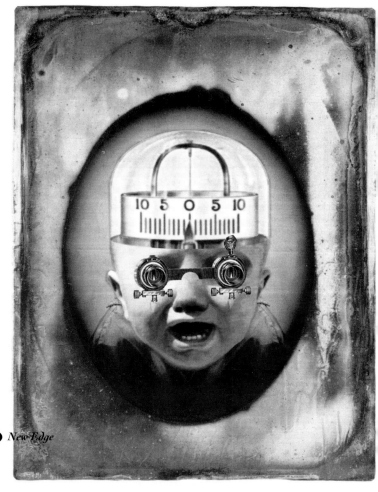

THE SINGULARITY

Vernor Vinge: When a race succeeds in making creatures that are smarter than it is, then all the rules are changed. And from the standpoint of that race, you've gone through a Singularity. That's because it's not possible before that point to talk meaningfully about the issues that are important AFTER that point.

I think a lot of people have had this notion, this sense that SOMEDAY it was going to happen. I think we're beginning to realize that SOMEDAY is really close. Von Neumann appeared to have a similar notion, so the idea has really been around for a long time. It's a case of something becoming more and more obvious until it kind of looms over everything.

If we don't blow ourselves up, then in twenty to a hundred years we will go through this technological Singularity. There may be humans afterwards—they will not be the principal players—and it's essentially impossible to talk about what's going on with them. Their art would not be art that you or I, at this time, could understand. To me, that's the hard reality.

"YOU THING RIKE JELLY-FISH PRETTY SOON NOW"

I think that certain biologic mutations would definitely be necessary in order to inhabit space. We know already that if you don't use it, you lose it. I mean, a skeleton doesn't have much function in space. In fact, it's an encumbrance where weight is an essential factor. And we know that the calcium tends to go. If people were in space for a year, they might lose all their teeth, be subject to spontaneous fractures, and over a period of time wouldn't have any skeleton at all. The end result would be

John VON NEUMANN helped build the first computer, ENIAC, in Princeton in the 1940s. In the late forties and early fifties, von Neumann became obsessed with the problem of whether or not machines could learn how to reproduce themselves. With the help of Stanislaw Ulam (coinventor of the hydrogen bomb), von Neumann worked out a cellular automata-based proof of the feasibility of machine reproduction—meaning that you really can have robots which build factories that make more robots. If this autonomous process is indeed initiated, then Vinge's predictions about superintelligent machines (or bioengineered humans) may come true.

"YOU THING RIKE JELLYFISH PRETTY SOON NOW": This comment is from a *MONDO* interview with one William Seward Burroughs. Textual surveys indicate that the single modern writer referred to the most often is none other than William Seward Burroughs. Like it or not, Burroughs is our Shakespeare. His two wonderful early autobiographical novels are called *Junky* and *Queer*—the guy has had it all hanging out since day one. His most famous novel, *Naked Lunch*, was given its title by Jack Kerouac, who was visiting Burroughs in Tangiers at the time. This great classic remains unspeakably toothsome and indescribably loathsome and has recently been made into a really fine movie. An interesting alternate view of the Tangiers which inspired *Naked Lunch* can be found in a novel by Paul Bowles, *Let It Come Down*. Burroughs has published a zillion small-press books, and has appeared on many tapes and records. Just one selection: *Letters From Tangiers*. A very good recent biography of Burroughs is *Literary Outlaw* by Ted Morgan.

something like a jellyfish.

MORIBUND

In the near future, the now-merging methods of computer and biological technology will make the human form a matter totally determined by individual choice.

As a flesh-and-blood species we are moribund, stuck at a "local optimum," to borrow a term from mathematical optimization theory.

PASSED OUT IN THE STREET

Bruce Sterling: I don't see much point in just whiting out and transcending the body. That brings its own level of debilitating trouble. I think that if you *could* become a cyborg for reasons of intellectual ecstasy, one day you'd discover that you've passed out in the street, and there are roaches living in your artificial arm. **E**

JELLYFISH: One of Burroughs's most notable jellyfishlike creatures appears in his book *The Ticket That Exploded*. **▲** "You win something like jellyfish, Mister. Or it win you," says someone, and then, on page 22: "Skin like that very hot for three weeks and then—wearing The Happy Cloak." Burroughs got the phrase "The Happy Cloak" from Henry Kuttner's forties SF novel *Fury*, and Rudy picked it up from Burroughs to use in his cyberpunk SF novel *Software*.

MORIBUND: These words come from a collaboration between Timothy Leary and Eric Gullichsen. Eric Gullichsen is one of the original virtual reality hackers, starting at Autodesk. He is a cofounder of Sense8, a competing company devoted to selling "turnkey," ready-to-use virtual reality systems. Sense8 is also creating programming tools to make it easier for developers to build their own cyberspaces (see "Virtual Reality"). Its recently released VR software product is WorldToolKit. **▲**

MATHEMATICAL OPTIMIZATION THEORY is just what you might think it is. It attempts to mathematically define the best (optimum) and worst possibilities in a situation given all known facts in both a limited (local) and an infinite field.

BECOME A CYBORG: Sterling and our own Rudy Rucker squared off on the issue of cyborgization and postbiological evolution on a recent "CBS Nightwatch" episode devoted to the theme of cyberculture. R. U. Sirius and Rudy Rucker appeared in a roundtable discussion with William Gibson and a keyed-up Sterling. The broadcast also included an interview with Mark Pauline of Survival Research Laboratories, as well as a segment with the Electronic Frontier Foundation's John Barlow.

Sterling has a gift for sneering polemics and psychotic invective that is more pleasant to experience in print than it is to encounter in person. In the early days of the cyberpunk science-fiction movement, he was known as "Chairman Bruce."

FASHION

THE WORLD OF COVERT DESIGN

Resistance to corporate fashion has sprung up in London. Fighting fire with fire, a covert-design movement hopes to undermine the monoliths and make the insidious march of corporate fashion explicit. Covert merchandising rides the wave of corporate fashion, reclaiming mass media images for its own ends. As one covert designer puts it, "When Coke or Nike makes a T-shirt, they are using carefully managed image-filters. We undermine that management process, not by copying what they do, but by accelerating it. The corporate domination of fashion is inevitable. The one way to stay ahead of the game is to take control by being one step in front. The only way to compete with the power of their icons is to access them for your own ends— 'hack' them, if you will." Covert designs are *not* copies. No original exists. "Copying a Chanel or Gucci T-shirt would be like exhuming a corpse. There are no 'originals' for our designs, except the clothes themselves."

In recent months, Sony tracksuits, Atari sweatshirts, and even Nintendo Super Mario Brothers jeans have appeared to an enthusiastic reception in London's clubland. From the Bank of Saudi Arabia to Apple, no corporation is safe. Inspired by the corporate future-shock imagery of *Blade Runner* and cyberpunk fiction, the clothes are so difficult to distinguish from officially sanctioned products that a booming export trade from London to Tokyo has resulted. In the postmodern world of covert designing, *nothing* is a forgery. "Devaluation through perfect imitation" is the covert designer's slogan.

COVERT DESIGN: Mark Heley was writing about things cyber for British pop magazines like *ID* when he became obsessed with the house/rave revolution. As part of the mobile cadre dedicated to internationalization of the movement, he came to San Francisco, where he and Diana Jacobson have launched the ultrasuccessful roving cyber-rave party known as Toon Town. The original proposal that created Toon Town was written by Sarah Stärä (formerly Lady Drew) and R. U. Sirius, a little-known historical fact.

▲ PHOTO BY AHMET SIBDIALSAU/CLICK IMAGE, CONCEPT AND STYLING BY JOSEPHINE GRIEVE AND HEIDE FOLEY, MAKE-UP BY SUSAN KOZAK, HAIR BY KAREN HARVEY, PHOTO ASSISTANCE BY TED THOMAS, PHOTO ASSEMBLAGE BY BART NAGEL.

MODEL: LYLI WONG ▼ PHOTO BY BART NAGEL ASSISTED BY HEIDE FOLEY; MODEL: JUSTINE HERBERT

At the vanguard of this assault is London designer Angel Biotek, whose new range of clothing is arranged around the theme of information anxiety. Her designs jumble image cues like flipping between adverts on cable—an uncompromising mass of twisted logos and slogans as aggressive as a walk through Times Square. This is appropriationist art, one step further down the spiral toward inevitable corporate apocalypse, where every sensory imprint will come complete with a trademark and copyright sign.

HOLOGRAPHIC: Normal imaging records only the intensity (amplitude) of light waves coming from an object. But by recording the phase of the light waves in addition to the intensity,

CYBER-SUITS

If functionalism has its day, as it surely will, the cyber-suit may be THE LAST GARMENT. Fabric technologies being developed by the likes of petrochemical giants such as ICI are already coming up with materials that will keep you warm, keep out the rain, and let you sweat. These materials are also comfortable and flexible enough to be body-tight without being constricting. These cyber-garments could literally become second skins within the next twenty years. With material-bacterial symbiosis, they could even become self-cleaning—*eating* dirt, perspiration, and stains.

4-D "DEEP" HOLOGRAPHIC CLOTHING

The London design house Space Time worked with heat-sensitive liquid-crystal designs that change color according to your body temperature and with patterns that appear only under ultraviolet light. But its major achievement to date has been the development of the world's first holographic fabric, which the designers already use on their full collection, from jeans and jackets to organza tracksuits.

The designers, Mia Manners and Richard Sharpe, are trained holographers. Together with award-winning holographer Patrick Boyd, they're now designing 4-D "deep" holographic clothes that change according to the angle of view.

holography can store and reproduce three dimensional images. This is done by splitting an intense coherent monochromatic light source (a laser). One part, the reference wave, goes directly to the film. The other part illuminates the object. The resulting interference pattern produces the hologram. Holography's major current use is in art and advertising as well as in high resolution imaging, information storage and security coding.

Holographic Clothing: Photo by M. Cairns, background by Francis Dosé

Holographic fabric also allows the exploration of completely new body textures and surfaces. Space Time's ultimate holographic suit would allow wearers to program pattern changes according to mood or whim. "Fashion" becomes entirely a matter of software. Designs would take on the quality of customized tattoos.

WEARABLE SYSTEMS

The work I'm doing now aims to amplify the individual psyche through technological means. I can create personal cybernetic adornments that are both wearable and capable of interacting in complex ways with environmental stimuli.

Rather than LEDs, I use direct-drive, twisted nematic LCDs that I design and fabricate in my studio. The spatial and temporal configurations of these LCDs are controlled by programs stored in on-chip EPROM of Motorola single-chip micros. I've been working with sixteen-segment LCDs (arranged as pie segments, bars, whatever) because it's easy to control with two one-byte I/O ports. The programs are written in a proprietary language that I commissioned so I wouldn't necessarily have to learn assembler. The graphics are generated in realtime, and the tiny (2k) memory allows about three minutes of novel imagery. Movement and change are *everything* in the new jewelry paradigm.

FUTURE FASHION

A tail might be sexy. *F*

WEARABLE SYSTEMS: This is from a piece called "Cybernetic Jewelry—Wearable Microsystems: From Hardware in 3-Space to Software-In-Time," by Vernor Reed, an Austin-based high-tech jewelry maker. He is obsessed.

LCDS: LED is Light Emitting Diode. LCD is Liquid Crystal Display.

EPROM: The Erasable Programmable Read-Only Memory chip. The data inside an EPROM can be erased and the chip reused for other data or programs.

SIXTEEN-SEGMENT: Most computers use a linearly addressed segmented architecture, meaning that the available memory is like a long ribbon of small cells that can hold zeros and ones. The "segmentation" aspect has to do with the fact that a program will usually need three kinds of memory: data (for long-term memory), stack (for short-term "scratch-paper" memory), and code (for the instructions of the program). When you load a software program into your computer's memory, the machine will normally allocate three long swatches of memory for your program: a data segment, a stack segment, and a code segment

An I/O PORT is an input/output gate.

SEXY TAIL: With characteristic aplomb, Debbie Harry, actress and rock vocalist, looks forward to twenty-first-century fashion trends.

PHOTO BY BART NAGEL, ASSISTED BY HEIDE FOLEY

Fiber Optics

WHAT IT IS

A fiber broadband network refers to an upgraded telephone network that replaces the dual-strand copper wire physically connecting your home or business telephone with the phone company's central office. Fiber-optic cables use light to transmit data.

WHY IT IS

What's happening today is that all forms of information, from text to sound to graphics to video, are being digitized—transformed into ⟨bytes⟩ of computer-readable information. When information is digitized, it can be easily transmitted, whether by telephone wire or direct connections between computer networks.

Copper wire will never be able to match the incredible capacity of a fiber-optic network, which can transmit at speeds up to twenty gigabits—that's twenty billion bits of information—per second. The best speed that can conceivably be hoped for from copper is twenty kilobits—twenty thousand bits—per second. So copper is a million times slower than fiber.

WHAT IT'S FOR

One application for a fiber network is the ability to retrieve music from a music server. There's about three billion bits of information on an hour-long CD. With a three-gigabit-per-second network, in one or two seconds you could ⟨download⟩ the whole CD. In a few minutes you could download a whole movie.

If you've got a video camera in the house, and a fiber to carry video to wherever you are, you could keep an eye on your kids from somewhere else.

A fast fiber-optic network would make it cheaper and easier to subscribe directly to electronic news services. Some entrepreneur would write a program to filter out all the stuff we weren't interested in, and we'd get to choose—from a much wider variety of sources—the news we wanted to read.

FIBER OPTICS: These items are excerpted from an article by Denise Caruso, who edits *Digital Media.*

BYTES: Bits and bytes are the units used to measure computer information. A bit is a single zero/one or yes/no decision. The game of "Twenty Questions" could well be called "Twenty Bits." A byte is a group of eight bits. Though there are only two possible bits (zero and one), there are 256 (two to the fighting eighth power) possible bytes. This is a generous enough number so that one can conveniently code up all the letters and punctuation marks by giving each of them its own byte-sized code. The most widely used version of this one-byte-per-letter code is known as ASCII. Programmers occasionally deal with half-bytes of four bits each, and they find it amusing to refer to these half-bytes as nybbles.

To DOWNLOAD something means to get an electronic copy of it from a computer network. Since all computer networks are ultimately connected, they are collectively known as the Net. When you put some information onto the Net you are uploading, and when you get info off of the Net you are downloading.

WHY NOT NOW?

It's the classic chicken-and-egg dilemma. The phone company doesn't want to make a big investment in fiber to the home until there are applications, and the companies who have the smarts to grow applications on fiber don't want to invest the time and money until they're sure there will be a successful venue for them to exploit.

Another factor is that the companies who have invested in existing ways to deliver information into the home—i.e., the cable television companies and traditional publishers such as newspapers—aren't looking forward to having to change the way they do business. **F**

LARRY GOODE

FRINGE SCIENCE

FRINGE SCIENCE

The task of science is to explore the unknown, to increase and consolidate our knowledge of the mysterious world in which we live.

While some knowledge involves a mere extension of what we already know, there certainly are wide intellectual territories that cannot be reached by presently known paths. To increase the chance that these unknown paths may be found, at least some scientists should be as unrestricted as possible in their choice of research topics, should be isolated from economic, political, and cultural pressures which encourage safe, fashionable, and immediately productive research. Ideally, universities and some industrial research laboratories are supposed to provide a supportive environment for research along the strange as well as the more familiar paths.

However, even in the secure atmosphere of the university laboratory, most researchers, timid creatures of convenience and fashion, do not search where the darkness is deepest. They look where they judge there is enough light to

FRINGE SCIENCE: These musings are from Nick Herbert, a bona fide physicist who prefers fringe science. His Doubleday Anchor book, *Quantum Reality*, ▲ is one of the best treatments of quantum mechanics. Nick once carried out an interesting experiment called "The Metaphase Typewriter." Here a printer was connected to a Geiger counter and a speck of radioactive matter. The printout contained the surprising message, "I am tired."

give them a reasonable chance of success. And who could blame them for this? Which of us would be brave or crazy enough to devote his or her life to an enterprise that will almost surely fail?

Here is where the fringe scientist comes in. Out of some uncommon sense of duty, strange obsession, or simple perversity, the fringe scientist is inexorably drawn to a corner of the Mystery where human ignorance is most complete and success least likely.

One is likely to find such characters, for instance, working on methods for communicating with the dead, with discarnate spirits, or with extraterrestrial intelligences. Many are exploring new theories of consciousness. Consciousness, they feel, with an intensity lacking in the usual psychology lab, is an intellectual black hole; our knowledge of consciousness is close to zero compared to the amount of mystery that yearns to be revealed. Consequently, we often find fringe scientists consorting with mediums, with psychics, with "channels" of dubious reputation who claim to communicate with extraterrestrial and extradimensional beings. Fringe scientists are interested in time travel, telepathy, psychokinesis, tantric sex, hypnosis, psychedelic drugs, wild-card models of mind, God, and universe, a universe that they passionately believe to be home to innumerable sentient beings, many not so far away, beings whose minds are, in H. G. Wells's famous words, "to our minds as our minds are to those of the beasts that perish."

Of course, the most interesting fringe scientists are those whose research is too obscure to be described in familiar terms, researchers who struggle to create unearthly geometries, who seek to decode and appreciate strange music and even stranger mathematics, who are experimenting with as yet unspeakable forms of being, knowing, and interacting.

Among these unclassifiable types of work one must certainly include recent feminist-oriented inquiries into the structure of reality, research which emphasizes participation, connectedness, and pleasure instead of analysis, separation, and power. On account of research in this dark and feminine direction, our descendants may well inhabit a world rich and varied beyond our wildest dreams.

Arthur Koestler has described Johannes Kepler, a kind of sixteenth-century fringe scientist, as a "sleepwalker" who lived half in the ordinary world and half in the world of his dreams of cosmic harmony. "Sleepwalker" is a good term for the fringe scientist, whose work is usually carried out in a darkness blacker than that faced by the ordinary scientist. Plying his obscure trade, the fringe scientist can be seen to be pursuing a kind of "pure research," the kind of research Wernher von Braun had in mind when he said: "Pure research is what you do when you don't know what you are doing."

TIME TRAVEL: GÖDELIAN UNIVERSES

The first space-time map containing time-machine trajectories was devised by the celebrated Princeton mathematician Kurt Gödel. To picture Gödel's solution, imagine an infinite universe lightly sprinkled with a fog of matter. Because of the everywhere-attractive force of gravity, this universe is unstable: It will tend to collapse upon itself. Now start this whole universe spinning at such a speed that centrifugal force exactly cancels out the tendency of the matter to collapse. The resulting model is called Gödel's Universe.

The most surprising fact about Gödel's Universe is that sufficiently long round trips along the direction of the universe's rotation are actually closed, timelike loops that lead into one's own past. The denser the universe, the smaller the diameter of the round-trip paths into the past. For better or worse, we apparently do not happen to live in a Gödelian universe.

Frank Tipler, a mathematician at Tulane University, has proven that closed, timelike paths into the past can be found in the space-time around an infinitely long, massive cylinder rotating so that its surface travels faster than half the speed of light. Probably finite cylinders would work as well. But Tiplerian time machines cannot be built, because matter is simply not strong enough. A massive enough Tipler cylinder would experience gravitational collapse and become a rotating black hole. A rapidly spinning black hole is called a Kerr object and may be a more likely source of paths into the past.

The fact that certain solutions of Einstein's relativity equations permit time travel is a tantalizing turn of events, suggesting that in the complexity of these equations may lurk the key to easy journeys into the past. The search for realistic solutions of the Einstein equations which allow time travel seems to be a worthy use for today's supercomputers.

SEE LIKE A BEE

Light from the sky is partially polarized in a direction and with an intensity that vary with the sun's position. The eyes of honeybees are sensitive to skylight polarization, presumably to help bees navigate to and from their hives on cloudy days. It is a little-known fact that human eyes can also sense skylight polarization, but most of us never bother to exercise this vestigial talent.

To experience bee sight, it is best to begin by viewing light that is totally polarized, such as that obtained by looking at the sky through a sheet of Polaroid plastic or polarized sunglasses. Polaroid plastic is a transparent, gray material that only passes light polarized in one particular direction—the direction of the Polaroid's optic axis.

As you look through the plastic, you will soon become aware of a "polarization icon" in the shape of a Maltese cross about five times as large as the full moon. One arm of the cross is blue, the other yellow. The cross has the visual character of an afterimage, and, like an afterimage, tends to fade away after a few seconds. To revive the icon, blink your eyes, shift your gaze, or rotate the Polaroid. When you turn the Polaroid, the icon will rotate, too, looking as though it were fastened to the plastic—a big, blue-and-yellow cross slowly turning in the sky.

After you know what the polarization icon looks like, try to see it in the sky without the aid of the Polaroid. Best results are achieved at twilight against the background of a dark-blue sky. Sometimes the sky appears to be covered with a latticework of yellow-and-blue crosses, an unforgettable sight.

Why was such an obvious phenomenon—amounting to an entirely new human sense—overlooked by hundreds of generations of artists, explorers, and curious laymen until its relatively recent discovery (1846) by an obscure Austrian rock doctor ? What other hidden human senses are awaiting discovery by alert sensory adventurers? *F*

AUSTRIAN ROCK DOCTOR: The polarization icon was first noticed by the Austrian mineralogist Wilhem Karl von Haidinger. The polarization icon is also known as "Haidinger's brush."

EMILY COHEN

Geek Humor

St. Jude & Gareth Branwyn: **GEEK** n. 1. ONE WHO EATS (COMPUTER) BUGS FOR A LIVING, ONE WHO EMBODIES ALL THE DREARIEST HACKER STEREOTYPES— AN ASOCIAL, MALODOROUS, PASTY-FACED MONO- MANIAC WITH THE CHARM OF A CHEESE GRATER. MAY BE EITHER A FUNDAMENTALLY CLUELESS INDI- VIDUAL OR PROTO-HACKER IN **LARVAL STAGE.** SEE ALSO **CLUSTERGEEKING, TERMINAL JUNKIE** 2. INSIDER PSEUDONYM FOR **NERD.** CANNOT BE USED BY OUT- SIDERS WITHOUT IMPLIED INSULT TO ALL HACKERS.

Computer-systems programmers and hardware designers—genus *nerd*—are a diabolically ingenious lot. They deal with permutation and invention in their work, and their playfulness with English is only to be expected: They have their own style of humor, and they endlessly reinvent a jargon that embodies it.

Take the word *geek.* Earlier in the century a geek was the freak-show wino in the Wild Man of Borneo getup who bit the heads off chickens. Nerds picked the term up from a couple of underground cult books about carny life. Geek as an intensive form of freak found favor because of the nerd's appreciation for allusion and metaphor. After geek, the noun, was adopted widely, it became "verbed." Typically in nerdspeak, popular nouns come to be verbed, just as useful verbs are "nouned"—so TO GEEK means to abase oneself. "I know you dropped that book on purpose: You just wanted to make me geek for you." Then geek was rehabili- tated as a secret synonym for nerd, and TO GEEK OUT means…well, read on.

But geek is the proud, insider term for nerd. If you are not a dedicated techie, don't use this word, honky.

Geek humor has its living monument in the Jargon File, an enormous dictionary of funny tech and twisted terminology that has been floating around on the Nets since before the beginning—in fact, it was originally distributed by Sneakernet. Nerds whose memory extends to the sixties may remember printouts of phony computer commands such as HALT AND CATCH FIRE and absurd computer room signs that were copied from installation to installation. You can still find them in the Jargon File, which now runs half a meg. Here are some choice bits:

BIG ROOM, THE n. The one with the blue ceil- ing and intensely bright light (during the day) and black ceiling with many tiny night-lights (at night), found outside all computer instal- lations. "He can't come to the phone right now; I think he's out in the Big Room."

CASTERS-UP MODE n. One of many synonyms for broken or DOWN.

CRUNCHA CRUNCHA CRUNCHA interj. An encourage- ment sometimes MUTTERED to a machine bogged down in a serious GRIND.

CYBERCRUD n. Obfuscatory tech-talk. The computer equiv- alent of bureaucratese.

DOCUMENTATION n. The multikilos of macerated, steamed, bleached, and pressed trees that accom- pany most soft- or hardware products. Hackers seldom read paper documentation and often resist writing it; they prefer terse and on-line. A common comment on this is "You can't GREP dead trees." (See also SOFT COPY and TREE-KILLER.)

EXAMINING THE ENTRAILS n. The process of groveling through a core dump or hex image in the attempt to discover the BUG that brought a program or system DOWN.

FEATURE SHOCK n. A user's confusion when con- fronted with a package that has too many features and poor introductory material.

SEBASTIAN HYDE

FUGGLY adj. Emphatic form of ugly—funky plus
ugly. Unusually for hacker slang, this may actually derive from black street jive. To say it prop-
erly, the first syllable should be growled rather
than spoken. Usage: humorous. "Man, the ASCII-to-
EBCDIC code in that printer driver is FUGGLY."

GEEK OUT v. To temporarily enter techno-nerd mode while
in a nonhackish context—for example, at social gatherings held
near computer equipment.

GREP [from qed/ed editor idiom: Globally search for this Regular Expression and Print lines containing it] vt. Rapidly scan
a file looking for a particular string or pattern. By extension, to look for something by pattern. "Grep the bulletin
board for the system-backup schedule, would you?"

HAMSTER n. A particularly slick little piece of code
that does one thing well; a small, self-contained
hack. The image is of a hamster happily spinning
its exercise wheel.

HEISENBUG [from Heisenberg's Uncertainty Principle in quantum physics] n. A bug that disappears
or alters its behavior when one attempts to probe or isolate it.

LIVEWARE n. 1. Synonym for wetware. Rare 2. [Cambridge]
Vermin. "Waiter, there's some liveware in my salad..."

MANDELBUG [from the Mandelbrot set] n. A bug whose underlying causes are so complex and obscure as to make its behavior
appear chaotic or even totally nondeterministic.

MONGOLIAN HORDES TECHNIQUE n. Development by gang
bang (possibly from the sixties counterculture expression MONGOLIAN CLUSTERFUCK for a public orgy).
Implies that large numbers of inexperienced programmers are being put on a job better performed
by a few skilled ones.

CLUCK

NEOPHILIA n. The trait of being excited and pleased by novelty. Common trait of most hackers, SF fans, and members of several other connected "leading-edge" subcultures, including the pro-technology "Whole Earth" wing of the ecology movement, space activists, many members of Mensa, and the Discordian/neo-pagan underground. All these groups overlap heavily and (where evidence is available) seem to share characteristic hacker tropisms for science fiction, music, and Asian food.

SNEAKERNET n. Term used (generally with ironic intent) for transfer of electronic information by physically carrying tape, disks, or some other media from one machine to another. "Never underestimate the bandwidth of a station wagon filled with magtape, or a 747 filled with CD-ROMs."

TROGLODYTE MODE n. Programming with the lights turned off, sunglasses on, and the terminal inverted (black on white) because you've been up for so many days straight that your eyes hurt (see RASTER BURN). Loud music blaring from a stereo stacked in the corner is optional but recommended (see also HACK MODE and LARVAL STAGE).

WAVE A DEAD CHICKEN v. To perform a ritual over crashed software or hardware which one believes to be futile but is nonetheless obligatory so that others may be satisfied that an appropriate degree of effort has been expended. "I'll wave a dead chicken over the source code, but I really think we've run into an OS bug."

WIREHEAD n. [prob. from SF slang for an electrical-brain-stimulation addict] 1. A hardware hacker, especially one who concentrates on communications hardware. 2. An expert in local area networks. Wireheads are known for their ability to lash up an Ethernet terminator from spare resistors, for example.

IN THE BEGINNING

In the beginning the Giver of Data generated Silicon and Carbon. And the System was without

IN THE BEGINNING: These excerpts are by Saint Silicon, a Bay Area comedian who wears a computer chip glued to the center of his forehead. His holy writ, *The Binary Bible*, ▲ is richly truffled with outrageous puns and cyber-wordplay.

SEBASTIAN HYDE

Architecture and was Uninitialized. And Randomness was upon the arrangement of the Matrix.

REVERSE POLISH

The path that is taken in life, although it appears to be a single path, is a complex path, and that is the difference between seeing it as a simple algorithm or seeing it as a heurism. Therefore all things are possible, but all things are not probable at a given time. That's what we call "Reverse Polish Salvation."

A computer's "ARCHITECTURE" has to do with the way that its calculating and memory resources are arranged. Most computers use a linearly addressed, segmented architecture, meaning that the available memory is like a long ribbon of small cells that can hold zeros and ones. The "segmentation" aspect has to do with the fact that a program will usually need three kinds of memory: data (for long-term memory), stack (for short-term "scratch-paper" memory), and code (for the instructions of the program). When you load a software program into your computer's memory, the machine will normally allocate three long swatches of memory for your program: a data segment, a stack segment, and a code segment.

REVERSE POLISH: The quirky but compact computer language Forth uses something called "reverse Polish notation," in honor of the 1930s Polish logician Jan Lusiciewicz. In reverse Polish notation, you push all the nonnumerical symbols toward the end of the sentence; so "5=2+3" would become "523+=".

An ALGORITHM is a procedure which always leads to an answer. The steps that you perform when adding with paper and pencil are the incarnation of an algorithm which was taught to you in grade school. The word "algorithm" is from the name of the Arabic mathematician Al-Khowarizmi, who wrote a book on algebra (called Al-jabr in Arabic) in 830 A.D. The Arabs kept mathematics alive after the Hellenic period ended and the Dark Ages enveloped Europe.

A HEURISM is a method of making educated guesses. Whereas an algorithm is supposed to always give the correct answer, a heurism might be right only two-thirds of the time...yet have the advantage of requiring less calculation to use. Somebody might say, for instance, "My heurism for getting good meals in restaurants is to always order the second special the waitperson mentions." In this context, an algorithm for food satisfaction would be more like, "I always order linguine with clams, and if they don't have that I get a medium-rare cheeseburger with hot peppers and Monterey Jack cheese, and if they don't have that I go to the next restaurant down the street."

The last shall be first. ASCII and ye shall receive. The freak shall inherit the Earth.

PMS WITH BROKEN WINDOWS—IT'S A

VIRTUAL MOTHER LODE OF PAIN

Somerset Mau Mau has burst upon the scene with a powerful new program that packs a wallop worthy of the old Marquis himself! It's brutal!! It's intense!! IT'S A WHOLE NEW WAY TO HURT!!!

PAINMAKER SADE WITH BROKEN WINDOWS is the surprisingly popular Operating System upgrade from Mau Mau's S & M & M NOT-SO-SOFT, the creators of DARK GODDESS-IN-THE-BOX and the VIRTUAL RITUAL MIRACLE MAKER. With SMMNSS and his KALIFORNICA RAM AND PROM currently recording profits in the gigadollars, CEO Mau Mau now stands astride the industry like a colossus of rogues, dominating mercilessly in the "Dark Soft Underbelly" market, that virtual subculture peopled by the malcontent chaos junkies, quasi-mutant pseudosatanists, subversive dominatrices, and dead people of cyberspace. (It just shows you how far Mau Mau will go to get customers, when he starts selling stuff to dead people...)

IT HURTS WHEN I WIGGLE MY MOUSE

I must confess, I had grave misgivings about getting involved with another Mau Mau package. Certainly, the first version of this operating system, CRACKED WINDOWS—with Bullets of various calibres, and Baseballs, Rocks, and Little Human Heads as icons—was a masterstroke of demented genius. But the text, crammed into the perpetually mutating Mandelbrot Fractal viewing environment, was virtually indecipherable. I procured a nasty case of carpal tunnel syndrome from constantly twisting the monitor around at my workstation.

ICONS ARE RELIGIOUS GRAPHICS

With this upgrade, we are again subjected to Mau Mau's dark, quirky vision. We are obliged, like it or not, to work with the Mau Mau Pen-

"ASCII" stands for "American Standard Code for Information Interchange." All computers except for the Macintosh use the ASCII format as a standard. (The Mac has to use something called RTF, for Rich Text Format instead—thanks for the community spirit, Apple.) ASCII is a system according to which each upper- or lower-case character which can be found on a computer keyboard is assigned a code number between 0 and 255. The high-valued ASCII characters include things like the yen symbol and various sizes of vertical and horizontal lines that can be used for boxing in menus. For more about ASCII, see "Fiber Optics."

VIRTUAL MOTHER LODE OF PAIN: Somerset Mau Mau started the psychedelic magazine *High Frontiers* with R. U. Sirius back in 1984. Mau Mau, when he's on, is brain-splatteringly funny. The WINDOWS in Broken Windows refers to the computer operating system "Windows." His tapes are available by mail order.

CARPAL TUNNEL SYNDROME is also known as a "repetitive stress injury" and is the hacker's worst nightmare—your hand starts hurting so much you can't type or use the mouse anymore. People with writer's block sometimes use it for an excuse as well, but most sufferers are overworked office personnel with ergonomically bad setups (e.g., no place to rest your wrists while you're typing).

dulum Finder. It's shaped like a broadaxe. The trash can is replaced by The Pit or Abyss, symbolized as a small black hole where you discard unwanted files represented as Little Bearded Men hanging by chains. A nice touch, I thought. However, the Platform holds some unpleasant surprises...

TERROR ON THE DESKTOP

You virtually have to *beg* for file information. And the

retrieval system is torturously clumsy and slow. Also, don't try to import in an unrecognized file format! The translation utility, Krazy Doktor, is capricious and full of bugs. The program often hangs up and leaves your Little Man hovering over The Abyss. You can't do a cold boot, you can't even pull the plug on your computer. If you try anything the program crashes and burns and takes your hard drive with it! YOU CAN'T DO ANYTHING UNLESS THE PROGRAM WANTS YOU TO!!

Help Me! I've Fallen and I Can't Get Up and Running!!

You may as well forget about help screens. There aren't any. The tutorial—Nazi Storm Trooper (sold separately)— is virtually bulging with disinformation, calculated to lead your Little Man and your precious files over The Edge and into The Pit where they are wiped from memory. But that's not the worst of it. Nasty Accident, the file manager, has the habit of eating your data for no apparent reason and then flashes the ubiquitous "TOUGH BREAK, CYBERSLIME!" message at the bottom of the screen. It's cruel and heartless and unforgiving and YOU NEVER QUITE KNOW WHERE TO PUT YOUR MOUSE!! If you click on the Thumbscrews, the keyboard spacebar becomes inop-

SEBASTIAN HYDE

erative. If you click on the Hand-
cuffs, you can't access the outer
keys. Click on the Whip or Clothes-
pins and the screen sputters for a
moment and then fades to black. You
must then free up a couple more megs of
memory just to buy your way back into the
environment. Your best bet is to click on the ?
icon, the BlindFold. The odds are 50/50 you can
at least get some work done and actually save a
file to disk, ferhevenssake! Though you are, for
all intents and purposes, virtually STROKING IN
THE DARK.

THE SILENCE OF THE LAMBSKINS

The communication package, GagComII
with Knuckle Sandwich, which boasts
D & S & S & M-Modem protocols, is
openly user-hostile. The features
MaleMerge, ShutUp!, ByteMe! and
Boot My Unit! are all hit or miss.
CornHole in the chat mode makes
for too-tight operating parameters
even with the help of HogTie batch
files with doors to DOS. It's so frus-   DOS is Disk Operating System.
trating going in for the first time that you just
want to scream and yet, it IS worthwhile and
even ENJOYABLE in an odd sort of way…

INQUISITIVE MINDS WANT TO KNOW

PMS comes bundled with a utility called the Iron Maiden
for compressing files. To decompress there's a little
program called The Rack. When the file is unzipped,
a short animation sequence shows blood squirting
out of the Little Man's orifices. And though
you CAN control the size of your cursor
(shaped like an erect penis in PMS), if
you run with the highest setting for too
long a bug in the system cuts it in
half right when you least expect it.

Once again, blood squirts out of the Little Man's orifices.

A NEW PARADIGM OF PAIN

After several hours of this digital abuse you might expect some sort of relief. Unfortunately, the discomfort merely continues to intensify. Then, just when you think you've reached your final threshold of mortification and embarrassment, when you are certain you can't take any more shame and degradation, PMS lifts you up to a new crescendo of self-loathing and anguish, onto a desktop and into an environment so repugnant and disgusting yet oddly compelling that it virtually reeks of dysfunctional computing and revolting table manners.

SUITE SURRENDER

Since virtually all avenues of escape from the program are blocked, my advice is to just give up and take your medicine. That is, after all, Mau Mau's consistent message through the years and one that he drives home with relentless fury in this challenging package. So just give up and buy some more software. Sell your car if you have to and move into a cheaper domicile.

Keep your eyes peeled for Mau Mau's new entry into the NecroFile market, due out next winter: BOARDED-UP WINDOWS—THE POSTAPOCALYPTIC COMPUTING ENVIRONMENT.

I VIRTUALLY shudder just thinking about it!! **G**

Hackers

St. Jude: Hackers are the elite corps of computer designers and programmers. They like to see themselves as the wizards and warriors of tech. Designing software and inventing algorithms can involve bravura intellection, and tinkering with them is as much fun as fiddling with engines. Hackers have their own culture, their own language (see "Geek Humor"). And in the off-hours, they can turn their ingenuity to sparring with enemies on the Nets, or to the midnight stroll through systems you should not be able to enter, were you not so very clever. Dark-side hackers, or crackers, slip into systems for the smash-and-grab, but most hackers are in it for the virtuoso ingress.

It's a high-stress life, but it can be amazing fun. Imagine being paid—well paid—to play forever with the toys you love. Imagine.

THE HACKER'S ETHIC

I don't know if there actually is a hacker's ethic as such, but there sure was an M.I.T. Artificial Intelligence Lab ethic. This was that bureaucracy should not be allowed to get in the way of doing anything useful. Rules did not matter—results mattered. Rules, in the form of computer security or locks on doors, were held in total, absolute disrespect. We would be proud of how quickly we would sweep away whatever little piece of bureaucracy was getting in the way, how little time it forced you to waste. Anyone who dared to lock a terminal in his office, say because he was a professor and thought he was more important than other people, would likely find his door left open the next morning. I would just climb over the ceiling or under the floor, move the terminal out, or leave the door open with a note saying what a big inconvenience it is to have to go under the floor, "so please do not inconvenience people by locking the door any longer." Even now, there is a big wrench at the AI Lab entitled "the seventh-floor master key," to be used in case anyone dares to lock up one of the more fancy terminals.

HACKER'S ETHIC: These excerpts are by Richard Stallman, who found his way to the M.I.T. AI Lab in 1971, toward the tail end of the big sixties hacking burst there. He is perhaps best known for having written the mother of all freeware programs, a text-editor known as EMACS. The open architecture and customizability of EMACS are such that versions of it have migrated to practically all of the Unix workstation-type machines used by heavy-duty programmers and academic scientists. Stallman has also authored a variety of other free software.

The idea of a "hacker ethic" is perhaps best formulated in Steven Levy's 1984 book, *Hackers: Heroes of the Computer Revolution.* Levy came up with six tenets:

1) Access to computers should be unlimited and total.

2) All information should be free.

3) Mistrust authority—promote decentralization.

4) Hackers should be judged by their hacking, not bogus criteria such as degrees, age, race, or position.

5) You can create art and beauty on a computer.

6) Computers can change your life for the better.

MARCUS BADGLEY

HACKING AND CRACKING

The term "hacker" has come to be associated exclusively with breaking security. That isn't what it is at all, but hackers were willing to state their total contempt for security people, because security was one form of bureaucracy. First-generation hackers would break security because it was in the way of doing something useful. Now a lot of kids do it 'cause it's naughty. Though it is true that showing you can break security that's said to be unbreakable is a nice hack, the original hackers did not break security just to be naughty. We broke security if somebody had locked up a tool that you needed to use.

FREE SOFTWARE

People discovered that by becoming obstructive, they could get rich. Imagine any other industry where one of the rules is that I won't sell my product to you if you're going to share it with anyone. It's ridiculous. And the sad thing is, good programs are going to waste because not enough people get to use them. If only half as many people get to use a program, it's half wasted. Software is very different from material objects where, say, if you grow a certain amount of wheat, it makes a certain number of slices of bread. Whether you sell it for five cents a slice or five dollars a slice, it still only makes so many sandwiches. That is not true with programs. You can copy a program, and you cannot, in the same sense, copy a loaf of bread. So anyone who tries to stop you from copying a program is doing real harm to society—setting up scarcity where there isn't any. They're also poisoning the spirit of scientific cooperation and the free interchange of ideas. People use pieces of all sorts of programs because that is, by far, the easiest way to get the new programs written. Now we're losing the ability to take a program and improve one aspect of it without having to redo the whole thing, the ability to adapt programs in new ways so you can use them, the ability to fix it yourself if it is broken.

HACKING AND CRACKING: A concise definition of a hacker is someone who would rather look at a computer screen than at a TV. In the fifties, "hacking around" meant something like "messing around." At M.I.T., the word "hack" came to mean some neat student trick—like taking a VW apart and reassembling it inside someone's room. And soon "a good hack" meant some cool computer programming shortcut. A "hacker" was a person who programmed a lot and produced interesting things. In violence-obsessed modern America, the word "hacker" is taken to mean someone who slashes away at the veils of security which protect the Man's war-game secrets, his shit-hoard banks, and his centralized surveillance systems. Breaking security is a type of hacking (known as cracking), but most hacking has nothing to do with the money or the secrets of the Pig.

FREE SOFTWARE: GNU and other free software are available from the Free Software Foundation.

Free software isn't a matter of price, it's a matter of freedom. Free software is about the freedom you have in using it and sharing it. I refuse to buy commercial software, but I would refuse to buy it even if the guy gave it to me at zero price, because I won't agree to the conditions. I won't agree not to share it with someone who would like a copy. And I won't agree to not have the sources and be helplessly at the mercy of the hoarder of the information. What I have decided is that rather than surrender to those terms, I will reject them and I will write myself the software I need. That is why I launched the GNU project.

BEYOND HACKER MACHISMO

Todd Rundgren: I want to get beyond the bit-twiddling, dealing with the machinery: That's just hacker's machismo. I mean, theirs is hard-won knowledge, yeah, but the real objective is not talking to this retarded machine—it's dealing with the higher conceptual levels of what you want to do.

WHY I HACK

The Hackers conference is to me what pop music once was. It embodies all the reasons why I got into music. It is breaking rules. It has a very broad horizon—what's acceptable to do and what's meaningful to do—and it requires an almost religious commitment to acquiring special knowledge. I've known people who are the equivalent of Eric Clapton on the computer because they have transcended technique.

CYBERPUNK SUMMER CAMP

The revolution isn't over. It's hardly begun. Now is the time to link up with the people we want to empower with the technology. The kids will be the ones to carry the process further—we need to provide something for their training and self-education. Cast-off computers still work, or can be made to work, and you learn a hell of a lot by doing it. How about maintenance and upgrade clinics staffed by eleven-to-seventeen-year-olds under the supervision of a few old grumps who remember the good old days? *H*

From Todd Rundgren's music video created on Newtek's Video Toaster

THE HACKERS CONFERENCE is an annual invitation-only event that was initially held as a celebration of *Hackers: Heroes of the Computer Revolution*. The Hackers Conference usually runs three days in October and is usually held at the Granlibakken Resort in Tahoe City, California.

CYBERPUNK SUMMER CAMP: This contribution is by Lee Felsenstein, political activist, mad scientist, and side-splittingly-funny lecturer. He briefly struck it rich in about 1978 when he designed the Osborne Computer, one of the very first home personal computers. He is currently president of Golemics, Inc., 2831 7th Street, Berkeley, CA 94710.

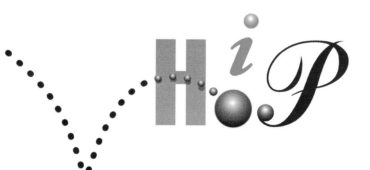

YO!

Rickey Vincent: The musical culture of rap music, known as hip-hop, has proliferated to the point where American tradition is forced to define itself in terms of this inner-city phenomenon.

Musically, a technological revolution in sound production has occurred, and the most prolific example of its possibilities is in the production of rap music. The surgical sound-grafting of sampling, the symmetric sound distortion of "scratching," the audio strobe effect known as "transforming," and a number of other recording and production techniques have opened up an entirely new and vital medium which serves as everything from news broadcast to pop art.

SCRATCHING involves putting a record on a turntable and moving it back and forth under the needle so that the sounds contained on the vinyl produce a peculiarly scratchy electronic noise and rhythm.

ROOTS OF HIP-HOP

This relentless technical revolution began in New York dance clubs in the 1970s, when disc jockeys began to gain fame manipulating records on a pair of turntables, adjusting their speed and mixing two songs "on beat" to create a new sound sensation all its own. They would then interject sound bits or lyrics from one disc onto another by rotating one record manually back and forth. This activity caused a "scratching" sound, and mutated the once-sacred recorded song into a twisted snippet of percussion, signifying whatever message the DJ decided to leave in your helpless, dancing soul. On a good night the DJ would render a live band obsolete and relegate the history of recorded music to a grab bag of gimmicks. Meanwhile, these musical medleys provided the backdrop for the rhyming, hyped microphone styles of the club MCs and soon-to-be-professional rappers.

**Opposite page:
Digital
Underground**

EMILY COHEN

LEADERS RESPOND

Civil rights leader Jesse Jackson concedes: "Hip-hop may very well be the most radical expansion of our culture since jazz." Baby Bam, one of the members of the Jungle Brothers, explains, "rap is a positive disease, and it's going to get beneath the skin of everybody." Pete Townshend of the Who, in his acceptance speech into the Rock 'n' Roll Hall of Fame, summed up rap music as the new rock by concluding "…it's not up to us to try to understand it. It's not even up to us to buy it. We just have to get the fuck out of the way."

THE SAMPLES IS THE HIT

Everybody's samplin' and bitin' off the funk, but there's no emphasis put on where today's music is coming from. Before, everybody would talk about like the blues, and slavery and blah blah blah, and gospel comin' out of the lack of our own religion and stuff. And rock 'n' roll was the outgrowth of all of that. Rock 'n' roll was the industrial-age blues. And then psychedelic is the white people's version of the same thing…you know—bustin' loose, turning the music up and jammin'. Now scratchin' and rappin', that's a whole 'nother outgrowth of all of this. Rap is definitely the new funk. But they ought to start studying the basis of the rap, you know. It started out with the beat box, but now you're using samples from other groups—James Brown and ourselves in particular. I mean there's like six different songs where "One Nation Under a Groove" has been sampled.

Some of them are clever, like Public Enemy. You can't tell where they get theirs from. You have to be studying really hard to find theirs. That's the best way—the cleverest, 'cause it's using the sounds and not necessarily the licks. But it don't bother me if they use the whole thing. And most of 'em be paying us. De La Soul pay real good.

SAMPLES IS THE HIT: The next three entries are bitten off from an interview with George Clinton, the Nasty and Complete Minister of All Funkadelia. He got his start as lead vocalist for a psychedelic soul group called Parliament. He spun off a partly distinct band called Funkadelic, leading to a touring P-Funk Jekyll & Hyde black music show that also featured Bootsy Collins. The show has been referred to as "the Black Grateful Dead." Clinton often refers to himself and his fans as "Maggot Brains." Clinton's sophisticated street-level surrealism and nigga psycho-socio-sexual sarcasm has been a primary influence on the hip-hop movement, and his is the music most sampled for the recent hip-hop beats. The entire Funkadelic and Parliament catalogues are now available on CD. ▲

MAGGOT-BRAINED AGAIN

The Secrets of the Pyramids was passed on to me, but I wasn't the Chosen One, 'cause I would be the first one out there tryin' to get some pussy. See, if I'm the Chosen One, I'm not gonna have no fun, man. I'll just deliver the message. I promised somebody I'd deliver the message.

We all are trying to straighten out a serious situation with faulty equipment. We have to acknowledge and understand that just like with the environment and the water and the air, our brains are polluted. So we gotta be real careful tryin' to analyze or figure out our current predicament. We gotta start off knowin' that we might make the wrong decision 'cause we're usin' faulty equipment. If we do that, then we can check and recheck our thoughts and impulses just to make sure we ain't reactin' to something that we don't know we're reactin' to. And I think that's the way we are now, in the nineties. We're Maggot-Brained again.

FUNK MEETS PISS WARS

We tested positive for the P-Funk. I'll pee in anybody's cup. May they cup runneth over. **H**

Bitin' Off the Funk with George Clinton, by Eric White

St. Jude: The kids felt left out. They missed the sixties. They wanted their own shot at saving the species. Fair enough.

There is now a worldwide movement around the idea of techno-hippie—the old love ethic with a new high-tech implementation. Hippie failed to revolutionize the planet, but techno-hippie will DO IT. Here's a new form of liberation theology, and the services involve ecstaticized, neon-painted dancing to the endless beat. It's the trance dance, to techno or house music, on a throbbing floor, wearing paisley, all night long. Most large cities have their clubs or gathering places. These kids are high on love. Look out.

There are differences, apart from tech, between then and now. The chemical support is new: These guys use "smart drugs" and the new staple, ecstasy, aka MDMA, for their all-nighters. LSD is still hanging in, but there is disdain for the primary "dumb drug," alcohol, along with all other downers.

Eco-organic types with MIDIs and lasers. Love it.

SUMMER OF LOVE, 1988

Mark Heley: When the first acid house records arrived in London from Chicago, they looked as innocuous as the first rabbit probably did landing in Australia. The effects on England's club culture have been just as speedy and devastating. House music was a cultural virus that found optimum conditions: general discontent with archaic licensing laws that closed all venues at 3 A.M., the shallow sterility of "youth style," and a breaking down of the traditional divisions between black, white, suburban, and cosmopolitan nightlife. But the most essential catalyst of all was the arrival of MDMA/ecstasy/E.

MDMA, otherwise known as ecstasy, is a nonhallucinogenic psychedelic drug that advocates claim helps people to feel what Aldous Huxley called "the essential allrightness of the world" and to communicate without their ordinary defensiveness. It was popularly used in psychotherapy, particularly in California, until the DEA declared it illegal in 1987. However, due to a bureaucratic error made by former Attorney General Edwin Meese, it is questionable whether the law is—in fact—in place, and a number of people have had their charges dropped as a result of this technicality.

MICHAEL SWAINE

120bpm
120bpm
120bpm
120bpm
120bpm
120bpm
120bpm
120bpm
120bpm
120bpm
120bpm
120bpm
120bpm
120bpm
120bpm
120bpm
120bpm
120bpm
120bpm
120bpm
120bpm
120bpm

The UK's 1988 "Summer of Love" created a synthesis that fused people together in a way few of them had experienced before. Acid house became the focus of a techno-shamanic ritual of deep power and purpose. In sauna-hot basements and studios, unrelenting, deafening sound systems blasted only the hardest dance music under a battery of frenzied strobe lights. You were *forced* to *trance-dance*. Fueled by equal quantities of MDMA and enthusiasm, dancers staggered out after eight or ten hours of intense, overwhelming sensory assault to dawn in a changed city.

THE BEGINNING OF THE END

The beginning of the end was signaled by the banner headlines—"Acid-House Drug Orgy"—splashed across Britain's influential tabloid press. Suddenly the secret was out. While thousands upon thousands of young people danced maniacally but peacefully in a field somewhere off London's orbital motorway, reporters dutifully fantasized floors littered with "ecstasy wrappers" and "crazed children strangling pigeons." This incoherent media frenzy soon turned into uncontrolled outrage. Acid house, a violence-free, stupidity-free party zone for hundreds of thousands of bored Britons, suddenly became a threat to national security. An initial burst of conciliatory talk about "licenses" and "permission" degenerated into the usual authoritarian backlash: police roadblocks, raids, and crude intimidation.

HEARTBEAT IN THE WOMB

House has branched out a lot since 120 beats per minute, especially with the advent of ambient house. We don't even call it acid house anymore, and even "rave" is almost out. But basically 120 is the baby's heartbeat in the womb—which describes the latent House Generation on the planet very nicely indeed! [*Laughter*]

TECHNO-SHAMANIC: Shamanism is an even more abused term these days than "cyber." Basically, a shaman is a kind of healer found in ancient cultures all over the world. The shaman is generally a visionary, a mutant (strange individual), and a powerful magician who helps lead people into alternative realities. Often the shaman uses psychedelic drugs. The idea of shamanism was popularized in the West in the character of Don Juan in the writings of Carlos Castaneda. People still debate whether Don Juan is a real or fictive character.

HEARTBEAT IN THE WOMB: The next two entries are from Fraser Clark. Fraser is a British countercultural troublemaker who goes way back. He currently publishes a yearly neo-psychedelic magazine called *Evolution*  and runs Evolution records, which releases house mixes, sometimes over sampled lectures from the likes of Timothy Leary and Robert Anton Wilson. Fraser is a *true-believer* type who thinks the rave movement is THE answer. This makes him a bit fascistic, but you just gotta love the guy.

Look. The nineties generation ain't the sixties generation, and it don't *sound* the same either. Rock 'n' roll, as a *sound*, is what grandparents listen to. House is a faster vibe for a faster era—time's speeding up, coming to its climax. Imagine twenty thousand young Westerners dervish-dancing to 120 bpm all night till the sun comes up. You get to feeling you're in the *same* womb! (Which we are—if you stop to think about it!) Everyone just *knew* that something important was being born. Amazing group solidarity—twenty thousand people *feeling* together! If that's not what the planet needs…wow!

NO MORE ROCK STARS

You can tell a rock crowd from a house crowd because the rock crowd are all looking in the same direction—at the big fat egos strutting on stages while everyone passively consumes. The house crowd is crucially different in that they're looking at each other! Music's back in the hands of the People now, or back in their feet.

HOUSE VS. DISCO

Deee-Lite: It's kind of like house music is one continuous song.

It's like you program a long MIDI number, and sometimes the MIDI channel fucks up and plays a whole new thing, all its own.

It's like tapping into the soul of a deep program.

A lot of people mistake house music, our dance music, for disco because of the tempo. But actually the whole persona of disco was escapist. The difference is the persona of house and modern dance music is much more humanitarian. And if you read between the lines, or if you skip between the beats, there are definitely new ideas being discussed, some very specific political thoughts. **H**

Deee-Lite:
Lady Miss Kier,
Dmitri and
Towa Towa

John Barlow: When Bush exulted "By God, we've kicked the Vietnam Syndrome once and for all," he meant merely that he had figured out how to give war a new lease on death—by keeping it at a distance and transposing another, denatured reality between the electorate and barbecued bodies.

The enemy then is mediated information.

This is a new, almost concrete form of abstraction that Jean Baudrillard referred to when he wrote: "Abstraction today is no longer that of the map, the double, the mirror or the concept. Simulation is no longer that of a territory, a referential being or a substance. It is the generation by models of a real without origin or reality: a hyperreal."

It is this hyperreality which has become the new and terrible American Dream. And it is a lucid dream, subject to selective mutation by the Dreamer. As long as we remain in it, no atrocity will be past us, for we have kicked the Reality Syndrome once and for all. *H*

JEAN BAUDRILLARD is a very au courant French philospher. Like most of the trendy European postmodernists, his writing is extremely dense. In Baudrillard's case, however, meaning *actually* outweighs obfuscation. IN FACT, I suggest you REREAD this quote. It says as much about the New Edge worldview as anything else in this book. His better-known books are *America* and *Simulations*.

BRONZE SCULPTURE BY JOEL PERIL

HYPERTEXT

The idea behind Xanadu is to have a common publishing repository for the writings of humankind. A published document becomes part of the universal repository that can then be accessed by anyone and to which anyone can make Links.

TED NELSON'S XANADU: These links arise from an interview with Ted Nelson. A graduate of Swarthmore and Harvard, Ted Nelson is a dynamic orator, a rogue intellectual, a magnificently theatrical idea-man, and one of the few real shamans of the personal-computer movement. In 1974 he self-published an amazing tract called *Computer Lib/Dream Machines,* which coined such great Tedisms as "Everything is Deeply Intertwingled" and "Simplicity is the Ultimate Sophistication." Ted's vision of Xanadu, or what will replace the printed word, was presented at the Eight World Computer Congress in 1980. An ever-evolving version of this talk is available as *Literary Machines.* Ted's interests also include social reform and personal sexual liberation.

XANADU is the company created by Ted Nelson to make an electronic alternative to conventional publishing. Xanadu's logo is the Eternal-Flaming-X symbol. Xanadu is currently incarnated as XOC (for Xanadu Operating Company) and is owned by Autodesk, Inc., the innovative computer-graphics and computer-aided design giant. The creation of the software for Xanadu has been of legendary difficulty. The problem is one of finding efficient ways to move about RAPIDLY in data bases as large as all the words in all the books in a big library—some trillions of words. It is said that the problems are now all nearly solved, and that Xanadu may be shipping product in the next year. Of course, Xanadu has been saying this for many years!

LINKS: One of the really innovative ideas in Ted Nelson's vision of Xanadu is the notion of a LINK. One begins with a huge raw data base with the text of many books. Users move around in the data base, reading something here, comparing it to something else over there, grouping it with a related topic, looking up references mentioned in a certain passage, and so on. These user actions can be recorded by the Xanadu system as links between different groups of bytes. A user can create a whole basket of links and "publish" this as a kind of sampler, anthology, or work of criticism. One of the really nice things here is that when you quote something by publishing a link to the document, the quoted text has the entire original document attached to it. There can be no quoting out of context. And the quoted author can be paid a royalty on each use of each of his or her words! The structure of the links is based on a high-powered mathematical concept called "Tumbler Space."

BART NAGEL

147

This radical notion of open hypertext publishing means both that your link can reach into the original document it points at and that FROM that original document you can find your link. So anyone can publish a footnote to any book.

The best way to look at it is as a system for delivering fragments from a document pool or delivering fragments from a pool of virtual documents that can share material and have links.

I started Xanadu thirty years ago thinking I would have this system in six months. So I started saving notes on the assumption that I would be able to use it as my principle writing method. So now I have two million notes hanging in fragments awaiting input. But that's my personal problem.

ZIG-ZAG HYPERGRID

My next major campaign seems to be against metaphors. I really dislike what has happened with so-called metaphors in computing. If you look at the Garbage Can and the Clipboard on the Macintosh — given their names and their behavior, I would submit that they're metaphors. And very bad ones. The Macintosh psychology is built around cluttering

HYPERTEXT: Although Ted Nelson may have invented the notion of hypertext, he did not trademark it, and many current computer companies are presenting their own versions of hypertext—for instance, the HyperCard software which Apple now ships with every Macintosh. The idea of hypertext is that one has an electronic document in which each page might have buttons leading not to one single next page but to many possible next pages. Hypertext can include sounds, images, film clips, and computer demonstrations as well as words. Some writers have attempted creating written forms of hypertext, and a wide variety of software "stacks" for the HyperCard program are available—a recent example is the *Beyond Cyberpunk* Stack.

A VIRTUAL DOCUMENT is, first of all, something which exists in computer memory rather than in print. A second feature of a virtual document is that it might in fact include no text written by its author whatsoever. It could instead be a collection of links to interesting sources. Somewhat like the *Whole Earth Catalog*, or like the book you're reading!

MACINTOSH: Computer people group roughly into four mutually slandering camps: PC, Macintosh, Amiga, and workstation (which splits into Sun and Silicon Graphics). One of the endearing things about Ted is that he can find something bad to say about every kind of machine.

the screen with a lot of icons that have diminished serviceability, excessive vividness, and that fill up the screen. You've got the Bird's Nest. The High-Button Shoe. The Frying Pan. The Yo-Yo. You've got to figure out what they're for—or what they meant to the person who programmed them! We'd be much better off if you didn't have an implicit comparison to start with. In my next software suite—or rather the software suite which I've been working on now for over a decade, called the Hypergrid or Zig-Zag Hypergrid—there ARE no metaphors. It is a space.

I never distinguished between technics and poetics. I've always assumed there was a continuum, and this is one of the things that has gotten me in trouble with a lot of people. I'm a monist. I refuse to acknowledge any dichotomy.

A MONIST believes that All is One. One of today's computer dreams is that we really will manage to sew everything together with the electronic fibers of the Net.

To me, software is an extension of self. In a movie, you have a virtual world that is created by many pieces under a common direction—a unified conceptual framework presenting ideas to the mind and the eye of the beholder. In software you're creating a unified conceptual idea for the mind and heart of the beholder, with interaction added. The decisions, the design decisions, are not decomposable and not delegated. 🄷

FROM INDUSTRIAL TO POSTINDUSTRIAL

Gareth Branwyn & R. U. Sirius: The industrial music & art movement began in the late seventies with crude garage electronic noise that echoed the sensibilities of the more mainstream punk rock and with the machine-age demolition robotics of Mark Pauline's Survival Research Labs.

Opposite page:

Mark Pauline of

Survival Research

Laboratories

POSTINDUSTRIAL MUSIC

Gareth Branwyn: This form of sonic assault has been offered as a massive wake-up call to the legion of drones who freebase television and Madison Avenue's trend du jour. The first sounds of "anti-Muzak" have echoed a great distance from the early garage electronics of Throbbing Gristle, SPK, and Cabaret Voltaire to the slick sounds of today's industrial. The current style is so different from the roots industrial of the late seventies and early eighties that "postindustrial" would probably be a better label. If there are any threads that connect these bands (sampling, a preoccupation with darkness and decline, and sociocultural ostracism), they are overcome by the diversity of musical styles and raisons d'etre. Perhaps the most sensible demarcation of postindustrial is between all the experimental work (noise, ambient, sound collage) and the many flavors of industrial dance (industrial-thrash, industrial-rap, techno-industrial, attack house, etc.).

SURVIVAL RESEARCH LABS (SRL) is a Dadaist robotic art group and the brainchild of Mark Pauline. Mark and the SRL members live in a warehouse in South San Francisco, working on their fabulous giant machines and preparing new spectacles. In person, Pauline is earnest, open, and down-home. He avoids the word "artist" and prefers to see himself as a worker with—and for—machines.

Ironically, Mark is not only internationally known as an artist; he's a cult god. Word-of-mouth and wrenchingly tragic posters promising MACHINE SEX or BITTER MESSAGES OF HOPELESS GRIEF or ILLUSIONS OF SHAMELESS ABUDANCE draw him overflow audiences. These he mystifies and bullies, sluicing them with stenches and flying glass, blackening them with unmetaphorical smut—and they leave his shows glittering with arousal and satisfaction.

KENT MARSHALL

EXPERIMENTAL INDUSTRIAL

Noise has overtaken information in our age. Signal and noise have switched places. We live in the value-dark dimension, a black hole of deconstructed values and exploded worldviews. Early industrial music looked at this cultural wasteland, gathered up some of the junk, and decided to make music with it. In the process, its pioneers discovered new possibilities for "art noise," explored the boundaries of music and antimusic, order and chaos, terror and bliss, beauty and bestiality. If the age of empire was dying, industrial music was busy scoring the funeral march. As industrial music has advanced, so has music technology. With the introduction of MIDI systems and sampling, the metal-on-metal rhythms of the junkyard were replaced by the cut-and-paste sounds of the videodrome. The night-marish hissings of the smokestack industry were replaced by the sound-collaged marketspeak of the culture industry. The fascinations of industrial artists have also shifted emphasis from control through subjugation and outward violence to the powers of pleasure-control and the mesmerism of the media simulacra. Through all this, noise, cut-up nonsense, and the cybernetics of feeding the garbage back into the system to hasten its decay have been employed as operating strategies.

Some EXPERIMENTAL INDUSTRIAL groups are: the Hafler Trio, Babyland, Muslimgauze, Zoviet France, and the Pelican Daughters. The work of these and other artists can be ordered from Silent Records. ▲

VIDEODROME ▲ is a film made by David Cronenberg that involves infectious snuff-film videos, people being biologically altered and brainwashed by video images, and Deborah Harry having a videotape inserted into her. Cronenberg is the ultimate cyberpunk filmmaker. His recent film version of William Burroughs's *Naked Lunch* ▲ must be seen at least three times.

From Baudrillard, the SIMULACRUM is the media-created reality that proceeds out of simulations of the real, without any ultimate base in actuality.

INDUSTRIAL DANCE MUSIC

Industrial is white-hot funky dance music, squeezed out of everyday white noise. Softened news and other fragments from the sound tracks of our lives provide the backbeat, over which snarls a demonic, from-a-sonic-distance narration of domination, control, and disaffection. Postindustrial dance (like early industrial) is built around the sounds our culture makes as it comes unglued.

There is something totally sublime about thrashing to industrial music on an urban dance floor with punks and goths and nerds and Rastas and other outcasts.

Some INDUSTRIAL DANCE MUSIC groups are Ministry, Clock DVA, Young Gods, Yeht Mae, Consolidated, and Front 242. More info can be found in *Technology Works*. ▲

THRASHING is a dance that comes out of the punk-rock movement of the late seventies. Basically, people jump up and down (pogo) and bang into one another to the frenetic rhythm. Usually it's done in a graceful manner so that everybody gets to release some anger but nobody gets hurt.

JORDIN ISIP

WHY I CHOSE INDUSTRIAL MUSIC

I was trained on the piano starting at five. When I got my first synthesizer, though, my piano playing came to an abrupt halt. Synthesizers seemed so much more than an instrument. I was also very into computers, electronics, and video—so it all seemed to fit. I got serious about writing music about the time that MIDIs and sequencers hit the scene. So, right from the start I was composing on computer and sequencer. Since I was a big fan of the American industrial movement—basically because it was electronic—it made sense for me to use this form. I had always been into electronic music, but I didn't feel it had much emotional intensity compared to rock 'n' roll. Then industrial came along. It was electronic, but it delivered as much power and intensity as any other musical form. It also represents the total misuse of technology, which really appeals to me.

ROBOT DANCE MUSIC

I started thinking that I should record in every city I'm in. I was booked to do a series of talks all over America. The series lasted about a month all together and I thought, it'll be so long since I actually did anything musical I might forget what it is I'm supposed to be talking about. So I had this idea, a bold notion of setting up a new band in every city that I went to.

WHY I CHOSE INDUSTRIAL MUSIC: This quote is from an interview with Trent Reznor. Trent Reznor created the 1990 industrial dance music record *Pretty Hate Machine* on his own with high-tech equipment. To go on tour, he got four musicians and formed the group Nine Inch Nails, who were part of a touring 1991 show called Lollapalooza.

A SEQUENCER is a computer software version of player-piano rolls. It digitizes electronic pitch, and notes can then be manipulated according to speed, sequence, and cycle. A fine example of the use of a sequencer on a popular album is the cut "On the Run" off Pink Floyd's *Dark Side of the Moon.*

ROBOT DANCE MUSIC: This is from an interview with Brian Eno, exemplar for a whole race of art-school persons displaced into music. He is a hero instrumentalist on what he contends is the most important new musical instrument since the electric guitar: the electronic recording console. His solo records include *Before and After Science* and *Here Come the Warm Jets,* and he has collaborated on albums by Roxy Music, John Cale, and other artists.

I tell each group the same story to begin with. I was in Japan recently. I was doing something for Toyota, and they took me to the factory where they make the cars. I was very impressed by the robots they have there. Six-armed robots —they look like the goddess Kali.

They're building cars. But they're quite rhythmic in the way they move. They go unt-unt-unt, zzt-unt-zzt-unt zzt-zzt-unt, zzt-zzt. And then the next car comes along. I was sitting watching this, and it had a good noise, the whole thing, and I thought this would be a nice kind of music really: music for car factories. And so that was my first idea. That I would like to make something that turned what they were doing into a kind of dance.

Mm, but then I thought the way they were moving needed a little bit of lubrication—actually they were very stiff 'cause they were Japanese, you know—so I thought, imagine if these industrial robots had been built in Nigeria. Right. What would they be like then? Well, they would be broken, for a start, like everything else in Nigeria. So my code word for this project became "Broken African Industrial Robot Dance Music."

That's the scenario I give to the band each time. And then having talked about this a little bit and what kinds of sounds might be involved in that, it's very easy to…1-2-3-4…and everyone starts playing.

And the only other rule is, if it sounds nice, something's wrong.

JAPAN: Pop culture is a big industry in Japan. Giant billboards for JAL, the Japanese airline, show Janet Jackson saying, "JAL. YES." Funkier things can be found in discos—weird cut-up videos and megamix house music.

SIX-ARMED ROBOTS: Industrial robots are dangerous to be around—recently the first human casualty at the hands of a robot happened in a Japanese factory. A fascinating science-fictional idea is the notion of a robot-operated factory which builds robots—just like an anthill is an ant-operated factory that builds ants. To push the notion, one would also need mining robots to get and smelt the raw materials for the factory.

TWO-HEADED MERMAID &
SOME ROTTING CHEESE

Mark Pauline: In Copenhagen, we went there a couple of weeks early to get a feel for what it was like. I talked to people there endlessly. And I was just like a news reporter asking, "What about this part of your culture…and what about this?" Et cetera et cetera.

What stands out is that all their monuments are like these grotesques, these really expressive kinds of things. But everybody is so glum-looking. Why aren't they more happy?

And then there's the mermaid, of course. The whole identity of the City of Copenhagen is tied in with that little mermaid…which is so weird. This tiny mermaid. I mean, it's only a couple of feet tall!

And then, Denmark is really a kind of dairy agriculture. They like to think of themselves as peaceful agricultural farmers. And it's very clean there. There are no smells there.

So how do you deal with this? Okay. We gave that little mermaid two heads about seven feet tall. We made it out of a cow carcass and put it in this device that would ride around and have its little legs crossed right next to a vat of boiling, rotten cheese—about two hundred gallons of rotten cheese with a huge coal fire underneath it. And we had these huge spires built. And all the structures were very angular, very much that kind of Danish-modern look. We had these wooden doors on an octagonal pedestal, all very regular, very organized, with an eight-foot-diameter glass skull on top. So there were smells, and there was this huge tugboat in the background that had pounds and pounds of this smoke powder. Then we had a boat that we dragged out of the wharves that had like a Viking disaster scene. And we put on this really intense emotional scene at the end.

It was all to bring out this idea of what their forebears had been and to ask why they were so sapped of that vital energy.

The fire department participated in it. It was like a free-for-all for them. They gave us like twenty pounds of smoke powder. They gave us these explosives. They were into it. They were shoving the stuff off on us. Then at the end of the show, all the firemen were there and they rushed in and started spraying everything with hoses. They were like screaming and laughing and stuff. They went to this tugboat that we had on stage…they went up there with axes and started smashing in the windows. It was this anarchic scene going on. These guys in uniforms and these really weird hats. The fire chief…his attitude was like—"There's never any fires here. And it's really great that you could come here and make all these fires for us to put out." They came to the party afterwards.

IT'S SAFER THAN YOU THINK

In the past, the shows were much more dangerous than they are now. But they appear to be much more dangerous now than they used to be. And that's because I think in the earlier shows I wasn't aware of the technology, and how to really control and harness these kinds of things. I mean, basically you're dealing with a situation where you've got a bunch of machines that are part of a show that's going on and people are watching it. And you have to have something to pull them into it. And you don't have an act in any traditional sense. You've gotta have something to keep the flow of action and hold it together. And in the past that had to be some pretty intense stuff.

I mean, that was how │ I hurt my hand, │ really. I was using unguided rockets with high-explosive heads. If they hit you they'd kill you. I mean we used those in shows in the first couple of years. And machines that spewed like raw gasoline…

The last show there wasn't any real explosive stuff at all. It was like all these gas-powered explosions that feel much more intense. They're bizarre, because it's like this six-barreled thing that's

I HURT MY HAND: Pauline blew off the thumb and three fingers of his right hand in an explosion. He had his big toe grafted to his hand, so that he can still pick things up with it. He has plans for eventually getting a full hand graft from a corpse…when the technology is ready. If possible, he'd like to try putting a LEFT hand on in place of the damaged right hand.

firing out these shock waves. It hits you and it knocks you back in your seat. And it's like, whoa!—that kind of fear you get from something totally unfamiliar. I don't even completely understand the principle behind it.

MACHINE LIBERATION

Each machine reflects the character of the people that put it together. And I sort of design the machines based on what I feel is the character. I'm an engineer. I can look at a device, and I can think what the mind-set of the person or people that invented it was.

I'll give you an example. The big arm, for instance. I've seen these backhoe arms, and I thought, these things are so stupid like this. They should be alive. You got some big fat guy with a cigar and dirty T-shirt running these things. What a horrible thing. It should be disassociated. It should never have to work again. I should get one, and I should make it not work 'cause they're always working. They're never sitting around doing nothing. You know, I should put something on so it can't dig. It needs a hand. It needs to be able to pick up stuff. It needs some way to know where it is so it doesn't have to have someone else driving it. It needs a computer, or encoders…position sensors on the joints. That's the way I looked at it. And it really was very anthropomorphic. I mean it wasn't anything physically very different from a backhoe arm. But with just these little touches and primps and a little bit of grooming it turned into this whole weird creature that served a real significant purpose in several shows.

Gave it a personality. It's like the closest a machine can have to intelligence is to have personality. I think that that's like really the best that you can do with these machines, that's the most intelligent life that you can give them, have them be very idiosyncratic and have a real personality.

THE BIG ARM can be seen in action in several of SRL's videos. The videos are available from *RE/SEARCH* magazine and directly from Survival Research Labs.

IS IT SCULPTURE?

If you're gonna give me money, and if you're gonna give me money because I did sculpture, I'd say that my machines were sculpture.

I mean, what does "sculpture" mean? Does that mean that they're designed to be separated and put in some sort of glass case somewhere and disassociated from the rest of the world? Or any other kind of world?

For me the definition of sculpture is tainted by the past and by the history of what sculpture has been. Unfortunately, most sculpture, like most art forms, has been out there serving the power structure. And I like to think that we don't serve those things.

Anyway, I think that they're performing machines. I think they're gonna be sculptures when I'm dead. And you'll be able to look up a lot of data on them—

"They were in this show and this show and that show."

IS IT SCULPTURE: Rudy and Mark were in Washington, D.C., to get taped for a CBS show on cyberculture. They walked over to the Mall and went to the National Air and Space Museum and the Museum of Industry. Mark wouldn't set foot in the Hirschhorn Museum and Sculpture Garden.

FORGET THE LIGHT SHOW,

HERE'S THE DARK SHOW

The project as it now stands consists of a number of independent sound designers, hackers, musicians, disc jockeys, engineers, vocalists, and the like who search out and destroy a collective past in order to chart out an uncertain future.

The creation is a dark show—the upside-down alternative to the sixties light show.

The analogy to the air-traffic control tower is apparent, with the audience roaming the runways between musical aircraft that land, take off, or crash through the sonic world.

JOHN BORRUSO

HERE'S THE DARK SHOW: These comments are taken from an interview with Naut Humon, the conductor/curator for the Sound Traffic Control show. Naut was the originator of Rhythm and Noise. In his words, "R&N was first conceived in the late sixties as a theatrical type of group involved in audience-participation events. For instance, in our *Dancing on Dead Rock* (1969), we set up a section of the Seattle underground, an old area of the city that the current city was built on top of, as a darkened womb and made the spectators crawl through a mining tunnel to get to it. All the while we were hurling furniture around them and using giant wind machines to create a torrential downpour. When they finally reached the end of the tunnel there was a void—no lights, no exit, nothing. As they started wailing, we would record their screams and amplify them. After a while, they were able to escape, and there were reporters who would take flash pictures and interview them about their experience.

"Other shows from the seventies dealt with further audience-abduction techniques utilizing factory assembly-line settings, moving the visitors by cranes in solitary cargo crates. Larger-scale productions fostered twelve-hour nocturnal excursions by bus, van, and boats through an entire county. The finale of our last eighties U.S. tour was an epic in L.A. with Comfort Control Systems of Phoenix. We integrated segments of the piece for body-machine interface—MIDI controlled, arc-welding Inquisition torture instruments."

THE HOVERDRUM

Timothy North's Hoverdrum is a giant percussion sculpture that hangs from the ceiling and swings back and forth to the unrelenting tempo of Tim's drumming. The structure hangs from springs that have microphones on them. This adds an eerie screech as he rocks back and forth and also puts the installation temporarily out of his control during certain portions of the show. Sometimes people in the crowd grapple with the apparatus and shove it around as well.

STANDING IN A POOL OF OIL

Barry Schwartz's sculptures are like giant electrical nightmares. He has one device called the Turntable that is a huge, rotating stainless-steel disc on which he drops a stylus of dry ice. Another device is the Harp—a monolithic upright bass with electrically charged piano wires. Standing in a pool of oil, Barry strikes the Harp with metal gloves that set off bolts of lightning that arc between the strings.

SHOCK SCIENCE

We'd hold things up like a gooey duck —which had a phallic, hallucinatory effect on people. And we did a staged assassination where a guy came out of the back room holding a gun loaded with a primitive flash system. We packed the thing with condoms and meat and charges, and this guy came running through the audience shooting at me. I hit the floor, and the thing shorted out on me. I was getting electrocuted, so I was vibrating pretty heavily. People just started screaming—it was cool! **I**

SHOCK SCIENCE: This is from an interview with Kevin "Ogre" Ogilvie of Skinny Puppy, a group from Vancouver, British Columbia. As well as putting on remarkable performances, Skinny Puppy has recorded a number of albums, including *Rabies* and *Too Dark Park.*

The GOOEY DUCK is a kind of clam in estuaries of the Pacific near Seattle and Vancouver. It has a hugely distended dicklike "foot," or "siphon," that dangles out of its massive shell.

HEIDE FOLEY

LONGEVITY

St. Jude: One of the master themes of cyberpunk is the extension of human possibilities by chemical and surgical interventions. And the bottom line is, of course, survival. Medical research into longevity proceeds with exquisite slowness, and present-day futurists are hovering like raptors, waiting for the next few millimeters of progress. If the rats can't be mustered because the funds have been allocated to military flourishings, if the journals don't care…well, then, we'll take things into our own hands. Pass that capsuling machine.

Self-experimentation seems logical. We'd better work with our own raw material: it's carrying an expiration date. Of course, self-experimenters are defensive people; the Food and Drug Administration wants to save us from our impulsive behavior, for our own good. The FDA makes exceptions for people whose expiration dates have been moved up by viruses. But the fact is, we are all suffering from an incurable disease: aging.

The obvious move is jiggering one's own biochemistry for personal fulfillment. After all, what an adult might consent to do to his or her own body in the privacy of his or her own lab must be extrapolated to be okay—this follows in the tradition of the United States Constitution and its popular spinoff, the Bill of Rights.

CRYONICS

R. U. Sirius: A Berkeley-based gerontologist, Dr. Paul Segall, and his team of scientists chilled Segall's family dog, Miles, in the doctor's ▢TransTime▢ Laboratory and then successfully revived him. Today, more than a year after his near-death experience, Miles is still, in Dr. Segall's words, "a fully functional dog."

"Cryonics is just the tip of the iceberg" when it comes to developments in life extension, according to Segall. The very near future will see "a radical assault on aging in seven parts: cryonics, interventive gerontology (studying the aging process to do something about it), transplants, artificial organs, resuscitation, regeneration, and ▢cloning."▢

Segall says that the general public is unaware of how much progress has been made. "Science is sending quakes throughout society. And you know what they can't handle? The real kick in the head is that all this is BECOMING REAL NOW. There's a fear that we're going too far—the gods will be offended. After all, the public perception is that we're

TRANSTIME ▲ is one of two existing cryonics companies in the world. The other is Alcor, ▲ in Los Angeles. In cryonics, a dead person's body, or sometimes just the brain, is frozen, in order to preserve it. According to cryogenic theory, it may be possible to reanimate these people in the future when we achieve sufficient technological know-how. Most of the hope for restoration of brain function amongst cryogenicists rests on the eventual achievement of nanotechnology (see "Nanotechnology"). Theoretically, the brain could then be repaired molecule by molecule.

Remember CLONING? It was the hot technological topic of the late seventies. In Woody Allen's film *Sleeper,* the "great leader" is cloned from his nose after an assassination. The idea is that the basic information pattern that is a person is contained in the DNA. Theoretically it should be possible to make genetic copies of people, but those people wouldn't have the same SOFTWARE as the original, i.e., memories, experience, education…

talking about immortality! People haven't figured out yet that they DESERVE it."

You don't need to be Walt Disney, Michael Jackson, or even Timothy Leary to get iced. While the full cost of cryonic preservation with TransTime is $125,000, healthy people in their twenties or thirties can get an insurance policy for around $30 per month.

REANIMATION CAPSULES

Timothy Leary: Why not have the option of jumping consciousness back into the body? The Egyptian tombs are really interesting. I see them as reanimation capsules. They used the highest science at the time. And now, microbiologists can get DNA from the bio-remains. So the Egyptian plan actually worked. Within ten years we'll be able to clone the pharaohs! Of course, the problem is there would be no memories. But that's why they included their software in the form of the jewels and artifacts. I admire that.

READ THIS OR DIE

St. Jude: Two of you who are impatiently browsing this book are going to drop dead this week. Too busy to read it, eh? Heh. With a couple of antioxidants you might have made it through the millennium to die of something more interesting. You, like most of us, will die from what are called, without irony, *natural causes*. The blood vessels naturally bloom microclots that organize into sludge. Your fouled conduits naturally blossom larger clots to strangle your heart or detonate your brain.

The Physician's Health Study, now in its sixth year, has announced a serendipitous discovery: Forty thousand IU daily of the antioxidant pro-vitamin ß-carotene combined with an aspirin tablet reduced by half the number of "major events"—stroke, heart attack, surgery, and, of course, death—in a subgroup with cardiovascular disease. **L**

DURK PEARSON

by Sebastian Hyde

ASPIRIN TABLET: Durk Pearson suggests that only a quarter of an aspirin per day is necessary for the home experimenter.

Robert Anton Wilson: Perhaps the most important idea Marshall McLuhan ever uttered is in the opening chapter of his very early work *The Mechanical Bride.* McLuhan simply reproduces the first page of a typical edition of a typical modern newspaper—a collage of our global village —and then shows what this Everyday Pop Art has in common with such avant-garde works as Pound's *Cantos,* Cubist painting, and *Finnegan's Wake.* We hardly regard this nonlinear communication as "modernistic" anymore, and wonder why critics went ape when Pound and Joyce first employed it. We quickly make sense out of bits of information rapidly delivered.

A PERIOD OF ANARCHY

McLuhan had an instinct for the vital nerve of Western cultural pretensions. In 1972 he wrote to Edmund Carpenter: "The Western psyche is a fragile, specialized product of the phonetic alphabet, which stands in terror of any snooping around for its credentials, whereas tribal men welcome such study. The tribal man says, 'Let's see what will happen and then decide to stay away from it,' whereas Western man says, 'Let's try it anyway and see what happens.'" Or again: "The suddenness of the leap from hardware to software cannot but produce a period of anarchy and collapse in existing establishments, especially in the developed countries."

MARSHALL McLUHAN (1911–1980) was a brilliant Canadian professor and writer. His 1964 book *Understanding Media* was a bible for enlightened cultural rappers in the sixties. The book has incisive chapters on things like "The Motorcar" and "The Telegraph." What does the motorcar mean? What does the telegraph symbolize? The motorcar is a mechanical bride. The telegraph is a social hormone. *Understanding Media* ends with a passage that peers forward toward us here and now (in reading it, understand that in those ancient sixties times, people used the word "automation" to mean "computers"): "Persons grouped around a fire or candle for warmth or light are less able to pursue independent thoughts, or even tasks, than people supplied with electric light. In the same way, the social and educational patterns latent in automation [computers] are those of self-employment and artistic autonomy. Panic about automation [computers] as a threat of uniformity on a world scale is the projection into the future of mechanical standardization and specialism, which are now past."

"GLOBAL VILLAGE" is one of McLuhan's phrases, nearly as famous as "The Medium is the Message." Reading McLuhan is kind of like reading Shakespeare—you keep stumbling on phrases that you thought were clichés, ONLY THIS GUY MADE THEM UP.

A PERIOD OF ANARCHY: This thought is from Terence McKenna. Known primarily as the hottest pyschedelic drug philosopher since Tim Leary, McKenna's thoughts on media, postmodernism, human history, evolution, and the human future could stand on their own, without reference to psychedelic drugs whatsoever. He's an inspired public speaker and has also written a number of books, including the unusual and amazing talking book *True Hallucinations* and the recently released *Food of the Gods.* He has a software package called Timewave Zero that "plots the ingression of novelty through time." Whoa!

HARDWARE TO SOFTWARE: Hardware is, of course, the machinery itself, and software is the information, the creative content, and the usable result. Here McLuhan is speaking of the transition from the industrial (hardware) age to the information (software) age, in terms that the rest of us wouldn't start using until the mid-eighties. This guy was *way* ahead of his time. Read everything by him that you can find!

FROM THE COLLECTION OF THE MARSHALL McLUHAN INSTITUTE

ME: Well, we needed someplace to stick a few of the cute things some people said in *MONDO*. The New Edge is not particularly personality-oriented. You stick around about only as long as you remain interesting. They say the youth of the seventies and eighties were the "me generation." Hacker hero and Apple founder Steve Wozniak tried to convert it into the "us generation," only to be ripped off by his rock-star heros and made to look like a fool regarding his Us Festival. The nineties may be the "it generation," as technology takes over. Personally, I like a bit of personality. The nerds feel that *MONDO* has TOO MUCH.

WHERE THE FUCK IS MY UNICYCLE?

Ted Nelson: At one time I was under the delusion a unicycle would be a practical vehicle. It was minimalist. It seemed unencumbered. You know how the young seek to be unencumbered. I'd seen Bongo Bear in Walt Disney's *Make Mine Music* zipping around, and I figured if he can do it, so can I. I got to the point where I could carry a notebook—but never a briefcase, because it had to be rigidly held in my hand to keep the balance. But I did actually use it for transportation at Harvard. And I still have it. Where the fuck is it? I haven't seen that unicycle lately!?…Yeah, I guess the unicycle's gone.

HOW TIMOTHY LEARY BEGAN

Timothy Leary: I began as a hopeful, optimistic sperm. Floating up Fallopian Highway 101 looking for an egg. I was conceived, as I can calculate back nine months before my birth, on the day that alcohol was prohibited in America. The first twelve years of my life I watched the grown-ups, all of them middle-class doctors, dentists, lawyers, army officers, abusing an illegal drug. So that was my beginning.

THANKS, TIM

Almost every day, someone will come up to me and say, "I really thank you for what you've done to my life." These are usually valet parkers and waiters, rather than the owners of the restaurant. When I was in prison, I'd go into a cell block and half the guys would say, "I owe it all to you!" I've never had someone with several million dollars come up to me and tell me how much he owes me.

OBSESSIONAL BEHAVIOR

Mark Pauline: I'll be the first to admit that there are engines that drive what I do that are very akin to the things that drive any kind of obsessional behavior. So that obsessiveness is a tool that I use. How does anybody get themselves to do anything besides sit around and smoke cigarettes and drink beer all day? Any way that you can trick yourself into doing anything is valid.

ALL IS ONE

Rudy Rucker: I've always felt touched by destiny. I feel I can achieve something in my life. My intellectual breakthrough occurred when I was about fourteen, and I suddenly realized that I'm going to die someday. My novel *The Secret Life* starts on that theme. Here you are. Aren't you having fun? You're going to die. What are you going to do about it? If you don't come to terms with your own mortality, people can take advantage of that hidden fear. The world at large exploits your fear, and you are supposed to run out and buy things to cover up the fear you have of death. Eventually I got to be less scared of death by learning to think of myself as part of a universe which is a single connected whole. This was largely due to the sixties and psychedelic experiences—feeling at one with God. *M*

Timothy Leary with his favorite No. 2. photo by Yvette Roman

THE MEAT

William Gibson: For me, given the data in the books, the key to Case's personality is the estrangement from his body, the meat, which it seems to me he does overcome. People have criticized *Neuromancer* for not bringing Case to some kind of transcendent experience. But, in fact, I think he does have it. He has it within the construct of the beach, and he has it when he has his orgasm. There's a long paragraph there where he accepts the meat as being this infinite and complex thing. In some ways, he's more human after that.

WHAT'S REAL

Kathy Acker: When reality—the meanings associated with reality—is up for grabs, which is certainly Wittgenstein's main theme and one of the central problems in philosophy and art ever since the end of the nineteenth century, then the body itself becomes the only thing you can return to. You can talk about any intellectual concept, and it is up for grabs, because anything can mean anything, any thought can lead into another thought and thus be completely perverted. But when you get to the actual physical act of sexuality, or of bodily disease, there's an undeniable materiality which isn't up for grabs. So it's the body which finally can't be touched by all our skepticism and ambiguous systems of belief. The body is the only place where any basis for real values exists anymore.

MEAT: The cyberspace-addicted hackers in Gibson's *Neuromancer* refer to the human body as "the meat." This expression communicates the frustration that people dealing with an infinitely expandable infosphere feel at the limitations imposed upon the wandering mind by the demands of the body. While some theorists—such as the inimitably strange Hans Moravek—look forward to the possibility of downloading human consciousness into a more versatile medium, others of us are exploring the limits of the body's mutability and the meaning of the body in the context of the information glut.

Ludwig WITTGENSTEIN wrote several classic and idiosyncratic works of philosophy, including his *Tractatus Logico-Philosophicus* and his *Philosophical Investigations*. The *Tractatus* has a very singular organization, being broken up into paragraphs that are numbered according to the paragraph they dangle off of, so you have things like paragraph 2.4.11.7. Many of the passages stand alone and have a mystical, aphoristic quality, like this classic: "We feel that even when ALL POSSIBLE scientific questions have been answered, the problems of life remain completely untouched. Of course there are then no questions left, and this itself is the answer. The solution of the problem of life is seen in the vanishing of the problem." *Philosophical Investigations* puts more stress on Wittgenstein's notion of language as being a game that is played according to internal rules that need have no connection with any absolute or objective reality.

NORI EZO

BODYBUILDING

My problem isn't so much being stared at as of finding who to hang out with. All my old art friends either went dead or rich! [Laughs] I certainly do feel comfortable in that milieu of bodybuilders and tattoo people. But I always needed to be able to move a lot, so I like to have at least five milieus that I can go back and forth to. So it's not like the bodybuilding scene, say, is my only thing these days. Bodybuilding, of course, also concerns my work, because it's work with the body. I like the atmosphere when I'm hanging out at the gym. There's an almost Zen-like focus people have that's kind of pleasurably stupid, mindless. You find the same thing with tattooists and motorcyclists.

TATTOOS are an ever-more-popular part of California life. Many also go beyond piercing their ears to piercing their noses, lips, nipples, or genitals as well. Lots of info on this can be found in the *RE/SEARCH* book, *Modern Primitives* or in the series *Tattotime*, also from *RE/SEARCH*. ▲ For more on piercing, see *PFIQX* ▲ *(Piercing Fans International Quarterly).*

SAVING YOUR OWN SKIN

Durk Pearson: What you see when you look at your skin is really a bunch of dead cells, called the stratum corneum. The only time you see live skin is when you get a scrape—you know you've hit live skin because it bleeds. As you get older, your skin gets thicker, because it takes longer for the cells created in the basal layer to get shed on the surface, so your skin looks older and more beaten up. Also, as skin gets thicker, it's more likely to crease. Wrap a piece of paper around a pencil and it will curl. You try a piece of cardboard, it will buckle and crease. So if you reduce the thickness of that dead outer layer back to what you had as a child, you will see the wrinkles go away.

This can be done using a variety of alpha-hydroxy acids, neutralized by ammonia to a reasonable pH; we're talking about lactic acid primarily, but also malic and tartaric acid. This will loosen the bonds within your skin so it sheds. If you use a white washcloth you'll find it's a lot dirtier because the dead skin is coming off. Remember as a kid when your skin was wet it would squeak? Well, now you've got such a thick layer of dead skin that it gets slimy when it's wet. Get rid of that old dead skin and you'll squeak again. You'll be squeaky clean.

PLASTIC PEOPLE

R. U. Sirius: The process of choosing a mate has deep biological roots. With the revolution in birth control and in vitro birthing, the bio "logic" behind this natural selection recedes and choice becomes an issue of aesthetics. Still, the biological instincts remain deeply imbedded. As we enter the age of popular plastic and physical reconstruction, there's a tendency to recoil at this genetic deceit.

This crime against history, plotted to service beauty contestants and the aging rich, is now committed by the *People* magazine-reading middle class—another radical disjuncture, another reality hack emerges from consumerist frenzy. **M**

PLASTIC SURGERY: Technology is just beginning to offer people the opportunity to alter their physical appearance. Recent disasters (or potential disasters) have revolved around the use of steroids (mostly by male athletes and bodybuilders) and silicone implants for women. It's interesting that both of these self-enhancements lend themselves to exaggerated stereotypes of masculinity and femininity. Meanwhile, it's easy to forget that alterations as deep and powerful as sex-change operations have been taking place since the 1960s.

MEDIA PRANKS

Opposite page:

MONDO VANILLI—

Simone Third Arm,

R. U. Sirius, and

Scrappi Düchamp

R. U. Sirius: It's an article of faith among denizens of the New Edge that we are living in media saturation, where simulations of the real have utterly replaced the real. For us, the media—both the one-way broadcasting media and the interactive media—are a playground and a battleground for competing fantasies. Media pranksters use the mass media's appetite for the sensational, and its inevitable reduction of experience and information to lowest-common denominator clichés, as a way of getting attention for our own activities, and as a way of exposing the utter fraud of modern politics.

Media pranking goes back to the 1920s and the Dadaists, who used to send out false announcements of art events to the print media, getting reporters to show up for non-events. Abbie Hoffman's Yippies were a powerful political force in the radical movement of the 1960s. The entire political strategy of the Yippies revolved around media tricks, such as throwing dollar bills off the balcony of the stock exchange or holding marijuana "smoke-ins" in the New York subway. The press was always informed of Yippie actions.

In the seventies, Malcolm McLaren turned radical pranksterism into a money-making art form. His band, the Sex Pistols, built their reputation around acts of public offense that generated publicity BEFORE the band had any music to show for it.

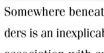

THE LAST WORD

Somewhere beneath the media representation of the Brom murders is an inexplicable human tragedy. Our act of creating a false association with such a tragedy will remain open to ethical interpretation.

We all swim in an ocean of mass media that fills our minds with people and events with which we have no actual connection at all. We commonly absorb these media presences as part of our own "reality," even though any media experience consists

THE LAST WORD: The Negativland record *Helter Stupid* ▲ comes with a chronology explaining their media hoax:

10/20/87: Negativland releases their fourth album, *Escape from Noise,* ▲ and begins preparations for a national tour. The album includes the cut "Christianity Is Stupid," which features the "found" vocal of Reverend Estus Pirkle from a sermon recorded in 1968.

2/20/88: Story appears in the *New York Times*, national wire services, and radio and TV network news relating the arrest of sixteen-year-old David Brom in the ax murders of his father, mother, sister, and brother two days earlier in Rochester, Minnesota. The *New York Times* article mentions that David and his father may have argued over a music tape David had listened to. The Broms are described as a devout Roman Catholic family.

3/10/88: Negativland cancels a U.S. tour when it becomes apparent that the tour will lose money. The group decides to send their American label, SST Records, a phony press release for distribution which attributes the cancellation of the tour to pressure from "Federal Official Dick Jordan," who has advised the band not to leave town pending an investigation

only of one-way, edited representations of reality. Negativland uses this electronic environment of factual fictions as both source and subject for much of our work, keeping in mind that to experience a picture of a thing is not to experience the thing.

Our lie was intended for and directed to the *media*, and it proved very effective in exposing the unreliable

Hal Eisner
EYEWITNESS NEWS

process of cannibalization that passes for "news." Negativland chose to exploit the media's appetite for particularly sensational stories by becoming a subject they could not resist—the latest version of a ridiculous media cliché which proposes that rock song lyrics instigate murder. Common sense suggests that murderers purchase records that appeal to them, just as they purchase the weapons they use.

Helter Stupid is about the media menu of illusions we all eat from, as well as an attempt to materialize our perception of Negativland as a bogus subject of the voracious media meat grinder.

YOU KILLED THAT KID IN MINNESOTA

The number of people who've heard about our connection with this story is far greater than the number of people that will hear the record. The number of people that hear the record are going to outnumber the people who actually buy the record.

into the Brom murders. The press release implies that David and his parents had been arguing about Negativland's song "Christianity Is Stupid" just prior to the murders. The *Times* article is distributed with the press release.

From here on it was off to the races, with *Bay Area Music*, the *Village Voice*, the *San Francisco Chronicle*, and several television stations reporting the situation as fact. Throughout the process Negativland steadfastly refused to comment. Eventually they were called by the lawyers for the convicted murderer, David Brom. They put a photo of David Brom on the cover of *Helter Stupid*. The album collages materials taken from the media coverage of the crime, media coverage of Negativland's "connection to the murders," samples from the song "Christianity Is Stupid," and other relevant materials.

Since then, Negativland have gotten into even more trouble. They put out a record parodying the righteous radical Irish rock band U2. The record, called simply *U2*, featured sampled bits from U2 and a big U2 on the cover. U2's record label, Island, sued the shit out of Negativland and their record label, SST, winning a $90,000 settlement against them. U2 was made to look like a humorless, headless corporate monster, and the extremely liberal rock media reacted with full sympathy for Negativland. What Negativland had done—in effect—was expose righteous rock 'n' roll politics as a simulation, mediated by giant music industry conglomerates and their lawyers.

This statement, "The Last Word," was also part of the package that Negativland included with *Helter Stupid* and was reprinted along with an interview with Negativland members Mark Hosler and Don Joyce in *MONDO*.

The number of people who buy it will outnumber those who really listen to it and read the liner notes. The number of people who read the liner notes and really get what we're saying and think about it will be outnumbered by those who don't. So—in fact—what's going to happen is we're going to end up perpetuating this hoax and this myth about ourselves to a large number of people.

I mean twenty years from now, I'm going to run into someone who's going to say, "Oh yeah, you killed that kid in Minnesota."

ENTERTAINMENT CRIMINALS

We have made the catastrophic discovery that it is legal to torture and murder people with entertainment. The mass audience is in danger of total extinction through "enjoyment." An international consortium of *entertainment criminals* has, through telegenetic engineering, created meta-viruses in the form of pictures and sounds. These *meta-viruses* are virtually indistinguishable from normal pictures and sounds. After entering through the eyes and ears, they devour the imagination of their victim and replace it with the imagination of one of the *entertainment criminals*.

ENTERTAINMENT CRIMINALS: This rant is from Rob Brezny and his band World Entertainment War. While the band is not known for doing hard-core media pranking, sticking to unconventional but stage-bound performances, their "ideology" expresses the attitude of media pranksters toward the entertainment industry.

META-VIRUSES: The idea that ideas spread themselves like viruses through a kind of osmosis is known as memetics and was first proposed in Richard Dawkins's seminal book on DNA, *The Selfish Gene*. This idea-virus concept is one of the central conceits of media activists in the New Edge culture. The New Edge itself, then, is a media virus (see also "Virus").

A BOOK OF PRANKS

John Shirley: It's a big world. It's a swollen world. It's a tumescent world. It's an overburdened, overflowing, data-loaded, high-content, low-clarity world, soaked in media and opinion and, above all, lies. What's important in all this input? Who decides? Which filters have you chosen? Have you mistaken the filters for the truth?

To upset the status quo, here comes *RE/SEARCH*'s latest, *PRANKS!* subtitled "Devious Deeds and Mischievous Mirth" from Timothy Leary, Paul Mavrides, Mark Pauline, Earth First!, Karen Finley, Abbie Hoffman—various politico-pranksters and performance artists. I'll let *RE/SEARCH* speak for itself: "Pranks constitute an art form and genre in themselves...here

PRANKS!: This book is a MUST READ for anybody interested in this subject.

WHAT DO YOU SAY AFTER PO-POMO? OR (THE MANIFESTO ART DAMAGE)

Art Damage is Camp with a Ph.D. Attitude with brains and a wink...

It's Read proof!

It's Self-irreverential!

It's a joke on the zeitgeist.

Out of the primordial tarpits where Kim Fowley meets Dada, came art school graduates with interchangeable last names and vaulting ambitions. Some aspired to avant-garde musicianship and rock godhood. Others consciously used Art Damage to mask guerrilla ontological agendas. And some were just Devo wannabes who discovered they could recycle far more than old Led Zeppelin riffs. Part sampling, part burlesque, Art Damage is all around us. But there is good Art Damage and bad Art Damage—and there are people who wouldn't recognize ironic distance at two feet.

Art Damage could not *exist* until now. It took a peculiar convergence of forces before it could even appear: the global village, marketing psychology, media sophistication, and the Borgesian Library of All Time and Space.

So plunder that library! Seize the raw materials to furnish the Playground of Ideas. Transmute unalloyed dreck into digital gold. Tickle America's self-loathing funny bone!

PO-POMO means Post-postmodern. It's essentially meaningless, except that the "rules" of postmodernism, such as they are, don't need to be followed. In other words, you can try to create wholly original works if you WANT to, provided that it's hip enough.

ART DAMAGE (THE MANIFESTO): On the cover of M2 #5, we reversed the names of the avant-garde guitarists Glenn Branca and Elliot Sharp. Upon noticing this, we decided that this was INTENTIONAL and reinvented Art Damage (see just below). Looking at the cover we decided that the whole thing was designed as a "double take." For instance the heading at the top of the cover says "Guaranteed Read Proof!" and, on first glance, it looks like the fellow with the voluptuous Dr. Fiorella Terenzi has his hand up her dress. Silly, you say? You bet it is. Art damage is whatever you can get away with.

KIM FOWLEY is best known for creating the seventies all-girl, all-underaged, cocktease rock band, The Runaways. Fowley is more infamous around L.A. for his vampire-like appearance, his extremely decadent parties (they often involve sex with animals), and his general LACK OF SUCCESS at becoming a rock Svengali. Some journalist used the term "art damage" in some rock magazine back in the 1970s to describe him, and this somehow logged itself in Zarkov's memory banks.

GOOD ART DAMAGE	BAD ART DAMAGE	NOT ART DAMAGE
Logitech Baby Ad	Benetton Baby Ad	Gerber Baby Ad
New Viennese School	New Wave	New Age
David Cronenberg	Brian DePalma	Jeffrey Dahmer
Madonna	Michael Jackson	Paula Abdul
Perry Farrell	Metallica	Axl Rose
Absolut Vodka Ads	Infiniti Ads	Jack Daniels Ads
Poison	Egoiste	Giorgio
MTV station breaks	MTV	VH-1
Nietzsche	Derrida	God
Public Enemy	Consolidated	Hammer
MONDO Vanilli	Devo	Milli Vanilli
MONDO 2000	*Spy*	*The New Yorker*
Laibach	Boyd Rice	Patrick Buchanan
Howard Stern	Dennis Miller	Jay Leno
Hustler	*Penthouse*	*Playboy*
Negativland	Kostabi	U2
Bowie	Bowie	Tin Machine

STEVE SPEAR

(pranksters) challenge the sovereign authority of words, images, and behavioral convention.
Some tales are bizarre, as when Boyd Rice
presented the First Lady with a skinned sheep's
head on a platter."

BOYD RICE is a performance artist who has—in recent years—either decided to portray, or has ACTUALLY become a hardcore Satanist and neo-Nazi skinhead. Nobody is sure whether he means it or not, perhaps not even Boyd himself.

MONDO VANILLI

MONDO 2000 magazine cofounder and Editor-in-Chief
R. U. Sirius would like to introduce you to his new project,
MONDO Vanilli. MONDO Vanilli is the first VIRTUAL REAL-
ITY ROCK BAND, the house band of the simulacrum. Here
are some things to know about MONDO Vanilli.

A) AUTHENTIC INAUTHENTICITY: In a weird flashback to the American Bandstand fifties, lipsynching is
suddenly an issue in mainstream rock 'n' roll. For
those of us who have been investigating the digital edge of cybermusic—as represented by
house, industrial, hip-hop, and techno—where
it's the song not the singer and where the DJ
fixes it in the mix, this all seems rather silly. So
here comes MONDO Vanilli to take the implica-
tions of Milli Vanilli and do it right.

As the first virtual reality rock band, MONDO
Vanilli makes no pretense that its performance/media
presentation is based around the concept of musicianship. Make no mistake about it, the music is intended to
stand on its own. But the public presentation will be a performance theater in which live music will be STRICTLY verboten.

B) TECHNOLOGICALLY-ASSISTED PERSONAL MUTATION,
THE MORPHING OF R. U. SIRIUS & PERFORMANCE SURGERY.
The first live performance of MONDO Vanilli will be "The Mor-
phing of R. U. Sirius." IN THIS PERFORMANCE, MV MAINMAN
R. U. SIRIUS WILL UNDERGO SURGICAL ALTERATIONS
BEFORE A VIDEO CREW, PHOTOGRAPHER, AND AN
AUDIENCE OF JOURNALISTS. Photographs will
appear along with an article by R. U. Sirius in a
future issue of *MONDO 2000*. Combining plas-
tic surgery, smart drugs, body building, GH

MONDO VANILLI: This is the first press
release for MONDO Vanilli, and it was exten-
sively quoted in the San Francisco Weekly.
MONDO Vanilli is the first band to make a
point out of lipsynching, as can be seen from the
release. They were scheduled to perform in
Pasadena on November 15, 1991, as part of a Cyber-
Arts program and then again at Klub Kommotion in
January in San Francisco as part of a "Cyberpunk Circus"
but cancelled both shows at the last minute. They are calling this their "False Starts" tour and are planning a few more
non-events followed by the release of a False Starts T-shirt with
a list of the performances and dates with a red line through
them and a red "CANCELLED" above each date. In spite of
their non-appearance, a rumor is circulating San Francisco
that their performance at Klub Kommotion was "excellent."
An album and an eventual series of ACTUAL
performances are planned under the title "READ
MY LIPS." We don't know as of yet which
record label this will be released on.

releasers, and other technologies, R. U. Sirius
is performing a public mutation of human form.
He calls this path "Technologically-Assisted
Personal Mutation." He is to be considered a poor
person's (and a smart person's) Michael Jackson.

C) READ MY LIPS & THE WORLD OF MONDO
VANILLI: The first MONDO Vanilli album will be called
"Read My Lips." Eight songs will be combined with audio
collage and MONDO Vanilli product advertisements. This
will function as an introduction to the virtual world of
MONDO Vanilli. In
this world, MONDO
Vanilli is a massive
multinational corpo-
ration that markets
smart drug foods
(MONDO Vanilli Beans
& Synapse Snaps),
cryonic suspension,
sneakers, and omi-
nous toys like the
Klaus Barbie doll,
among other things.
MONDO Vanilli Corp.
also has its own mer-
cenary army, prints
its own currency and
offers it in a straight
dollar-for-dollar
exchange with U.S.
currency, and has its
own religion called

"The Administration." MONDO Vanilli also has an enemy
group, a bunch of high-tech pagan hippies called the Merry
Tweeksters, who make incursions into MV's media
products. The virtual world of MONDO Vanilli will
exfoliate slowly via records, video, film, performance and the actual marketing of products. *M*

MULTIMEDIA TAG TEAMS

Ed Mullin of Sony Corporation is fond of saying: "What is multimedia? The definition shifts depending on what the definer is trying to sell you…"

It's a real wrestling match out there, with chips, storage media, greed, and aggressive marketing all pummeling each other for fun and profit. We may not be able to predict who will take whom to the mat, but we can identify some of the more colorful contenders. They break down into several tag teams:

• The Optical Storage contenders

• Smart TV developers (the marriage of computer and television)

• The Compression seekers (the quest for video images over the phone)

• Computer-as-Media hawkers (publishing by, of, and for the computer)

OPTICAL STORAGE

Here's what's getting most of the press these days. You can store great gobs of data on one of these shiny discs. Any kind of data: a shelf full of books, a day of AM radio, an hour of CD audio, a small bit of full-motion video, a larger bit of not-so-full-motion video…it's up to you to pick and choose among a cornucopia of formats. Optical storage comes in several flavors:

ANALOG STORAGE

This silver disc is the big brother of all these squabbling media siblings. Available since the seventies, analog videodisc allows computer control of video for the creation of interactive videodisc programs. Analog seems to be the media that won't die. The new kids sneer at this older brother, calling analog storage old fashioned. Horsepuckies. Standing

MULTIMEDIA: This entry is from Peter Sugarman, one of our street tech reporters. Gareth Branwyn defines multimedia as the integration of communication elements drawn from different media (text, sound, video, animation). The coordination of these elements and the corresponding interactions with the user are accomplished through a computer. Elements may reside within the computer, or the computer can control other storage/playback devices such as VCRs, videodisc players, and TV monitors. (This is all repeated in "Street Tech.")

the test of time, this is the only videodisc medium actually in use today. And then there's the Baskin Robbins of optical storage...

THE COMPACT DISC

There are SO MANY DIFFERENT flavors of these lil' silver discs. They include:

CD AUDIO—CD audio was the fastest adoption of a new technology in history. It killed vinyl.

CD+G—basically CD Audio plus graphics. Titles in this format have been published for several years, but are still waiting for the hardware that will show them on your TV.

CDV—a format which hasn't caught on, but refuses to die—basically a "45 single" analog videodisc.

CD-ROM—holds up to 550 megabytes of digital information. CD-ROM is driving all the fevered multimedia hoopla. It's portable, dense enough to hold big data, and able to share, to some degree, the economies of scale afforded by its predecessor, CD audio. The only hang-up is needing a CD-ROM player to access the information. Still, costs of these units are dropping rapidly as the technology battles its way onto the business desktop.

CD-I—announced prematurely five years ago, CD-I stands for Compact Disc Interactive. Can you say "couch potato"? This is multimedia for the home. It won't look like a computer—more like a stereo component—and will play on your TV set. This will teach us old folks what young Nintendoids have known all their lives: Touch the TV and the TV touches you. Due imminently, this tech could finally put interactive multimedia in the hands of the masses ("couchware," here we come!).

CD-ROM XA—CD-I will be able to do tricks that plain vanilla CD-ROMs can't. CD-ROM XA (for extended architecture) will bridge the gap. By publishing in CD-Rom XA, programs will be able to run on either CD-ROM or CD-I systems.

CDTV—Commodore Computer stole some of CD-I's thunder by bringing its competing product, CDTV, to market first. At the Microsoft CD-ROM conference, this unit was described as the "Trojan Horse" that will insinuate itself into the lives of the computer illiterate. It's essentially an Amiga computer cross-dressed as a mild-mannered entertainment device.

All these different CD-ROM formats are waiting for new and better compression schemes to permit them to show full-screen, full-motion video. In the meantime, they make do with text, graphics, sounds, animation, and video which is either smaller than full screen or slower than thirty frames per second.

DVI—Digital Video Interactive. Developed by Intel (the same fun guys that put the guts in IBM's CPU), this technology is aimed at the professional market rather than the living room. Many new media savants find DVI in competition with CD-I. Probably not, as the target markets differ. DVI is not so much a different flavor CD—more a different way to store the information onto disc.

OTHER BATTLES

• SMART TV—There are other arenas, besides optical storage, where science and the marketplace are spoiling for a fight. As we all know, computers have gone from room size to palm size. As soon as computers start ducking inside our appliances, the Smart TV will move into our living rooms. It'll be your media agent, taking notes on your viewing habits, and taping what you missed, even when you didn't bother to find out what was on. Your interests will be its commands. Besides the improvement in the human/machine interface, program quality will also improve because of the digital signal. And, you'll be able to manipulate the pictures and sounds to your heart's delight. Today's football widows have given us a taste of what's to come.

• VIDEO COMPRESSION—The search for new and better ways to compress video data is the commercial equivalent of the race to the moon. The stakes are tremendous. When video shrinks to fit inside a phone cable, it'll be a whole new ballgame. Why buy a movie if you can get it downloaded into your Smart TV? Every film in the vaults of major Hollywood studios could be a phone call away. The mind boggles.

• COMPUTER PUBLISHING—Actually, we don't have to wait for our computers and TVs to mate and breed Smart TVs. Often overlooked is the fact that computers themselves represent a new medium, a new platform to publish on. Using the computing power of the display vehicle, these documents can respond to the user, and in that interaction, present a new experience with each use. Touch the Computer and the Computer touches you...

WHAT WILL SURVIVE?

The answer is simple. Nothing. Should this inhibit your adoption of the new media into your life? Of course not. If you have an itch, scratch it. If multimedia can help you solve a problem at work, or provide home entertainment which encourages something better than legume emulation, go for it. Don't worry about whether there will be a newer, sexier, faster technology waiting in the wings. *There always will be.* If you wait for it, you'll never get the pleasure from what's here for you now. *M*

NANOTECHNOLOGY

NANOTECHNOLOGY: This piece is sampled from an article by Ed Niehaus. "Nano" is a prefix which means "one-billionth," and nanotechnology talks about machines that are on the order of one-billionth of a meter large...the size of molecules and atoms. The idea behind nanotechnolgy is that it should be possible to assemble a desired molecule one atom at a time, like a Tinkertoy. Support for this dream comes from the existence of the Scanning Tunneling Microscope (STM for short), a thin, highly charged wire that is mechanically scanned back and forth over a surface of interest. The surface is charged as well, and the idea is that the wire is always just on the point of sending a spark down to the surface, and by tracking the electric potential between the two, you actually measure bumps in the surface that are the size of one atom. By computer-processing the STM data, one can in fact generate pictures that seem to show the atoms in some crystals all lined up like oranges in a supermarket display. It is also possible to use the STM to actually pick up individual atoms and move them around. Recently the doughty engineers of IBM used an STM device to spell I-B-M out in atoms.

GETTING SMALL

In his book *Engines of Creation*, Eric Drexler coined the term "nanotechnology" to mean the inexpensive and complete control over the structure of matter. His predictions of the future of engineering are both disturbing and profoundly hopeful. Nanotechnology may offer inexpensive solutions to many of the major problems facing mankind, including hunger, housing, and pollution. Nanotechnology could also result in world domination by whoever first achieves the breakthrough to "self-replicating assemblers," the virus-sized, computer-controlled, man-made robots Drexler predicts will become our servants/saviors in the next century.

BUILDING THE CORNUCOPIA

Nanotechnology has been described as the manufacturing technology of the twenty-first century. Some argue that it will be able to manufacture almost any chemically stable structure at low cost. If realized, such precise fabrication abilities could be used both to improve existing products and to build products that are impossible within present constraints. Based on estimates of parts count and power dissipation, components of molecular size could make a single desktop computer of the future more powerful than all the computers in existence today combined. Devices smaller than a red blood cell might circulate through the body and attack and remove both fat deposits and infectious organisms. **N**

SELF-REPLICATING ASSEMBLERS: There is a regular meeting of nanotechnology-interested people in Silicon Valley. The great missing link in nanotechnology is the assembler, that microscopic machine that can assemble whatever molecule you want it to. Program the assembler, give it some carbon and water, and it'll build you a beefsteak...or a new human kidney. Since building an assembler is so inconceivably difficult, the hope is that you can use assemblers to construct more assemblers. This is, in a way, what living cells do. At this point, nanotechnology is a fairly science-fictional concept. The big dream which many (often overweight and unhealthy) nanotech enthusiasts express is that there will someday be tiny nano-machines which they can inject into themselves. These little helpers, it is hoped, will clear the cholesterol out of their arteries, the Alzheimer's-disease-producing aluminum out of their brains, and so on.

MARIA GIBERT

THE NET

Gary Wolf & Michael Stein: Today, people are using their computers to travel the globe. Technically, it's simple. A small, inexpensive box, called a modem, converts your computer's digital signals into audible pulses that can zip through the phone system. Now, with the right combination of malice and know-how, you can release a virus that will dim lights and scramble air traffic around the world.

More humbly (and more legally), a modem permits you to hook up with an international web of computer networks and bulletin board systems (BBSs). These networks and BBSs are virtual communities, electronic meeting places for a far-flung, multilingual membership.

What happens on a BBS? People dial up or "jack in," read their electronic mail, scan the ongoing public discussions, leave their own traces (or not) and vanish, either racing off to another BBS or dropping back into their gravity-stricken physical lives. This world of on-line communication is known as THE ETHER.

Most recent estimates put the number of BBSs at more than 30,000. Huge "electronic highways" allow data to flow between systems. Want to find out what's happening on-line? Check out "Boardwatch," a jewel of a journal that scans the ether with the dedication of a medieval astronomer tracing the epicycles of Mars. "Boardwatch" costs $18/year and can be ordered by calling (303) 973-6038.

The WELL, an all-purpose net laden with writers, Mondoids, and computer wizards, was started by *Whole Earth Catalog*, founded by Stewart Brand. At ten bucks a month and two bucks an hour, it's one of the main lines for cyberheads. If you want to find us, that's where we'll be! Voice: (415) 332-4335. Data: (415) 332-1396.

For some ultra-weird stuff, check Private Idaho, the BBS created by Robert Carr, the man who brought you the famous Mac programs Momonoids from the Deep, Porno Writer, and MacJesus. Be sure to read the warning Carr posted for federal agents who might be spying on his system—it's hilarious. Data: (208) 338-9227. **N**

GARY WOLF & MICHAEL STEIN: Gary Wolf is an up-and-coming journalist who wrote an infamous story for *Rolling Stone* about smart drugs. He and Michael Stein are writing an electronic travel guide to computer networks and BBSs. Email your BBS suggestions to gwolf@well.sf.ca.us

PEG PASTERNAK

FASTA
El Coche
PALOMA GRANDE
THE FOOT
Captain Steubing
Ramona
DA LETTA
THAN
PASTERNAK
TO-LANE-LOVE-PEG

No Madness

THE DIFFERENCE BETWEEN

MOVING AND NOT MOVING

I have some interesting toys, but I have some real objectives, too, which mostly have to do with erasing the difference between moving and not moving. None of it is there just to be nifty.

I want to be able to do R & D work, writing, consulting, without having to stop and set up an entire lifestyle someplace. Now, what that means in essence is that I want maximum autonomy in terms of computing power, electrical power generation, and communications capability and maintainability anywhere in the world.

POWER

Power has to be autonomous. I have eighty-two watts of solar panels, regenerative braking, the ability to charge off of any publicly available grid, or off of somebody's car. All of those things are integrated into a power management system with distributed batteries and redundant systems and so on, so I have a good chance of always having power.

COMPUTERS

The high-level graphic interface is a Mac portable. The screen is mounted on the console on the front of the bike, and there's a cursor-positioning device on the helmet so I can move the mouse around while I'm traveling.

The Mac also connects to a Sun computer back behind the seat which I use as a mapping workstation and a communications node. Underneath the Mac screen there is also a PC clone. I'm using that for computer-aided design, a lot of my mapping stuff, satellite tracking for the ham radio satellites, my big data base, and so on. While I'm mobile I use a tiny monitor that's mounted on my helmet. It's a Private Eye.

COMMUNICATION

The main business conduit is a cellular phone with two modems and a fax. I'm on the network

NOMADNESS: Steve Roberts is a tall, bearded "ungineer" (he dropped out of engineering school) who spends his life riding around the world on his huge, computer-laden bicycle. He is the author of two books, and publishes a magazine called *High-Tech Nomadness*. ▲

A REGENERATIVE BRAKING system slows a vehicle by hooking its wheel to the crank of a dynamo that generates electricity which can be saved…this instead of just clamping onto the wheel to generate friction and heat.

SUN and Silicon Graphics are the two companies making the most popular machines that are a notch larger than Macs and PCs. The Sun Sparc and the Silicon Graphics Indigo are big hits.

THE PRIVATE EYE ▲ is a very small headset-mounted display that creates a hanging sheet of monochrome cyberspace right in front of your eye. The resolution is 280 pixels wide by 720 pixels high. The thing works off a single row of 280 tiny red-light-emitting diodes. A counterbalanced mirror sweeps up and down while the diodes' pattern changes for each line. In effect the device paints a computer-screen image onto your retina one scan line at a time.

two or three times a day to communicate with
my base offices.

I'm also a very active ham radio operator.
I can be out in the middle of Asia and still send
and receive email. I have access to the new
Microsats, which are ham radio satellites. I can do
this all while mobile, with my flip-up antennas. And
there's a small amateur television station, too, that I use
with my little Sony camera. I'm doing a bi-weekly feed
to a cable TV show called "Silicon Valley Report." Having
all that capability on the bike means that it's simply a
matter of adding one circuit board to have an amateur
television station.

EMAIL: For an explanation of email see the notes to "Electronic Freedom."

BEHEMOTH
designer Steve
Roberts, photo by
Robert Waldman

THE BIKE

The bike itself is an eight-foot recumbent with a four-
foot trailer. The whole thing weighs about 350
pounds. It's got fifty-four speeds, which helps,
and the granny gear is really, really low. I call
it BEHEMOTH: Big, Electronic, Human-Ener-
gized Machine, Only Too Heavy.

WHY?

Basically, all I'm doing here is chasing a dream,
living my passions. I believe that passion is one of
the strongest motivators for doing anything, certainly for
learning. A lot of the reactions I get from people are, "Hey,
you know something I've always wanted to do..." Of course,
my response is, "Well, go for it!"

The thing about all these communications tools is that they
erase boundaries; it doesn't really matter where I am. I have very
little respect for national borders or other such political artifacts.
I live in dataspace —dataspace is my real home.

The beauty is, I have these growing circles of friends who
are just out there somewhere. I have no idea what they look
like or anything else, but we all have this brain-to-
brain contact. It's a meta-community which is very
alive and energetic and complex. N

DATASPACE: In the words of John
Perry Barlow, "Cyberspace is where I
am when I'm on the telephone." When
you're on the Net as well, the construct
gets a further element of reality and perma-
nence...you can go back and read the same email
again, even though you can't usually hear the same
phone conversation twice.

Personal COMPUTING

St. Jude: War has been touted as the main spur for technological advance, but technology is also driven by desire. We want the sweet tech, neat toys, tech of our dreams. When the first warehouse-sized electronic computers appeared, the techies joked about having their own personal computers— maybe even the size of televisions, heh heh. It's been a long haul to the ultralight notebook computers that are fast and vast and talk to anything...

THE BIRTH
OF THE PERSONAL COMPUTER

The first personal computer—named Altair after one of the brightest stars—was featured on the January 1975 cover of *Popular Electronics* magazine. The day the issue came out MITS was a company of twelve people and Bill Gates was a student at Harvard. From that moment on the world was changed forever.

People are always amazed when I tell them it all began in Albuquerque, New Mexico. Not Silicon Valley, not Route 128. That's right, personal computing was born in the Land of Enchantment, the land of turquoise jewelry and blue-corn enchiladas with an egg on top. I know because I was an eyewitness. I was in the actual goddamn delivery room.

As head MITS propagandist—and on a nearly nonexistent ad budget—it was my job to get the word out about this revolution to hobbyists throughout the land. It was also my job to write instructions telling them how to put these things together, as the majority were sold in kit form.

MICROSOFT

The other day I was in Stacey's bookstore in Palo Alto when I saw something that had me laughing uncontrollably and nearly rolling in the aisles. It was

BIRTH OF THE PERSONAL COMPUTER: This reminiscence is by David Bunnell, who was an early employee of a company called MITS. "MITS" originally stood for "Model Instrumentation Telemetry Systems," and it originally made equipment for model rockets (a light-flasher so that you could take a time-lapse photo of your rocket's trajectory and estimate how fast it was going). MITS founder Ed Roberts was the first to have the idea of taking Intel's new 8080 processor chip and soldering wires to it to make a small computer—as opposed to keeping the wonder-chips ensconced in basements full of Hulking Giant equipment. Thus was born the Altair.

BILL GATES, the president of Microsoft, Inc., is probably the youngest self-made billionaire the world has ever seen. Gates got his start by writing a version of the interactive computer language BASIC which would run on the Altair. To Gates's fury, an early version of the program (which was sold on a long, punched, paper tape) was stolen during a demo, and many pirate copies of it were made. Gates's big score came in 1982 when IBM gave him the contract to design the software for its new personal computer. This was PC-DOS, for "Personal Computer Disk Operating System." IBM made the wise decision to make its computing architecture "open," meaning that other manufacturers are allowed to make IBM-PC-compatible machines, which are called "PC clones." The PC clones all use MS-DOS, for "Microsoft Disk Operating System," and there are millions of them. Microsoft has definitely not sat on its laurels—its new operating system, Windows, is a shoo-in to find a place on every PC clone that's powerful enough to use it.

MICHAEL LLEWELLYN

the Microsoft MS-DOS Encyclopedia—or more precisely, it was a photograph in the introduction of this three-thousand-plus page tome. There was the world's youngest self-made billionaire, Bill Gates; his rock 'n' roll partner Paul Allen; and the original Microsoft crew as they appeared in 1977 when they were in start-up mode in Albuquerque.

Yes, Microsoft started in Albuquerque, too. As did *Personal Computing Magazine* and the now-defunct U.S. Robotics Society. Bill wasn't so rich then, though Microsoft was already the number one microcomputer software company. The funny part is that Bill and the gang looked so outrageously scruffy and young and very unlike a future Fortune 500 company. Long hair, beards, sloppy, casual dress—these people looked like they were just coming down off a ten-year acid trip.

ACID ROCK

When Gates and Allen started the MITS software division in 1975 prior to striking out on their own, they played the loudest, hardest-driving music they could find, and they played it full blast all day long while sitting at their keyboards writing code.

Personal computing has become just another business. Bill Gates wears a jacket and tie. Apple Computer is the darling of Wall Street, and hardly anyone remembers MITS at all. However, something incredibly important transpired along the way: Computer technology was liberated. It is currently in the hands of millions worldwide. The participants who created the industry may have turned into business toads, but users, God bless their nerdy hearts, are carrying on the vision.

THE STONE AGE OF COMPUTING

Todd Rundgren: When the only tool you have is a hammer, every problem looks like a nail—that's the way we use computers in this, the Stone Age of computing.

THE DAWN OF PERSONAL COMPUTING

Lee Felsenstein: "Computer Power to the People" was our slogan back then—never mind that the people weren't clamoring for it. We knew that Americans could handle the most complex gizmos provided that they believed that the gizmos were actually simple and that it was only a bunch of self-serving elitists trying to convince them otherwise. Ten thousand of us sent in $2 for the plans to the "TV Typewriter" when a how-to-build-it article appeared in *Radio-Electronics* in 1973. The editors considered twenty letters a large response to such an article. Something was moving! Even IBM came around to our "open architecture" way of sharing information. It had to. The closed-architecture personal computer it first fielded was a failure.

THE NEW EDGE

R. U. Sirius: It's obvious that the New Edge, both cultural and economic, lies in the evolution of creative, interactive technology. From desktop video to hypermedia, from art software based on Mandelbrot sets to virtual reality, from the completely portable office-in-a-suitcase containing fax, computer, modem, and phone to the power of supercomputing on a desktop, the computer/high-tech industry has already reached beyond the limits of what a dulled, prosaic, practical-minded, slow-moving, middle-of-the-road public is going to find useful. Call it a hyper-hip wet dream, but the information and communications technology industry requires a new, ACTIVE consumer, or it's going to stall. This is one reason why we are amplifying the mythos of the sophisticated, high-complexity, fast-lane/real-time, intelligent, active, and creative reality hacker. **P**

David Bunnel, Founder of PC WORLD, photograph by Robert Waldman

POLITICS

A THANKSGIVING PRAYER

RONALD REAGAN & REALITY

Before the Reagan Era, people had more conscience about being utterly deceptive, and now it's taken for granted. It's really disturbing to me. I think that Reagan probably instituted a level of unreality that's going to be a long-term part of American culture. There are some cultures in the world that are fundamentally deceitful, and I think ours is going to be one of them now. It's a hard thing to crawl back once you've slunk into that particular pit.

ABSTRACTED WARRIORS

John Barlow: Watching TV reports, the closest one got to the action was the occasional footage of people scurrying around in the darkness following a Scud warning, followed by a blurry flash of distant fireworks as the Patriot took out the Scud.

Which was, in a way, a perfect metaphor for the apparent abstraction and bloodlessness of this new form of combat. A missile would emerge without any tangible point of origin, its senders anonymous and devoid of human characteristics. A machine would detect it, another would plot its trajectory, and a third would rush out to kill it. It was like an academic argument.

A THANKSGIVING PRAYER: This festive benison comes from William Burroughs and can also be found in his small-press book *Tornado Alley*, currently available (along with most other Burroughs books) from City Lights Books. For info on Burroughs see the *User's Guide* entry on "Evolutionary Mutations."

"Thanksgiving Prayer" was produced as a video by KPDX and Island Records. The video shows the spectral Burroughs's face in front of all the American icons—flags, monuments, astronauts, armies, factories, war.

RONALD REAGAN & REALITY: This is from an interview with Jaron Lanier, who is the plump, dreadlocked genius-inventor of the DataGlove and the Eyephones, among other things. His company, VPL (which stands for Visual Programming Language), is the undisputed leader in ready-to-run virtual reality installations. Jaron has a collection of some three hundred ethnic musical instruments and says that his original inspiration for the DataGlove was a desire to build the ultimate air guitar. His father was a science-fiction writer. Much more of Jaron in "Virtual Reality."

Thanks for the wild turkey and the passenger pigeons, destined to be shit out through wholesome American guts.

Thanks for a continent to despoil and poison.

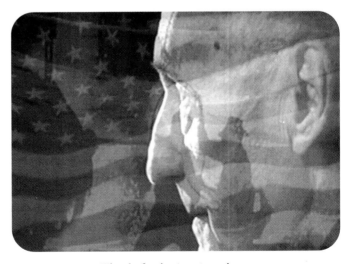

Thanks for Indians to provide a modicum of challenge and danger.

Thanks for vast herds of bison to kill and skin leaving the carcasses to rot.

Thanks for bounties on wolves and coyotes.

Thanks for the American dream,

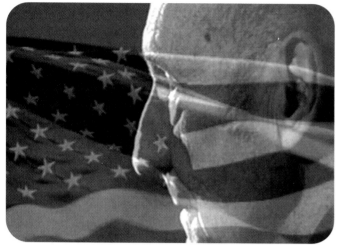

to vulgarize and falsify until the bare lies shine through.

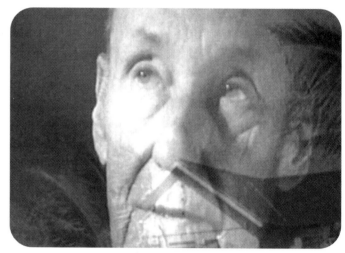

Thanks for the KKK.

For nigger-killin' lawmen, feelin' their notches.

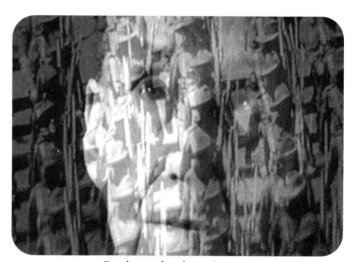

For decent church-goin' women,

with their mean, pinched, bitter, evil faces.

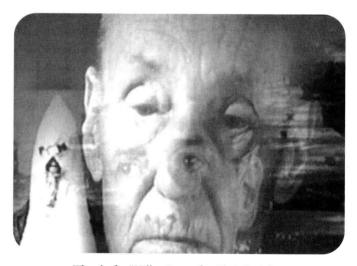

Thanks for "Kill a Queer for Christ" stickers.

Thanks for laboratory AIDS.

Thanks for Prohibition

and the war against drugs.

Thanks for a country

where nobody's allowed to mind their own business.

Thanks for a nation of finks.

Yes, thanks for all the memories—

all right let's see your arms!

You always were a headache and you always were a bore.

Thanks for the last and greatest betrayal

of the last and greatest of human dreams.

KPDX PRODUCTION
CENTER
WILLIAM BURROUGHS
"THANKSGIVING
PRAYER" 124
ISLAND RECORDS
director GUS VAN SANT
editor Wade Evans
camera Bob Yeoman
date June 17, 1930

THE SANCTUARY OF THE SCREEN

Trying to surrender to the Italian television crew through whose cameras they were beamed to us, the Iraqi soldiers looked hapless and confused. The were devastated refugees from the real world, trying desperately to enter the sanctuary of the Screen, a sanctuary we had enjoyed throughout this affair, whether in an armchair in Terre Haute or at the bombardier's workstation in a B-52.

The massacre, in which we may have incinerated as many as 400,000 soldiers and civilians while losing 179 of our own troops, was pronounced a great and courageous victory. Not since Agincourt, when the technology of the English longbow thoroughly undid the French, has there been such an unfair fight. At least the English had the grace to mourn the French. But they had been in direct contact with the humanity they had snuffed out. For us, it was a statistical exercise.

POLITICS IS THE
ENTERTAINMENT BRANCH OF INDUSTRY

I haven't decided to run for president, but I HAVE been thinking about it. If I do it, I would do it without party affiliation. The problem is, you need maybe $2 million just to get your name printed on the ballot in all the states, and that's without any cash for any kind of campaign. And the minute you're in the megabucks category that you need to campaign, you owe somebody a favor. So I've considered the possible strategy of the noncampaign where I say, "Okay, I'm available as a candidate. I've got my name on the ballot, and when you get tired of everyone else, just vote for me." So it's pretty straightforward and awfully cheap.

My idea is the only way you can exert influence over the media is to be president. I always say that politics is the entertainment branch of industry. A president can make things happen. Not by laws, but by force of personality.

WOODSTOCK NATION REVISITED

It just shows the flexibility of the human organism that people who would willingly sit in the mud and chant "no rain" between badly amplified rock groups turn out to run the economy. **P**

POLITICS IS THE ENTERTAINMENT BRANCH OF INDUSTRY: These two entrys are from Frank Zappa. Zappa's long career has combined rock and avant-garde music with scathing social satire. Zappa emerged in the rock firmament right around the same time as all of the early hippie bands like the Grateful Dead, Jefferson Airplane, The Doors, Buffalo Springfield. But Zappa, though he looked like another hippie, satirized the hippie culture. His third album with the Mothers of Invention, *We're Only in It for the Money,* was a particularly NASTY look at the counterculture scene.

Psychedelic Drugs

R. U. Sirius: The links between psychedelic drugs and the New Edge culture are deep and subtle. Due to the regrettably silly fact that they are not only illegal, but classified as narcotics along with such SEVERELY detrimental substances as heroin, cocaine, and amphetamines, the role of psychedelic drugs in these zero-tolerance times tends to be down-played. Still, the fact remains that psychedelics have greatly influenced high-tech's evolution.

Setting aside for a moment the varieties of spiritual and psychological experiences that have been reported by psychedelic trippers, one might look upon psychedelics as temporarily allowing the human brain to process greater quantities of information. This is QUITE literal.

As with the "smart drugs," psychedelics cause the brain to release vasopressin, a brain chemical which seems to speed up and sharpen the brain's processes. On top of that, psychedelics INHIBIT the release of serotonin. Serotonin may be what Aldous Huxley intuited when he theorized that the brain has a "reducing valve." HIGH levels of serotonin in the brain limit the firing of information across brain cells. These limits are important for us. When too much information enters the brain, it becomes difficult to focus on basic tasks. One might, in the rush of vastly fascinating and complex mindstuff, put the baby back in the refrigerator and the turkey in the crib.

On the other hand, the high serotonin levels necessary for our functioning in hard industrial reality may be accountable for the overall "smallmindedness" of modern man. NOW, as we spend less time in hard reality and more time in virtual reality—or information space— we tend to seek those things that allow the brain to process more information.

Peter Stafford, author of *The Psychedelic Encyclopedia*, has compared the use of mind-altering substances to changing the filters on your "perceptual" camera. In other words, you are forced by the drug to

LITERALLY see things from a different perspective. Being able to access multiple points of view is an important part of the creative process, thus the popularity of mind-altering drugs with creative artists throughout the ages. Interesting solutions to creative and technological problems often result from these different angles and vantage points that are brought on by mind-altering chemicals, thus the popularity of mind-altering drugs with today's technological hackers.

DMT MACHINERY IN DEEP SPACE

Terence McKenna: I think the experience of the tryptamine hallucinogens is qualitatively different from any other hallucinogen. It exceeds the model of Jungian-Freudian psychology by quite a bit. The tryptamine hallucinogens don't seem to convey you into a part of the human psyche, personal or collective. It's more like they convey you into a parallel universe or an alternative dimension that has a reality outside of the human psyche.

The other aspect of the tryptamine hallucinogens is that there is felt to be an intelligent presence that you can interact with and dialogue with. The messages are insights from a point of view not that of the ego, but they come into the mind with great clarity and diction. They're like listening to yourself think, except it isn't yourself thinking.

Most people just explore the area right over the threshold of activity, and think that that's all it is: this amphetaminelike lift, flat geometric visual hallucinations, accelerated thought process. Those are the things which happen with a light dose of these compounds.

On an effective dose, you get these hyper-dimensional hallucinations that are more like sculptured geometric patterns that can be viewed from all angles. You get the sense of the contact with a hierarchy of organized intelligence. You get these extremely pristine hallucinations of machinery in deep space, alien architectures, bizarre planetary ecosystems, just a very galactic kind of tapping-in to the information field. But that is not happening unless people take committed doses…

PSILOCYBIN UFO EXPERIENCES

The UFO is the central mystery symbol of the psilocybin experience, because the psilocybin

TRYPTAMINE HALLUCINO-GENS contain the chemical dimethyltryptamine, or DMT. DMT resembles certain hormones made in the brain, and there is speculation that the brain secretes DMT to produce its own "drug-free" visionary experiences. Synthetic DMT has been available on the black market for years. DMT is also found in a variety of South American plants. South American Indians make a DMT snuff called yopo; they also add DMT-bearing plant leaves to a psychedelic brew they make with the yage or ayahuasca vine. Parts of McKenna's *True Hallucinations* deal with yage. A "classic" account of the search for yage is found in *The Yage Letters* 🔺 by William Burroughs & Allen Ginsberg.

SEBASTIAN HYDE

experience blends imperceptibly into the UFO-contact experience if the doses are high enough. Now that's a fairly radical claim. These two fringe concerns, UFOs and psychedelic drugs, have never really been connected in the public mind, probably because linking a taboo to a pariah is not good sociological strategy. Nevertheless, experientially they are definitely linked, and it is almost as though the UFO experience is a psychedelic experience induced by something other than the direct ingestion of a chemical agent. It's breaking through from the collective psyche, a totality-symbol organized around the idea of the hyper-dimensional rotating vehicle, which is linked to earlier images of the soul, earlier images of angelic flight and that sort of thing. In its modern expression it's the UFO, which looks like a mushroom, strangely enough. These are like visual and topological puns.

"PSYCHEDELIC" still means "mind-manifesting."

I'm talking about five dried grams for a 140-pound person to experience these more intense psilocybin-induced things. I think if you're going to bother to take a hallucinogen, you should take it at a sufficient amount that you can tell it from any other hallucinogen. At a very low dose, you're just sort of buzzed. But as you pile it on, then the special characteristics of each one begin to become apparent.

PSYCHEDELIC ANTIFASCISM

Psychedelic drugs decondition you from the prevailing myth of whatever culture you're in. That is a political act, to decondition yourself from a cultural mythology, and political acts are closely watched and controlled because they have consequences. The people at the top of the pyramid reserve the right to control political acts. This is the real controversy about psychedelic drugs. It's not whether one in 50,000 people steps out of a second floor window. No, the issue is what happens to the other 49,999 people. How their attitudes toward authority, their own lives, and their ability to take control of their own lives are subtly altered. It's a tremendous force for antifascism.

LSD FLOWERS

We used to get crystal flowers that were three to six inches in diameter. The LSD crystals were suspended in gelatin. We'd have this absolutely flat three-foot-square glass plate at the right temperature. We had a roll of foam tape about an eighth of an inch thick. We had the glass scribed for the shape and the dimensions, and we had it leveled. We'd get all the tape on and then we'd mix up a coffeepot with Knox gelatin, the LSD, a little alcohol, and water and stir it up with a stirrer for quite a while. Then the chemist would pour it around and get it so it would run into the corners. Looking at it under ultraviolet light, you'd get different intensities. Acid crystals...acid flowers. Probably not many people in the world have seen those.

LSD FLOWERS: This is from memoirs by Captain Clearlight, who was responsible for the distribution of some quarter of a billion 250-microgram hits of LSD in the sixties and seventies.

JFK: THE FIRST PSYCHEDELIC PRESIDENT

Jack waved away the concerns of the S.S. men at the door. "I have a right to some privacy, dammit, and I'm good and well going to get it. Now."

As his chauffeur drove him away from the White House, Kennedy leaned back against the seat in relief. His thoughts wandered to the woman he was on his way to visit. Although she would be difficult to live with, as he had remarked more than once to her brother-in-law Ben, she was certainly dynamic. He really liked her. She was hot in bed, too. Up there with Marilyn and Judith. And she had a way about her. Persuasive. He still couldn't believe she'd gotten him to smoke marijuana in the White House! He laughed. Now she'd persuaded him to try her new "wonder love drug."

PSYCHEDELIC PRESIDENT: This is by Nan C. Druid and is based on material in Timothy Leary's *Flashbacks*, Benjamin Bradlee's *Conversations With Kennedy*, and Victor Lasky's *JFK*. If Oliver Stone is right in saying that JFK was assassinated for being about to bring peace, might it also be possible that LSD showed Jack what peace is? Did the CIA kill JFK for LSD? It makes a nice sentence, anyway.

EVERYTHING IS LOVE

Mary Pinchot smiled at Jack as he looked at her in wonderment. "You're feeling pretty high now, aren't you, Jack?"

The president nodded. "A little bit thirsty, too." He looked at her in expectation and she smiled again. "How about some orange juice?"

"That's the absolutely perfect thing. That sounds great. Orange juice!"

Mary rose to her feet and padded into the kitchen. Jack watched her body flow upwards and noticed how cat-like she moved as she left the room. The kitchen light was too bright. As she switched it on he flinched and shut his eyes. The pain was gone, but he kept his eyes closed. "Technicolor," he thought.

Mary was back with the juice. "Here you go, Jack." He opened his eyes and reached for the glass. "This juice tastes good…" Suddenly oranges became terribly significant. "My God," he said. "The world's insane. We're contemplating madness."

Mary put her arms around him. "Jack, you can change that. You have the power to manifest a vision of peace."

TARANTULA VENOM

JANET ROSS'S ACCOUNT:

SICILY, 1890

There are various kinds of the insect of different colors; the women in the fields are the most liable to be bitten, because they wear so little clothing on account of the intense heat. A violent fever is the beginning of the disease. The person bitten sways backwards and forwards, moaning violently. Musicians are called, and if the tune does not strike the fancy of the tarantata (the person who has been bitten), she moans louder, crying "No! No! Basta! Not that air." The fiddler instantly changes, and the tambourine beats fast and furious to indicate the tempo. At last the tarantata approves of the tempo, and begins to dance frantically.

Her friends try to find out the color of the tarantula that has bitten her, and adorn her dress and her wrists with ribbons of the same tint as the insect: blue, green, or red. If no one can indicate the proper color, she is decked with streamers of every hue which flutter wildly about her as she dances and tosses her arms in the air. They generally begin the ceremony indoors, but it often ends in the street, on account of the heat and the concourse of people. When the tarantata is quite worn out she is put into a warm bed and sleeps, sometimes for eighteen hours at a stretch.

TARANTULA VENOM: Tarantism is the condition produced in a person by the bite of a tarantula spider. It's a painful, heavy trip that usually wears off—if you dance enough. People under the influence are tarantata (singular) or tarantati (plural), and they like to dance to the tarantella. This contribution was researched by Queen Mu. She advises the reader, "Don't try tarantula venom. It permanently imprints the nervous system with a manic-depressive syndrome—and it's probably carcinogenic."

AUGUSTUS HARE'S ACCOUNT: IN THE BOOT OF ITALY, 1910

Tarantism was an epidemic of melancholy madness, which pervaded the women in the boot of Italy, ending in frenzies like those of hydrophobia and sometimes in death, and was believed to proceed from the bite of the tarantula, chiefly because the disease appears in the season when this spider wakes up for summer life. It was believed that music is the best means of giving relief to the tarantati, inciting them to dance and causing them to throw off the poison of the tarantula in perspiration. The tarantata, dressed in white and crowned with flowers, used to be led out into the garden by her friend, and the musicians in attendance would play the air of the tarantella, which the tarantata would follow, leaving one partner after another until she finally fell down exhausted, when a pail of cold water was thrown on her, and she was put to bed. The epidemic, and the belief in the tarantula bite, spread over the whole of Italy. *P*

Rants

NEW WORLD DISORDER:
ALL IS NOT ONE!

R. U. Sirius: Back in our second issue, commenting on the end of the cold war, I warned of a "legalistic, megacorporate, one-world, peace-on-earth." Right. Welcome to the New World Order.

So here we are—decadent-softcore-commercial anarchists operating out of multinational Japan's favorite two-bit Banana Republic, this mercenary entertainment state with a big Hollywood Rambo ego, all glitter on the edges and PROFOUNDLY stupid in the middle. How can we RESIST the New World Order, irresistible as it is?

There's always been the idealistic hope, ever since the League of Nations, that in this time of increased interpenetration and communication, nations great and small could come together to blah blah blah ad nauseum. Forget it! The New World Order is the thousand year Reich of the international well-behaved center, with a small sexually pentup macho American adolescent core of police protectors and overseas mercenaries.

To resist the New World Order, spread chaos and confusion, first amongst yourselves. DON'T come together. Come apart. Don't identify with the nation state, the tribe, your race, gender, bulletin board, or dance club. That's how you get suckered. Be mercilessly politically incorrect. Be commercially successful by being pleasingly offensive. Subvert through media, not because you think you can "change the system" but because successfully tickling America's self-loathing funny bone is an amusing form of foreplay. And believe us, everybody's gonna get fucked.

These are RANTS. And YOU DON'T EXPLAIN RANTS!!! For books full of rants see *Rants* and *Apocalypse Culture*, 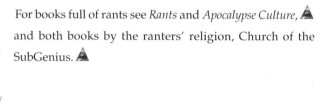 and both books by the ranters' religion, Church of the SubGenius.

BART NAGEL

BART NAGEL

Holocaust German-style,1940s: piled-up dead Jews, gypsies, and communists in a concentration camp. Holocaust American-style,1990s: Consumer goods spill out of the guts of bombed-out cars in a silent traffic jam in the Kuwaiti desert. With dead Iraqis hidden from view inside.

Johnny's come marching home. America is transformed in its pride. The American media completely capitulated to state censorship. THAT JOB IS DONE.

Have no illusions. Something has changed. You blinked your eyes and there was suddenly a juggernaut. Blink again and it's breaking down your door. Abortion. Drugs. Freedom of speech. You could wake up tomorrow and find out that if it ain't whitebread, it ain't allowed. We can now see how fast it can happen.

So the New World DisOrder—which is all you have left—starts within yourself. It starts when somebody says, "We should (or shouldn't) fight against Iraq" and you think, "What the fuck do you mean by *we*? I'm not gonna fight, you're not gonna fight, and I'm not a member of any militaristic state. There IS no

we." The New World DisOrder starts when you realize that safe sex is boring sex, cheap thrills are fun, AND YOU'RE AS ATAVISTIC AS THEY ARE. The New World DisOrder starts when you no longer can listen to debates about whether the nice guys or the mean guys can make the trains run on time. This ain't a reasoned debate. This is Jehovah against Dionysus. Let's drink that tired old self-righteous motherfucker under the table.

WALRUS GUMBO

Queen Mu: John Lennon knew. But then he was a prophet. Michael Jackson knows. But then he's been co-opted.

I've got this big jigsaw puzzle I've had ever since the sixties. Every once in a while I haul it out of mothballs and see if I can put it together yet. There are a few pieces still missing—and there are a few pieces that seem to belong to another set altogether. The puzzle is called Walrus Gumbo (evidence, I claim, for John's prophetic genius!).

Here's the picture in broad strokes. The border's pretty much there. Ron and Nancy, George Bush, and Elizabeth Taylor. It looks kinda like a garden party. Yoko, Sean, and Macaulay Culkin. The Elephant Man. Even the Simpsons. The central icon, dancing on the Ford, is surely Michael Jackson...but I can't find the face piece. I've got a piece that fits, but it's a fifteen-year-old *maiko* in rice powder paint. And I still can't fill in the face of the Walrus.

The basic driving message of the video is "It don't matter if you're black or white." That no one has remarked on the irony of Michael's performing it in *whiteface* says something. Amid all the moral tub-thumping and outrage, the fact that this was the most exquisitely wrought little piece of propaganda ever released seems to have been overlooked. Over seven million dollars was spent on the eleven-minute video—the first Michael Jackson video since he signed with Sony. A deal that may help explain his makeover into a *bishonen* or transvestite pretty boy. He has not only been cosmetified for Japanese consumption, but—as in the Daijosai Enthronement Ceremony—has become a "ritual female."

Propaganda Films produced "Black or White" with former snuff film director John Landis directing. Yet it was Michael's baby all the way. Produced at fever pitch in twenty-eight days, it amasses a powerful punch through the appropriation of high-tech special effects. "Morphing" is one of these—yes, it's now a verb. And the effect is disturbingly powerful.

The sequence—produced by Pacific Data Images— was the longest continuous "morph" sequence ever. Twelve dynamic transformations across gender and ethnic boundaries: a marvel of seamless matting and killer algorithms described as "costing $10,000 a second and worth every penny."

It is so blatantly propagandistic it verges on camp. "Come together, right now, under me," it seems to be saying. That "Come Together" is the first song Michael's recorded of the Northern Songs catalog he euchred Paul out of is the sublimest irony.

Never before has someone rejoiced in such megaphone capability. The debut of "Black or White" reached an estimated five hundred million people in twenty-seven countries. The deleted *masutabeshan* scene merely added to its draw. I mean if you were World Controller and wanted to insinuate your meme into the collective psyche of Middle America, what would you do? Right.

The phallic display persists on the aether and on countless bootleg tapes—like a phantom limb in all its mythic radiance. And as a guaranteed hook for Sweeps Week, it was unbeatable. But was it perhaps more than that—a magical act, a trigger, a sexual imprint on the world's prepubescent? Is Michael Jackson *more* than just our most successful export? Certain theatrical embellishments suggest magical acts. His patented crotch-grabs signal his shapeshifting (see "Moonwalker"), so important in Teutonic witchcraft.

"Black or White" has a weird, fractured quality that's hard to put your finger on—like Japlish, there's that eerie dissonance. I'll leave the precise exegesis to Greil Marcus, but no opportunity was lost in creating "the heaven of the spectacle."

Most compelling was the morph from Michael Jackson into his panther nagual. The algorithms leave one gasping. Between that and the crotch grabbing, no one stops to examine the flaming contradictions. Just like the *fascinum* of antiquity, the obscene and the technically dazzling are employed to rivet our attention, away from what's *really* going on. Michael is being marketed as both the savior and deliverer of the children of the world. But there are the added resonances of the dangerous, the orgiastic and the violent. Only a technique like morphing could deflect us from the basic cognitive dissonance.

The message "It don't matter if you're black or white" is the message of the Antichrist. It's *just* the sort of sanctimonious pap he's supposed to spout. Of course it matters! Cultural relativism—a fine thing—does not negate the biological reality of DNA, at least not yet. The hidden correlative of the refrain is that there is no *moral* black and white. And however fashionable ambiguity may be, I'm just Manichaean enough to believe that there are two poles, Good and Evil, and that most of us lie somewhere in between. What better cloak for Evil than ambiguity?

The notion that Michael Jackson is the Antichrist has been making the rounds for a while now. And though a fascinated observer of Apocalypse Culture, I don't fully buy into that one. The Far Right *does* seem intent on manifesting Biblical prophecy as their mandate, however. And every Antichrist needs his prophet, his John the Baptist—a John the Baptist with a fifteen-square-mile theme park in Paraguay.

Which brings me 'round full circle to *The Lost Prophetic Writings of John Lennon*. John, with his uncanny prescience, foresaw an era when the Walrus would cover the earth with theme parks. When "theming" would become a verb, when this blatant act of cultural imperialism would be embraced by the subject cultures and even hallowed. Spiritual theme parks like Akeno on Japan's Izu Peninsula or the Maharishi's Vedaland in Florida. Therapeutic theme parks, VR Aesculapia, high-tech incubation centers.

In cryptic verses he described how the theme parks of the future would cloak the "living laboratories" of the Industrial War Machine dedicated to mind control and behavior modification. The internment camps of the future would be Biospheres. Dermal patch technology—the protocols were established for nicotine—and subdermal microchip implants would guarantee the full experience. And for Po-mods, the full experience might be VR transsexualism, VR auto-castration—extremes of neurohormonal experience, as routine stimulus has numbed our response threshold.

Control is the program: benign, paternalistic, downright avuncular. The Walrus, the Antichrist are catch-all metaphors heavy with freight. John appears to use them interchangeably in his *Lost Prophetic Writings*. He understood the power of the media—simply "newspeak" for propaganda. Glamour, seduction, and mind control. The Walrus was the master media manipulator, the arbiter of pop culture and kitsch. But the Walrus was more than a metaphor. He was a real man. John Lennon knew who he was but, like the court jester, could only tell us in conundrums (see "I am the Walrus," inspired by "The Walrus and the Carpenter").

It remained, then, until the discovery of the *Lost Prophetic Writings* for us to get a clear picture of our prototypical arch bull-Walrus. Lewis Carroll dealt in doubles or complementary dyads. The Walrus and the Carpenter. If the Carpenter is Christ, who is the Walrus? Who, in this century, is the master of hypocrisy, petty morality, and the Ersatz? Who bastardized and sanitized the Brothers Grimm, leaving out all the good bits? Who has imprinted generations with counterfeit images stripped bare of real soul-stuff? Who ruled "Mauschwitz" with an iron hand with the galley slaves chained to the oars? (Clue: He's got a walrus mustache.)

Yoko Ono's stated objective was to bear the Messiah (a not uncommon delusion in the annals of New Age). She was uniquely fitted for this role through centuries of tradition and selective breeding . With John's Liverpudlian genes for hybrid vigor, Sean was an alchemical experiment, destined from the womb to be the new digital Maitreya.

To forge a World Mythos, a world leader requires a global PR campaign of such proportions that it boggles the mind. A universal icon needs to be created that amalgamates all races and genders through the glorious apotheosis of facial averaging. The myth also needs to amalgamate Messianic traditions, East and West. John the Baptist and Jesus Christ,

BART UCHWALD

the Youth of Lunar Radiance in Medieval China, Peter the Hermit, Stephen and the Children's Crusade, the Pied Piper, the Magical Child, Mickey Mouse, Rudolf Steiner and the ten-year-old Krishnamurti, and the various Maitreya figures of Japanese Nichiren Buddhism. See how they fly like Lucy in the sky, see how they run.

Michael Jackson's "Magic Kingdom" is the world turned topsy-turvy. A Disneyland of Chapel Perilous; a phantasmagoric Luna Park. The symbolism ranges from Bosch to carney, with Bubbles his pet chimpanzee being crowned atop it all. Edison (or is that Barnum?) wears a lapel pin that says 1992, while Tom Thumb stands on his head. There's enough material on the *Dangerous* album to keep pop iconographers busy until the snow thaws. The world turned upside-down is a prime apocalyptic theme. The holy fool is elevated, the freaks and the simpletons inherit the earth.

Our species has always had a taste for the marvelous. Special effects and simulations hold us in thrall. But now artifice alone has reached a point of mass cultural apotheosis. Skin jobs are in. Cyborgs are hot. There is no stigma at all attached to cosmetic surgery. David Duke readily cops to four or five. He can tell Michael Kinsley on *Firing Line* that he looks like a worm and should make a date with a scalpel. In fact, David Duke is beginning to bear an uncanny resemblance to Michael Jackson. I'm just waiting for the ultimate morph…

XANDOR KORZYBSKI LETTERS

Major meme shift message. Reality override. You must (whip it…no, wrong metaphor), you must get…that's it…get *The Secret Government* by Milton Cooper. Very major metaparanoia.

People of Earth: A little known fact that seems to have savagely eluded me is that insectoids from UFOs (synchronicity note: The radio just started

XANDOR KORZYBSKI LETTERS: *MONDO 2000's* Letters to the Editor section is full of rants. People particularly love the ones we've been getting from somebody out of New York City who calls himself Xandor Korzybski.

JULIA COLMENARES

playing "The Wasp" by Benjamin Britten as I write this) have taken over the earth and are living in splendor underground in Arizona, Nevada, and New Mexico. The U.S. and Soviet governments are collaborating with them. The NSA and CIA were set up to track and handle them. They like to eat people for their hormones and blood and conduct horrible genetic experiments. They controlled Hitler and manipulate us with occultism and religion. Headed by Krill, another UFO group, the Gray Aliens run the Trilateral Commission and the Foreign Affairs Council from seventy-five massive underground sites in the U.S. desert. There is no defense against them. The U.S./Russians have advanced colonies on Mars and the moon and use the space program to funnel money and hide the missions. The world will end in 1999, and scientists have time-traveled there to confirm it. Are you with me? The insects will take over in 1994 and make most of us slaves to build escape vehicles for the remaining chosen few, like George Bush, who will go to Mars just before the holocaust. One out of forty people have been taken aboard spaceships and given implants and will be turned against us, you see. The CIA is pushing drugs to provide the money for this major project and to keep the insectoids living in the style to which they have become accustomed. The CIA is giving ghettos guns and drugs to turn us against guns so we disarm ourselves so they can take over and put us in concentration camps and is spreading AIDS to reduce the population. Just thought you'd like to know.

Congratulations on the courage to publish my neo-paranoid letters, in which I have "explained" our planned enslavement by underground aliens as food supplies and slave labor to build escape spaceships, masterminded by kiss-ass "new world order" (Orwellian one-world government) Trilaterals fronted by lisping-lizard-liar Bush. Unfortunately, I was optimistic. It's happening much faster than I thought.

As I warned, our so-called government is run by traitors. I have evidence from a close friend at the meeting that the Iraq war scenario was created in 1977 by aerospace fanatics in a secret meeting in Washington. It was revealed by Ross Perot on a live CNN show (and never followed up) that the Department of Commerce allowed a supercomputer for creating nuclear weapons to be shipped to Iraq AFTER the war had started. In April, the *Financial Times* of London exposed traitors in the National so-called Security Council of the White House that knowingly allowed shipments of sensitive electronics systems and spare parts to Iraq via Jordan—up until December, believe it or not! So while our troops were fighting and dying, superTraitor Bush was supplying the enemy.

Now let's see if you dare publish this—or if you too are part of the government-controlled media: A *60 Minutes* freelance researcher revealed to a mutual friend that while viewing incoming satellite TV feeds, she saw something that CNN immediately censored: U.S. forces blowing up oil wells. The footage also revealed that *most* of them were blown up by the U.S. Ask *60 Minutes* (and CNN) why they are afraid to run this story! Hint: Shadow-government operative Bechtel Corporation expects a $100 billion contract with Kuwait.

Meanwhile, Bush, whose Skull and Bones fraternity at Yale included a secret Hitler altar (source: *New York Times*), over the protests of Schwarzkopf, refused to disarm the Iraqi military, coldly watching them napalm whole villages as millions of cholera-suffering Kurds were herded into U.S. concentration camps, with thousands dying every day—the same mass-murderer Bush that intentionally misled the Kurds into fighting his good buddy Saddam, whom he has protected (with his forces) from attack and for whom he has even tried to bargain safe passage out of the country, by his own hissing admission at a so-called press conference. His plan apparently is to allow Saddam to live in his under-construction, heavily fortified secret underground bunker in the Rockies, undoubtedly connected into the alien underground tubes throughout the West.

In case you haven't figured it out, let me spell it out: All this is tightly scripted, alien-controlled, Hitler-inspired experimental genocide to test various population-control techniques, plus global mind conditioning for the forthcoming enslavement, led by supersadist covert ops assassin George Herr Walker (watch his reptilian mouth and Cheney's sadistically twist whenever they lie, reflected in the hypnogenic lizard-mind activation command to "read my lips"), co-conspirator Saddam, who enjoys torturing and murdering kittens and hallucinates himself as the reincarnation of Nebuchadnezzar (who destroyed Jerusalem and deported the Jews to Babylon, now Iraq), plus superStalinist mind-controller Gorby (the Soviets' secret code name for the Iraqi operation is "Bleed the Dragon," referring to the U.S.).

Skeptical that slimy Bush would be that cold-blooded? Wake up! Take a look at the underground videotape now circulating (and censored by all TV networks) produced in Burma by top Vietnam War hero Colonel Bo Gritz (head of Delta Force and the real-life model for Rambo), who was sent by the White House to bring back the MIAs. He proves conclusively that Reagan and Bush have been keeping the MIAs in Indochina for fear the MIAs will reveal their massive Trilateral/CIA/KGB/mafia worldwide cocaine/heroin smuggling-racketeer conspiracy, which finances the parallel government and its supersecret illegal intelligence organization headed by Bush(wacker). (Ask *20/20* why they were afraid to show the U.S.-funded highways from the poppy fields in the Burmese jungles in their program about Gritz. Ask any journalist why they haven't written anything about this.)

Gritz has now learned about the gray aliens, and recently led an unsuccessful paramilitary raid on one of their secret underground entrances in New Mexico. Just ask any citizen of Dulce, New Mexico, which is close to a major underground alien base connected by underground shuttles to other alien bases throughout the desert, especially to Los Alamos nuke research center. More importantly, it is close to Dreamland, the top-secret government/alien UFO research center north of Las Vegas at Grouse Lake, where the Stealth bombers (the radar-invisible planes that demolished Baghdad) were developed and tested, along with other alien-designed vehicles seen by thousands of locals and covered up by the media.

Now consider these facts: In January, an "asteroid" approached the earth within 106,000 miles—the closest an asteroid has ever been seen. What was it? You figure it out. Also in January, meteorologists were shocked to discover "huge (100 kilometer) and mysterious pressure waves…rippling across the midwest," resulting in bizarre weather patterns, according to the *Wall Street Journal* on January 15. These, of course, are from scalar (Tesla) waves controlled by Soviet mad scientists who, like U.S. mad scientists, are controlling weather, knocking out crops, and inciting riots in cities. This is just one piece of evidence of the invisible ongoing electronic ELF war between four major countries, using alien-developed technology. Ask book publishers why they are afraid to publish Puharich's tell-all book. I don't blame them. They wouldn't live very long. (Neither will you, dear Mondoids, if you keep publishing these letters!)

Meanwhile, says the *New York Times* (April 14), millions are still threatened in the Soviet Union by Gorby's Chernobyl population-control experiment (ten times more fallout than Hiroshima, rivaled only by the 120 million gallons of radioactive waste deliberately dumped into the ground for over twenty years at the Hanford reactor in Washington State, according to a federal report released April 12) and in South America by a cholera epidemic threatening millions, according to medical authorities, and programmed to spread (via the programmed-earthquake Costa Rica cholera zone) to the U.S. later this year.

Fact: AIDS was created for the CIA at Fort Detrick, Maryland, and unleashed on "unfavorable" elements of society in Africa and the U.S. for population control. Fact: Other genetically engineered superdiseases are ready, combined with Bush/CIA-engineered drug addiction and the savings and loan collapse, to further destabilize the population and create widespread unrest and justify declaration of a "national emergency" and parallel-government (read: alien) takeover, internment of perceived troublemakers in the already-waiting Federal Emergency Management Agency concentration camps around the U.S. and creation of new traceable magnetic-fiber money for total Orwellian tracking of every transaction.

The clock is ticking on the Trilateral New World Order (read: loss of all constitutional rights). See Nixon's White House Executive Order 11490, which allows the FEMA to take over all media, energy systems, food, transportation, medical facilities, and housing, along with the total mobilization of citizens into work brigades.

Get the media-suppressed facts! Start with Bo Gritz, Box 472, HCR31, Sandy Valley, Nevada 89019 and William Cooper: BBS users, dial 602-567-6725 or write to him at Citizen's Agency For Joint Intelligence, P.O. Box 3299, Camp Verde, AZ 86322 (warning: use a pseudonym and a temporary non-U.S. Post Office mail drop, and if you have been contacted by an alien, do NOT tell so-called UFO researchers—the CIA is using many of them to collect names for future internment of abductees).

It's time to act NOW, before the secret government and their alien controllers destroy us all. Demand congressional investigations and the immediate impeachment of Bush and all other secret-government traitors! Start your own investigations. Demand to see government surveys, satellite data, the location of the supercomputer in Iraq and the names of the traitor hackers who are undoubtedly using it to covertly create the next monster weapon, the Dr. Strangelove SDI plans crafted by mercury-contaminated insane German scientists, and Majestic 12 (government alien coordinating committee) meeting transcripts. Force "them" to open up the UFO research labs. Back up your files and hide them before "they" rewrite reality.

The time is short. You know what to do. **R**

FAST, CHEAP AND OUT OF CONTROL

Kevin Kelly: Rodney Brooks runs the robot lab at M.I.T. He says that rather than trying to bring as much life into Alife (see "Artificial Life") as possible, he's trying to bring as much Alife into life. He wants to flood the world (and beyond) with inexpensive, small, ubiquitous, thinking things. He's been making robots that weigh less than ten pounds. The six-legged walker weighs only 3.6 pounds. It's constructed on model-car parts. In three years he hopes to have a 1mm (pencil tip-size) robot. His ultimate plan is to invade the moon with a fleet of shoe-box-size robots that can be launched from throwaway rockets. It's the ant strategy. Send an army of dispensable, limited agents coordinated on a task, and set them loose. Some will die, most will work, something will get done. In the time it takes to argue about one big sucker, he can have his invasion built and delivered. The motto: "Fast, Cheap, and Out of Control!"

As an example, Brooks built what he humorously calls "The Collection Machine"—a robot in an office space that collects empty soda cans at night. It's ingenious. It operates according to the Society of Mind approach to Alife robotics. The eyes of the Collection Machine spot a soda can on a desk and guide the robot until it is right in front of the can. The arm of the robot knows that it is in front of a soda can because it "looks" at its wheels and says, "Gee, my wheels aren't turning, I must be in front of a soda can." Then it reaches out to pick the can up. If it is heavier than an empty can, it leaves it on the desk. When it takes a can it finds its way all the way back to its station to unload it, then randomly wanders again through offices

ROB HAFERNIK

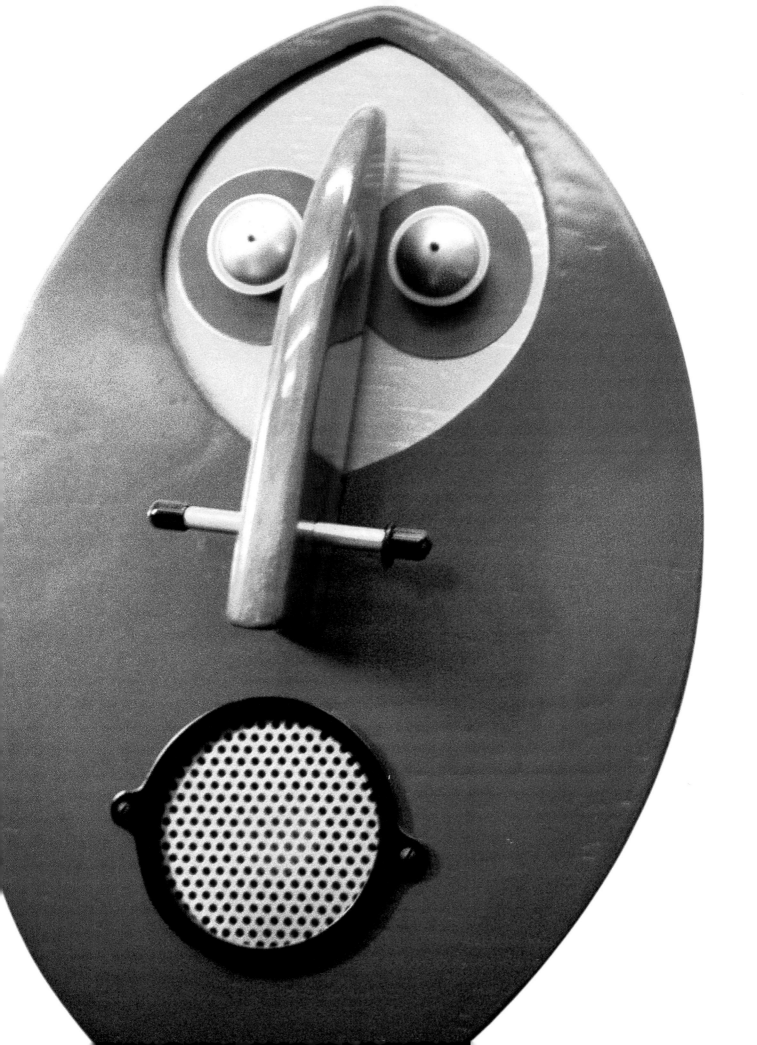

until it spots another can. Not very efficient per trip, but night after night it can amass a great collection of aluminum. During the day it sleeps.

Brooks has another small robot in mind that lives in one corner of your TV screen and eats off the dust when the TV isn't on. A student of his built a cheap, bunny-sized robot that watches where you are in a room and calibrates your stereo so it is perfectly adjusted as you move around.

ROBOTICS AS ART

We started with robotics as an art form, and then we got interested in the idea of artificial life. We don't want to do robots with a point, because robots with a point are boring. If you forget about having a point, then you get stuff like this.

I think that studying intelligence and making robots is the ultimate art form, because it's studying yourself. There's no way you can understand someone else's intelligence; all you have is yourself. It's the ultimate self-expression.

There's been talk about getting together with some of the folks that make latex human figures and animating them. We'd like to build a figure that would sit in an airport, apparently reading a paper. After a while people would realize that it's a piece of art and gather around to look at it. Once enough people gather, it would come alive and rip its face open and reveal the robot inside.

MECHANO-EROTICISM AND ROBO-COPULATION

Mark Dery: "I feel," sang James Brown, "Like being a sex machine."

The soul singer envisioned himself a plug-in stud, tireless as a punch press but still salty with sweat, soft to the touch; the emphasis, in "Get Up (I Feel Like Being a) Sex Machine," is on sex, not machinery.

Increasingly, however, the mass mind muddles sexy machines and machine sex, conflating them into the conundrum Marshall McLuhan

ROBOTICS AS ART: This was sampled from Alex Iles, who is part of the Robot Group, a gang of technical experimenters and artists based in Austin, Texas. Their projects include robot blimps that fly around indoors and a robot heavy-metal band.

suggested was "born of a hungry curiosity to explore and enlarge the domain of sex by mechanical technique, on one hand and, on the other, to POSSESS machines in a sexually gratifying way." This mechano-eroticism is evinced by the *Party Machine*, a TV discotheque in which miniskirted, midriffed models gyrate suggestively in front of giant cogwheels and pistons, and by videos for songs by Janet Jackson and C&C Music Factory incorporating Machine Age scenery that suggests a cross between Studio 54 and Vladimir Tatlin's "Monument to the Third International."

Even as machinery is eroticized, sexuality is mechanized. The "metamorphosis of man into a dynamo, the beauty of women considered as sparkplugs, cogs and pistons" augured by a 1919 Dada manifesto has become commonplace. Pop singers and Hollywood stars, with the aid of aerobic workouts and plastic surgery, chisel themselves into Futurist sculptures, all sharp edges and flat planes. Ads for Evian bottled water depict the postmodern ideal, glistening Aryans whose streamlined physiques look as if they were lathed and polished on some Nordic assembly line. It seems only appropriate that the cultural icon for the nineties should turn out to be Arnold Schwarzenegger, an affectless automaton whose acting ability falls just short of Disneyland's Mr. Lincoln, an Audio-Animatronic dummy brought to life by bursts of pressurized air.

Schwarzenegger, a hunky MENSCHMACHINE best known for his portrayal of a death-dealing cyborg, epitomizes sexual confusion in the technotronic age. When he confesses, in the BBC's five-part teardown of Tinseltown, "Naked Hollywood," that "Pumping iron is just like having sex," he speaks for many. "Can you believe how much I am in heaven?" he effuses. "I am, like, COMING day and night." His experience is hardly unique. Few who have sat in a state-of-the-art health club, surrounded by mirrors and straddling a gleaming Cybex apparatus, its moving parts slick with lubricant, would deny that the overall impression is one of automated

Craig Sainsott with members of Robot Band, photograph by Martha Grenon

intercourse. It is PHILOSOPHY IN THE NAUTILUS
ROOM—the Marquis de Sade meets Jack
LaLanne.

Stuart Ewen improvises brilliantly on these
themes in *Consuming Images: The Politics of Style
in Contemporary Culture.* "This machine-man is one
of a generation of desolate, finely tuned loners who
have cropped up as icons of American style. Their bodies,
often lightly oiled to accentuate definition, reveal their
inner mechanisms like costly, open-faced watches."

Technocultural sexuality is cyborgian, a marriage of
meat and mechanism. As Enzo Ferrari put it, "Between man
and machine there exists a perfect equation: 50 percent
man and 50 percent machine." Stephen Bayley anato-
mized the equation in *Sex, Drink & Fast Cars:* "The idea
of mechanical intercourse…lies only a little beneath
the surface of people who are fascinated by fast
cars." It celebrates what the French art histo-
rian Marcel Jean called "the sexual frenzy of factories," the psychosexual symbolism of
hydraulic fluids squealing through small orifices
under high pressure, of camshafts thrusting
ceaselessly. It follows, naturally, that tech-
nofetishism in the bedroom should lead to a cul-
turally-pervasive desire to couple with machinery.
The only thing better than making love LIKE a machine,
it seems, is making love WITH a machine.

In recent years, the subrational appetites of the collective
unconscious have given rise to a vast proliferation of mechano-
erotic imagery. Examples abound: the sexy replicant who beds
Rick Deckard, the hard-boiled protagonist of the movie *Blade
Runner*; the mechanoid whore with the "polyethylene cunt" and
"waterproof synthetic skin" in K. W. Jeter's cyberpunk novel, *Dr.
Adder*;  the robot odalisques of Japanese cartoonist Hajime
Sorayama—their chromium pudenda free of hair, holes, and
other female unpleasantries; and the servo-controlled
android geisha invented by Japanese roboticist Shu-
nichi Mizuno, who believes that eroticizing the
machine "will be essential for the coexistence
of man and machine in the future."

Mizuno's words may prove prophetic if cultural momentum propels events on their present course. Man-machine miscegenation—robo-copulation, by any other name—may seem a seductive alternative to the vile body, locus of a postmodern power struggle involving AIDS, abortion rights, fetal tissue, genetic engineering, and nanotechnology.

| RoboCop 2 | a hollow movie with a heart of brass and a head full of clocksprings, nonetheless contains one wholly unique scene, a brief vignette that offers a profoundly disturbing vision of things to come. In it, Angie, the girlfriend of the deceased drug lord Cain, finds herself face-to-face with the hulking, hawkish robot in which her lover's consciousness now resides. A computer-generated simulacrum of Cain's leering face, lips pulled back in a vulpine grin, peers down at the mortified woman from a video screen mounted in the automaton's head. Purring salaciously, he extends a pair of snapping, sawtoothed pincers; for a

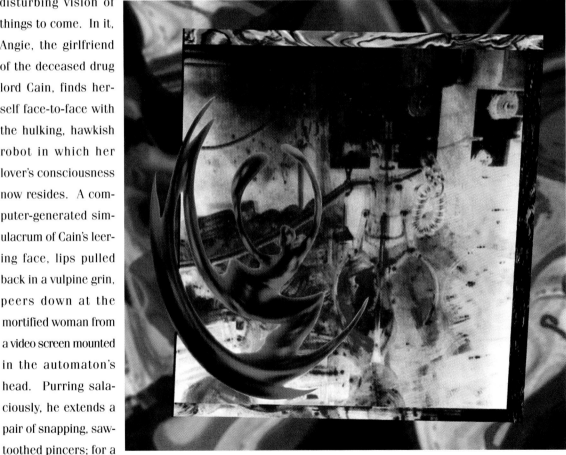

KHYAL BRAUN

second, they are angled in such a way that they bear an unmistakable resemblance to an erect male organ—a PHALLUS DENTATUS of sorts. Moaning, Angie runs a taloned finger along the mechanical protuberance's cold hardness, her glossy lips slightly parted. "It'll take some getting used to," she decides at last, "but it'll be GREAT!" **R**

The ROBOCOP movies, along with the TERMINATOR movies, represent Hollywood's usurping of the cyberpunk mythos. *RoboCop* particularly runs cyberpunk themes, such as the idea that the megacorps ARE the new governments, and that we're becoming cyborgs.

St. Jude: The media—mass and occult—are doing the hoopla over smart drugs: Better living through chemistry. More fun with your mind. And it's not even illegal. Do these drugs increase intelligence? Probably, although most of the effects are subtle. Bear in mind that the placebo effect is strongest in the most intelligent, and bright people are usually the ones who are self-experimenting.

Nevertheless, rats can get good results, too, and EVERYONE responds to Milacemide. It's just bothersome that our imagination moves so much faster than brain research.

Dosing for intelligence increase fits in nicely with the other crazes of the moment: cosmetic surgery and body-building. Onward, upward, and outward, on all fronts…

NEW DRUGS THAT MAKE YOU SMART

"Last year a friend took me to hear Sun Ra and his Intergalactic Arkestra as a birthday present. I had just received a bottle of 800 mg tablets of Piracetam from Interlab. My friend and I each took NINE of the tablets (an ATTACK dose, they call it in the literature) before entering the hall.

"The music began thirty minutes later. I found myself able to concentrate as never before. I was completely lucid with absolutely no sense of intoxication. My ears felt as though they were being stimulated from all directions at once, but the feeling was entirely pleasant. For the first time in my life I could hear each individual horn's timbre (Sun Ra has about ten horn players, often all playing massed harmonies). I was enthralled.

NEW DRUGS THAT MAKE YOU SMART: This article by John Morgenthaler, co-author of *Smart Drugs and Nutrients,*  is presented in its entirety. It appeared in *MONDO 2000 #2*, before all the hype. It's fairly inclusive and self-explanatory. Keep a bookmark on this page, and don't pester us with any phone calls. John Morgenthaler is the founder of the Cognitive Enhancement Research Institute (CERI).

SMART

"My friend has worked as a professional saxophone player. He, too, reported extraordinary hearing and concentration abilities. I recommend Piracetam as an alternative to getting 'high' before a concert or any other experience that improves with keen concentration."

The above testimonial is typical of people using Piracetam, an intelligence booster and CNS (central nervous system) stimulant with no side effects or toxicity. It is so remarkable in its effects and its safety that it prompted the creation of a new drug category called the nootropics. The term nootropic comes from the Greek word meaning "acting on the mind." Since the invention of Piracetam by UBC Laboratories in Belgium, other drug companies have been scrambling to develop their own nootropics. Some of them being researched now include vinpocetine, aniracetam, pramiracetam, and oxiracetam. As yet, there is no nootropic drug that is FDA-approved for sale in the United States, but there is plenty of motivation on the part of the drug companies to get that approval—financial analysts expect the U.S. market for cognitive enhancers, smart pills, to soon be in excess of $1 billion per year!

Nootropics are very interesting, partly because of their lack of toxicity, but they are not the only substances that increase intelligence. There are over thirty chemicals that have been demonstrated to improve animal and/or human intelligence (learning and data processing of particular types of tasks). In the remainder of this article, I present a practical, drug-by-drug guide to the use of the most inter-esting of these cognitive-enhancement compounds, and information on where you can get them is provided.

CENTROPHENOXINE (TRADE NAME: LUCIDRIL): Centrophenoxine is an intelligence booster and also an effective anti-aging therapy. It has been shown to cause improvements in various aspects of memory function and a 30 percent increase in life span of laboratory animals.

One of the most widely recognized aspects of aging is the buildup of lipofuscin in brain cells (lipofuscin is the stuff that age spots are made of). Centrophenoxine removes lipofuscin deposits from brain cells and reduces its rate of accumulation in young brain cells. It also rejuvenates the synaptic structure—the area where the actual transfer of information takes place between nerve cells.

Precautions: Centrophenoxine should not be used by persons who are easily excitable, people with severe arterial hypertension, or those subject to convulsions or involuntary musculoskeletal movements. The drug also should not be used by nursing mothers. Adverse effects are rare, but include hyperexcitability, insomnia, tremors, motion sickness, paradoxical drowsiness, and depression. There is no toxicity of centrophenoxine at therapeutic doses.

Dosage: Take 1,000 to 3,000 mg per day. Centrophenoxine takes effect very quickly. You'll notice an increase in alertness and a slight feeling of stimulation.

JIM CHERRY ▶

Sources: Centrophenoxine is not sold in the United States. It can be purchased over the counter in Mexico or by mail order from the address below.

CHOLINE/LECITHIN:

Choline can be found in several forms, including choline bitartrate, choline chloride, or phosphatidyl choline. Phosphatidyl choline (PC) is the active ingredient of lecithin. All of these forms of choline will produce memory boosting effects, but PC has some unique effects as well.

Choline compounds, including PC, are able to pass through the blood-brain barrier where the brain utilizes the choline to make acetylcholine (a neurotransmitter that plays an important role in memory). Thus, choline enhances memory by increasing the amount of acetylcholine available for memory and thought processes.

PC has some other important health benefits. It functions as a source of structural material for every cell in the human body, particularly those of the brain and nerves. It also aids in the metabolism of fats, regulates blood cholesterol, and nourishes the fatlike sheaths of nerve fibers.

Precautions: Any compound that acts like a precursor to acetylcholine, such as choline, PC, or DMAE, should not be used by people who are manic-depressive, because it can deepen the depressive phase. Choline bitartrate and choline chloride can sometimes cause a fishy odor or diarrhea. PC, however, does not have either of these effects.

Dosage: Take 3 grams of choline per day in three divided doses. If you're taking lecithin you need to take a lot more, because only part of the lecithin is choline. Often the label will provide information on the quantity of choline per tablespoon. All forms of choline should be taken with one gram per day of vitamin B-5 so that the choline can be converted into acetylcholine.

Sources: Choline and lecithin are considered nutritional supplements and can be found at healthfood stores or drug stores. Commercial lecithin usually contains other oils and phosphatides besides phosphatidyl choline. Look at the label before you buy and make sure the product contains more than 30 percent phosphatidyl choline. Also, you should taste your lecithin and make sure it does not taste bitter (this indicates rancidity). Much lecithin on the market is rancid. The best form of lecithin I know of is Twin Labs brand PC 55—it contains 55 percent PC, and it's always very fresh.

DHEA:

Dehydroepiandrosterone (pronounced dee-hi-dro-epp-ee-an-dro-ster-own) is a steroid hormone produced in the adrenal gland. DHEA is the most abundant steroid in the human bloodstream. Research has found it to have significant antiobesity, antitumor, antiaging, and anticancer effects. DHEA levels naturally drop as people age, and there is good reason to think that taking a DHEA supplement may extend your life and make you more youthful while you're alive. Additionally, DHEA may be an important player in cognitive enhancement.

DHEA is involved in protecting brain neurons from senility-associated degenerative conditions like Alzheimer's disease. Not only does the neuronal degenerative condition occur most frequently at the time of lowest DHEA levels, but brain tissue contains more DHEA than is found in the bloodstream. In an experiment with brain cell tissue cultures, Dr. Eugene Roberts found that very low concentrations of DHEA were found to "increase the number of neurons, their ability to establish contacts, and their differentiation." DHEA also enhanced long-term memory in mice undergoing avoidance training. Perhaps it plays a similar role in human brain function.

Dosage: Dosage of DHEA ranges from 50 mg to 2,000 mg per day. There is no solid information indicating an optimal dosage for humans but, if you want to get serious, you can get your DHEA levels tested every few months (for about $65), each time raising the amount of DHEA you take. When your blood levels of DHEA reach what is normal for a twenty-year-old human, then you're taking enough.

Sources: DHEA is now being used by many people with AIDS because of its immune enhancement and antiviral effects. DHEA is not FDA-approved, but AIDS buyer groups are able to sell it to members, because the FDA has a policy of looking the other way when it comes to the activity of these organizations. Try contacting these buyers groups: Alliance 7, (619) 281-5360 in San Diego; or Healing Alternatives Foundation, (415) 626-2316 in San Francisco.

HYDERGINE (ERGOLOID MESYLATES):
Research in other countries has shown that Hydergine increases mental abilities, prevents damage to brain cells, and may even be able to reverse existing damage to brain cells. Hydergine acts in several ways to enhance mental capabilities and slow down or reverse the aging processes in the brain. Among its wide variety of effects, it:

1. Increases blood supply to the brain.
2. Increases the amount of oxygen delivered to the brain.
3. Enhances metabolism in brain cells.
4. Protects the brain from damage during periods of decreased and/or insufficient oxygen supply.
5. Slows the deposit of age pigment (lipofuscin) in the brain.
6. Prevents free radical damage to brain cells.
7. Increases intelligence, memory, learning, and recall.
8. Normalizes systolic blood pressure.
9. Lowers abnormally high cholesterol levels, in some cases.
10. Reduces symptoms of tiredness, dizziness, and tinnitus (ringing in the ears).

One way that Hydergine may enhance memory and learning is by mimicking the effect of a substance called nerve growth factor (NGF). NGF stimulates protein synthesis that results in the growth of dendrites in brain cells. Dendrites facilitate communication throughout the central nervous system and are necessary for memory and learning. New learning requires new dendritic growth.

Precautions: If too large a dose is used when first taking Hydergine, it may cause slight nausea, gastric disturbance, or headache. Overall, Hydergine does not produce any serious side effects, it is nontoxic even at very large doses, and it is contraindicated only for individuals who have chronic or acute psychosis.

Dosage: The U.S. recommended dosage is 3 mg per day; however, the European recommended dosage is 9 mg per day, taken in three divided doses. Most of the research has been done at levels of 9 to 12 mg per day. It may take several weeks before you notice the effects of Hydergine.

Sources: Hydergine is available in the United States and you can buy it if you have a doctor's prescription, but keep in mind that your doctor may not be familiar with the uses I have discussed. It can also be purchased over the counter in Mexico or by mail order from overseas (see below).

PIRACETAM (NOOTROPIL):

Piracetam is a cognitive enhancer under conditions of hypoxia (too little oxygen) and also improves memory and certain types of learning in normal persons. It is used in the treatment of stroke, alcoholism, vertigo, senile dementia, sickle-cell anemia, and many other conditions. The subjective effect described by a lot of people is that it "wakes up your brain."

A chemical analogue of the neurotransmitter gamma-amino-butyric acid (GABA), Piracetam seems to promote the flow of information between the right and left hemispheres of the brain. We know that communication between the two sides of the brain is associated with flashes of creativity.

Piracetam is so safe that one FDA employee has been quoted as saying that it can't possibly have any pharmacological effects because of its very low toxicity even in huge doses; hence, the substance must be physiologically inactive.

The effect of Piracetam can be improved if taken with DMAE, centrophenoxine, or choline. When choline and piracetam are taken together, there is a synergistic effect that causes a greater improvement in memory than the sum of each when taken alone.

Precautions: Piracetam may increase the effects of certain drugs, such as amphetamines and psychotropics. Adverse effects are rare, but include insomnia, psychomotor agitation, nausea, gastrointestinal distress, and headaches. Piracetam has virtually no toxicity or contraindications.

PIRACETAM: Although we're STILL not sure how it works, Piracetam is the HIT of the smart drug scene. It's effects are noticeable yet opaque—no side effects.

Dosage: Piracetam is supplied in 400 mg or 800 mg tablets. The usual dose is 2,400 to 4,800 mg per day in three divided doses. Some literature recommends that the first two days a high "attack" dose should be taken. I have noticed that when people first take Piracetam they do not notice any effect at all until they take a high dose (approximately 4,000 to 8,000 mg). Thereafter, they may notice that a lower dose is sufficient. The drug takes effect within thirty to sixty minutes.

Durk Pearson & Sandy Shaw of VRP (Vitamin Research Products) psychoactive soft drinks and designer foods.

Sources: Piracetam is not sold in the United States. It can be purchased over the counter in Mexico or by mail order from the address below.

SULBUTIAMINE (ARCALION):

Sulbutiamine is a new compound that has been described as being like Hydergine, only better. It has been shown to facilitate wakefulness, improve long-term memory, increase reaction time, decrease anxiety, and increase overall resistance to stress.

ERIC WHITE

Sources: Sulbutiamine is not sold in the United States. It can be purchased by mail order from the address below.

VASOPRESSIN (DIAPID):

Vasopressin is a brain hormone that is released by the pituitary gland. It improves attention, concentration, memory retention, and recall (both short-term and long-term). Vasopressin facilitates more effective learning by helping to "imprint" new information in the memory centers of the brain, a function which cannot be achieved without the action of vasopressin.

Cocaine, LSD, amphetamines, Ritalin, and Cylert (pemoline) cause a release of vasopressin. Frequent use of these drugs can cause depleted levels of vasopressin, making you slow and dopey. If you feel burnt out, a whiff of vasopressin can transform your experience in about ten seconds, because it is a direct application of the specific brain chemical that has been depleted.

Alcohol and marijuana, however, inhibit the release of vasopressin. A whiff of vasopressin when using these drugs will compensate for much of the dopiness caused by them.

Dosage: To combat fatigue, take two 200 mg tablets per day, always with breakfast or an A.M. meal, for a period of twenty days. Do not exceed three tablets at any time, as this very powerful substance may cause severe headaches. Other than this, Sulbutiamine has no known adverse side effects.

Vasopressin is very useful in situations where there is a large amount of new information to learn. It increases your ability to memorize and recall specific factual information.

Precautions: Vasopressin occasionally produces the following side effects: runny nose, nasal congestion, itch or irritation of the nasal passages, headache, abdominal cramps, and increased bowel movements. Vasopressin has not been proven to be safe for use during pregnancy.

Dosage: Vasopressin usually comes in a nasal spray bottle. Most studies showing memory improvement have been done with a dose of 12 to 16 USP per day or about two whiffs three or four times per day. Vasopressin produces a noticeable effect within seconds.

Sources: Vasopressin is available in the United States. You can buy it if you have a doctor's prescription, but keep in mind that your doctor may not be familiar with the uses I have discussed. It can also be purchased over the counter in Mexico or by mail order from overseas (see below).

VINPOCETINE (CAVINTON):

Vinpocetine, like Piracetam, is a nootropic drug and a powerful memory enhancer. It facilitates cerebral metabolism by improving cerebral microcirculation (blood flow), stepping up brain cells' production of ATP (the cellular energy molecule), increasing the brain's use of glucose, and increasing the brain's oxygen utilization.

Vinpocetine is often used for the treatment of cerebral circulatory disorders such as memory problems, aphasia, apraxia, motor disorders, dizziness, and headache.

Precautions: Adverse effects are rare, but include hypotension and tachycardia. It has no drug interactions, no toxicity, and is generally very safe.

GREG NERSESSIAN

Dosage: One or two 5 mg tablets per day.

Sources: Vinpocetine is not sold in the United States. It can be purchased by mail order from the address below.

MAIL ORDER:

A little-known FDA ruling now allows the importation of a three-month personal supply of drugs as long as they are regarded as safe in other countries. Ordering safe but unapproved drugs is now legal under the new FDA pilot guidelines, Chapter 971. This compromise was made under pressure from AIDS political action groups because they were being denied access to potentially life-saving substances.

Interlab, a mail-order pharmacy in England, was established in response to this new FDA ruling. Interlab carries a wide variety of drugs for cognitive enhancement, life extension, and the treatment of AIDS which are not available in the United States. It even carries Retin-A.

All of the drugs I have discussed here can be purchased without a prescription. You can request a price sheet by writing to: Interlab, BCM Box 5890, London, WC1N 3XX, England. Prices are reasonable and on some items quite low. If you want to order right away, send a personal check for the amount of the item(s) you want, plus $10 for shipping (or $15 for accelerated shipping). See page 290 for new information.

Centrophenoxine (60 x 250 mg tablets) $29
Hydergine (100 x 4.5 mg oral tablets) $39
Piracetam (60 x 800 mg tablets) $16
Sulbutiamine (20 x 200 mg tablets) $11
Vasopressin (12 ml nasal spray) $32
Xanthinol nicotinate (60 x 150 mg tablets) $9

You must include the following signed statement with your order: "I hereby declare that the products I am purchasing are not for commerical resale. They are for my own personal use only. The supply ordered does not exceed three months' usage and is used with the consent of my physician."

Other cognitive enhancers include: Xanthinol nicotinate, fenozolone (Ordinator), idebenone, ginkgo biloba, acetyl-1-carnitine, DMAE, pyroglutamate, RNA (ribonucleic acid), isoprinosine, phenylalanine, amphetamines, phenytoin (Dilantin), pemoline, Ritalin, vitamin B-12, ACTH 4-10, L-prolyl L-leucyl glycine amide, caffeine, niacin, vitamin C, ginseng, GH3 (Gerovital), PRL-8-53, R-58-735, ISF-2522, THA, metrazol, and strychnine (the last two are very dangerous).

HYDERGINE

St. Jude: Hydergine is a member of the ergot family, generally a fun bunch. Albert Hofmann, the man who gave us LSD, is responsible for hydergine. He takes three or four of them daily, just on the off-chance they might be useful. Hydergine is interesting because it seems to reverse nervous system entropy. Ordinarily your neurons just pop like overstressed condoms, until you die. Hydergine makes your dendrites—the little end-bristles on your neurons—more profuse and bushier. This means they may reach out and touch neurons they couldn't get at before. It appears that enriched connectivity amps up the read-and-write functions.

PHENYLALANINE

Sandy Shaw: Phenylalanine and other noradrenergic agents are good for memory. Agonists for the noradrenergic, serotonergic, and dopaminergic neurosystems, they all enhance memory and improve intellectual performance.

SMART DRUGS ARE MAINSTREAM

The September *Neurology* introduces us to a substance that speeds access to stored memory BY SECONDS, in people both old and new.

PHENYLALANINE is the main ingredient in Pearson & Shaw's Rise and Shine which, in turn, is the main drink currently being offered in the newly fashionable "smart bars." In case you haven't been reading the papers, smart bars are the latest thing on the club scene. Generally found at all-night raves (see "House Music"), the smart bars have become the most visible public manifestation of New Edge culture, thanks to media excitement. The inevitable backlash is ensuing.

SMART DRUGS ARE MAINSTREAM: In the midst of all the hype about smart bars, and all the cynical denials by the medical establishment, articles of a scientifically valid study on a new intelligence drug, milacemide, hit the FRONT PAGES of major urban newspapers, only to disappear from the media in the quest for more smart drinks at all-night house parties with cute babes with names like Earth Girl. And who can blame 'em.

To quote the abstract: "We administered milacemide, a glycine pro-drug, or placebo, to young and older healthy adults, who performed a word-retrieval task. Milacemide administration increased the number of words retrieved and decreased the latency with which these words were retrieved for both young and older adults."

The latency—the lag time for retrieval—which ran six to eight seconds on placebo, was diminished one or two seconds with milacemide. Consider. A couple of seconds quicker regurge can mean the difference between a verbal choke—all UHs and *YOU* KNOWs—and consummate eloquence. Save a couple of seconds on each memory access, and after a few dozen exam questions you've gained forty IQ points. Aiieeeee! Order me up a drum!

MILACEMIDE, people.

Is this merely a speed effect? To quote from the discussion: "Performance on the word-retrieval task requires activation of general knowledge, namely activation of semantic memory...It is possible, however, that glycine did not have a specific effect on semantic memory, but rather had a generalized facilitative effect on cognitive functioning by increasing alertness or motivation. Some evidence against this interpretation, however, is provided by an additional test, namely recognition memory...Nevertheless, to completely rule out the possibility...it is necessary to examine directly the effect of milacemide on a variety of measures of attention."

What is this drug?

Milacemide is 2-N-pentylamino-acetamide HCl, an acylated glycine derivative which enhances NMDA-mediated (that's N-methyl-D-aspartate) neural transmission in the brain.

Let's back off a moment: Milacemide sneaks across the blood-brain barrier and is converted to glycine. Glycine increases the sensitivity of the NMDA receptors in the cell walls of neurons. The excitation of these NMDA receptors facilitates learning and memory.

Milacemide, on its way to becoming glycine in the brain, goes through its glycinamide phase. By sheerest coincidence, of course, the ass end of vasopressin, proline-arginine-glycinamide, is heavily implicated in vasopressin's effect on data storage and requisition. See how it all fits in?

No, forget it: Probably not—it may be decades before this is sorted out.

STRUNG OUT ON SMART DRUGS

Are you bobbling around, drooling and scratching, waiting for your shipments from—no, no, not Mendocino, not Medellín—Switzerland and England? Now that the bottles are empty, can you feel the hole left by every single IQ point? It's time to own up to it, baby: You've got a habit. Another case of smart-drug dependency.

It started so innocently: just a snort of vasopressin before sex, or before getting down with your keyboard. Then you discovered that 800 mg of Piracetam helped you remember obscure Japanese technical terms—*kyogen!* that's the word!—never noticing how all-out unnatural it is to recall stuff like *kyogen.*

But now you're strung out, spinal tendrils twitching like beached jellyfish, browned-out brain itching like a phantom limb, ears tuned to the UPS truck that is always late. The first thing that you learn is you always gotta wait. **S**

"THE FIRST THING YOU LEARN IS YOU ALWAYS GOTTA WAIT" is from William Burroughs's *Naked Lunch.* It was later repeated by Lou Reed on *Andy Warhol Presents the Velvet Underground* in the classic heroin song "I'm Waiting for the Man."

STREET TECH

Gareth Branwyn: The most important rallying cry for cyberpunks must surely be "The street has its own use for things." Bill Gibson said it in *Burning Chrome*, and the nineties have underscored it with a vengeance.

Street tech is about commercial low-end development and technological improvisation. It's about the fringe worlds of monkey wrenching, from brilliant hacking to low-life cracking.

MONKEY WRENCHING is a kind of guerrilla disruption of technological activities deemed by ecological radicals as environmentally unsound.

DESKTOP VIDEO

The following system will give you the ability to record broadcast-quality video images with hi-fi stereo sound, edit them into a finished production with clean edits and a few unique special effects including slo-mo, posterization, and titling, and then duplicate your production onto VHS videocassettes for distribution. The components of this basic system cost about $5,000.

DESKTOP VIDEO: This was researched and reported by Allan Lundell. The equipment he describes is available in all large electronics stores.

HI-8

Hi-8 camcorders are small and inconspicuous with an ability to zoom in by a factor of 8 and with low-light capability. I prefer Hi-8 format, because the Hi-8 video images and sound are superb, the camcorder bodies are small and compact, and the videocassettes are about the size of an audiotape. The Hi-8s are

great in-the-field image-acquisition machines with a horizontal-line resolution of approximately 400 (compare with regular VHS or 8mm at 250 lines horizontal resolution). The Sony V-101 and the Canon H-680 are both excellent Hi-8 cameras. Overall, the Canon seems to be more rugged, designed for a camera user, while the Sony is stronger in combination with newer, higher tech. Each one has a list price of about $1,200.

EDITING VIDEOS

When you edit video, you are always working with two tapes at once, a source tape and a target tape. The idea is to patch together the good bits from raw source tape by copying them patch by patch onto the target tape. Since you work with two tapes at once, this means you need two videotape players, or VCRs. Generally you will want your target tape to be a VHS tape, as this is the kind of tape that fits into most people's VCRs. So you are going to want a Hi-8 videotape player and a VHS videotape player. Not just any VCR will do, as you want high-end VCRs that can smoothly inch the tape forward and backward. I use the EV-S900 H-8 VCR and the SLV-R5UC S-VHS VCR from Sony, $1,600 and $1,000, respectively.

So that you can see what's on the source and target tapes you'll need two monitors; I got two Sony 13-inch Trinitrons for $350 each. You can save expense here by using your existing TVs as the monitors.

The next thing you need for editing is a controller, which is the piece of hardware that you use to move the good bits from the source tape to the target tape. For this I use a Sony EM-300 controller, which lists at about $750. Since my controller and my two decks are all Sony, they are compatible. Both decks can be remote-controlled by the controller, which has an LCD window that shows you everything you need to know about where your system is at and gives you the commands to choose and change. The unit has two jog wheels which allow you to go forward or backward on either deck. Turning the jog wheel a few degrees moves a tape a few frames in that direction. A primary function of the EM-300 is cut-and-paste—marking the beginning and end points of segments you wish to use and then assembling them.

ADDING SOUND

Trying to edit a video's sound at the same time you are editing the images is a hopeless task. Instead you start by getting the images looking good, and then fix the sound later. This requires an equalizer. I use the $250 Videonics Equalizer. Its audio mixer allows you to combine the sound from your video with music from an audiotape. A microphone input is available for narratives and voice-overs. The digital paintbrush can change the color of a few objects—or the entire screen. The enhancer can improve the video signal quality, reducing noise and increasing image sharpness.

PACKET RADIO

Lee Felsenstein: The most revolutionary technological development in the last several years is packet radio, which offers the promise of efficient long-distance communication with no privately owned medium. In the case of packet radio, one of the most rigid government bureaucracies had to be fought in order to permit its legal development. And of course, once it's developed it still works whether it's legal or not. Good work, boys! **S**

PACKET RADIO: When you talk on the phone, your voice is converted into digital bits and bytes which are bundled into data packets that are sent over the phone net in bursts. Separate packets of your conversation may end up traveling over distinct lines. Ham radio users are now able to duplicate this process, but without having to use the phone company's lines. One can get a simple hand-held phone which bounces packets off the communications satellites, info which goes from user to user without ever having to enter the belly of the Babylon Beast.

Jas. Morgan: Synaesthesia comes from the Greek *syn* (union) and *ais-thesis* [sensation]. This is literally a merging or parallelism of sensory input where pieces of information occupy the same pencils of sensory space. Sound and light might merge at the same point of data—occupying the same piece of meaning.

The supercognition of synaesthetic communications makes possible a language of Gestalts, the bootstrapping of discrete sensory channels. Seeing and Hearing becomes SEE/HEAR, for example. Psychedelics offer us a taste of synaesthetic possibilities that are increasingly being realized by our external electronic communications technology.

THE COLOR OF SOUND

Roger McGuinn: I've always had a correlation between letters of the alphabet and colors and numbers. The key of E is blue to me. And the key of D is green. C is yellow, A is red, B is brown. When you get into an A-sharp or B-flat it's orange because it's changing from red to brown. So it makes sense; it's sort of a spectral thing. I don't know where it came from or what it is, but I've had it since I was three years old. My mother had it, and she had different colors associated with her letters and numbers. When I grew up, I was surprised to find out that not everybody had numbers, letters, and colors associated like that. It seemed like a normal thing to me. A minor key doesn't change the color, but it changes the hue a little bit. A D-major will be more of a lime green and a D-minor will be more like a teal. I don't really think about it that much. But it does help me when I'm playing. "My Back Pages" is a blue song; it's in E. G is kind of a grayish color, a dolphin-skin gray—songs like "Wild Mountain Thyme."

When I play a song like "The Bells of Rhymney," it's a green song. I see green the whole time I'm singing it. The same is true of "Mr. Tambourine Man" and "Turn, Turn, Turn." Those are all green songs; they're in D. It's not that visible, but it's very, very real. I just know that I'm in a green key. I think green. I don't see it visually. **S**

Synaesthesia

If everyone could see the things that I hear

Synaesthesia

A giant box of crayolas in my ear

—The Bobs (1989)

ERIC WHITE

TEMPORARY AUTONOMOUS ZONES

ISLANDS IN THE NET FOR REAL

The medieval Assassins founded a "State" which consisted of a network of remote mountain valleys and castles, separated by thousands of miles, strategically invulnerable to invasion, connected by the information flow of secret agents, at war with all governments, and devoted only to knowledge. Modern technology, culminating in the spy satellite, makes this kind of autonomy a romantic dream. No more mountain fortresses! No more pirate islands! In the future the same technology—freed from all political control—could make possible an entire world of AUTONOMOUS ZONES. But for now the concept remains precisely science fiction—pure speculation.

Bruce Sterling, cyberpunk laureate, published a near-future romance about political systems in decay. This decay led to a decentralized proliferation of experiments in living: giant worker-owned corporations, independent enclaves devoted to "data piracy," Green-Social-Democrat enclaves, Zerowork enclaves, anarchist liberated zones, etc. The information economy which supports this diversity is called "the Net"; the enclaves (and the book's title) are *Islands in the Net.*

THE PIRATE INFO NET

The Sea rovers and corsairs of the eighteenth century created an information network that spanned the globe; primitive and devoted primarily to grim business, the net nevertheless functioned admirably. Scattered throughout the net were islands, remote hideouts where ships could be watered and provisioned, booty traded for luxuries and necessities. Some of these islands supported intentional communities, whole mini-societies living consciously and determinedly outside the law if only for a short and merry while.

ISLANDS IN THE NET FOR REAL: These musings are from the man who calls himself Hakim Bey. Hakim has published a number of books, most recently an anthology of his writings called *TAZ: The Temporary Autonomous Zone,* available from Autonomedia. ▲

JAMES KOEHNLINE

PIONEER DROPOUTS

We were taught in elementary school that the first settlements in Roanoke failed; the colonists disappeared, leaving behind them only the cryptic message "Gone to Croatan." What really happened, the textbook implied, was that the Indians massacred the defenseless settlers. Later reports of gray-eyed Indians were dismissed as legend. However, Croatan was not some El Dorado; it was the name of a neighboring tribe of friendly Indians. Clearly what really happened was the settlement simply moved back from the Coast into the Great Dismal Swamp and was absorbed into the tribe. And the gray-eyed Indians were real—and they're still there, and they still call themselves Croatans.

So—the very first colony in the New World went native. They dropped out.

THE BUCCANEERS

Sectarians were able to thrive better under the looser and more corrupt administrations in the Caribbean, where rival European interests had left many islands deserted or even unclaimed. Barbados and Jamaica in particular must have been settled by many extremists, and I believe that Levelers and Ranters contributed to the Buccaneer utopia on Tortuga. Fleeing from hideous "benefits" of Imperialism such as slavery, serfdom, racism, and intolerance, from the tortures of impressment and the living death of the plantations, the Buccaneers adopted Indian ways, intermarried with Caribs, accepted blacks and Spaniards as equals, rejected all nationality, elected their captains democratically, and reverted to the state of Nature. Having declared themselves at war with the world, they sailed forth to plunder under mutual contracts which were so egalitarian that every member received a full share and the captain usually only one and a half shares.

BUCCANEERS: William Burroughs's novel *Cities of the Red Night* has many scenes set in homosexual pirate utopias.

RANTERS: Among the people who left England to come to the New World were members of a variety of strange religious/political sects such as the Familists, Quakers, Levelers, Diggers, and Ranters.

OTHER ENCLAVES

Throughout the eighteenth century, North America also produced a number of dropout "tri-racial isolate communities." (This clinical-sounding term was invented by the Eugenics Movement, which produced the first scientific studies of these communities. Unfortunately the "science" merely served as an excuse for hatred of racial "mongrels" and the poor, and the "solution to the problem" was forced sterilization.) The nuclei invariably consisted of runaway slaves and serfs, "criminals" (i.e., the very poor), "prostitutes" (i.e., white women who married nonwhites), and members of various native tribes. Thus we have the Maroons of the Great Dismal Swamp, the Ramapaughs of northern New Jersey, the Moors of Delaware, the Ben Ishmaels of Ohio, the Kallikaks of the New Jersey Pine Barrens, the Jukes of Tenessee, and the Issues of central Virginia.

IN THE AUTONOMOUS ZONE

Let us admit that we have attended parties where one brief night a republic of gratified desires was attained. Shall we not confess that the politics of that night have more reality and force for us than those of, say, the entire U.S. Government? Some of the parties we've mentioned lasted for two or three years. Is this something worth imagining, worth fighting for? Let us study invisibility, webworking, psychic nomadism—and who knows what we might attain? *T*

JAMES KOEHNLINE

TRANSREALISM

MY LIFE'S WORK

Rudy Rucker: I want to have my life's work on a CD with an access system that can call up any part of it, key on it with a cursor, and then go out into my journals, see what was happening, or get into my essays, see what I was doing then or find other stories that used a particular item and have it all be totally seamless. See, that's what I call Transrealism. If there is a category, Transrealism came first. That's what I'm into, but the label cyberpunk is what stuck. I'm trying to merge my life with my fiction and essentially create a word model of my consciousness. That is the basic concept in my novel *Software*. If your brain software is on the disc, the computer can simulate you, and you will be, in some sense, alive inside the computer. *T*

TRANSREALISM: The two basic principles of transrealism are 1) write about immediate perceptions in a fantastic way, and 2) base your characters on real people. Rucker's most recent book, *Transreal!*,  is a complete collection of his poems, stories and essays.

YVETTE ROMAN

VIRTUAL REALITY

**Opposite:
The Virtuality™
machine, a virtual
reality video
arcade game.**

R. U. Sirius: "Virtual reality is the name of a new technology that creates the illusion of being immersed in an artificial world, or of being present in a remote location in the physical world. To enter virtual reality (VR), a person puts on a head-mounted display (HMD) that looks like a SCUBA mask. A pair of tiny television-tubes, special optics and wide angle lenses, and a device that tracks the position of the user's head are mounted in the HMD so that when it is worn, the normal view of the outside world is completely blocked; in the place of the physical world is substituted a stereographic, three-dimensional computer graphics depiction of a 'world model' that exists in a computer. Besides being immersed in the artificial world, the person is able to navigate within that world, and to manipulate it using hands and fingers." These words, taken from Howard Rheingold's popular book by the name of *Virtual Reality,* might appear to be describing a mere device. In fact, MEGATONS of philosophical verbiage have been expended on the meaning and possible results of this technology over the past two years. And the fact that our pals at Spectrum Holobyte have turned out the first arcade war-game version will not make the discussion any less highfalutin'.

Some journalists seem to think that *MONDO 2000* is primarily dedicated to virtual reality. In

reality, of course, we represent a much broader gestalt, as expressed in the many topics in this book. On the whole, I think too much has been made of VR. But it IS a new media, and new medias are little cultural revolutions in and of themselves. Ultimately, what's far out about VR is that it will let people better share the contents of their minds. With every possible kind of visual image and sound digitally stored, and with the ability to put that into motion, you could beam your dream or your vision, however strange, surrealistic, or PERVERSE, right into the eyestalks of your virtual friend or enemy. FUN!

VIRTUAL REALITY IS THE TELEPHONE OF THE FUTURE

Jaron Lanier: My favorite story is the telephone. The telephone is a total win.

I want to propose a test of whether a technology is good or evil. Here's how the test goes. If the technology makes people more powerful or more smart, then it's an evil technology—because all of our problems except for a very few are self-brought. If a technology helps people to communicate, has a potential to promote empathy, but doesn't fundamentally increase power at the same time, then it's basically a good technology. The test tells you what's good and bad about computers and about telephones.

Virtual reality is going to be the telephone of the future. And that's the key thing.

ARTIFICIAL LIFE IS WITH PEOPLE

Virtual reality is made of other people. Period. All it is is a bunch of personalities that can be expressed through any form at all. But the actual meaning of those forms, which are infinite and ever-varying, is simply the personalities of the other people.

Without the personalities, there's actually nothing there, because the forms become infinitely easy and cheap.

VIRTUAL REALITY IS THE TELEPHONE OF THE FUTURE: Jaron Lanier was described earlier, in the "Politics" section. It's worth mentioning here, though, that Lanier has emerged as the premier spokesperson/philosopher of virtual reality.

MICHAEL LLEWELLYN

VR OVER THE NET

There are some types of virtual reality over a network that don't require much bandwidth at all. If your world is only made of synthetic imagery without any real-world imagery being brought into it, and if you have the right kinds of algorithms, you can really go quite low bandwidth, because all you're doing is sending changes to a data base about exactly where objects are and how they're tilted. And that doesn't have to take up a lot of information.

On the other hand, as soon as there are the fiber-optic lines and the ISDN standard is implemented, you can really take advantage of it in virtual reality by bringing in higher-quality realities that incorporate some real-world imagery. But we can actually do quite a strong level of virtual reality over the present phone system.

WHY NOT CREATE?

In virtual reality each building is as easy as the other from a practical point of view. From an artistic point of view, of course, it still takes more work to make a beautiful building, but that's work that will be enjoyed. All you can do is be creative in virtual reality. There's really nothing else to do.

That's a thing that must sound very alien and strange. Everybody has this reaction: "Who'd want to be creative? It's so much work. I just want to, like, be lazy and have this stuff presented to me." That's a weird concept to me. That's just an illustration of the sickness of the twentieth century, where people grew up with television. There will never be another generation that has that attitude.

BREAKING THROUGH THE STUPOR

The American Stupor. The stupor of the twentieth century that allows us to ruin our very lives in order to be wealthy and powerful and safe…that kind of blindness and

BANDWIDTH is the hacker term for the rate of information transfer. The bandwidth of a communication channel can be measured in terms of bits per second. Telephone lines do not have particularly high bandwidth, although if you use a modem you can indeed zap a fairly large document over the phone lines in a minute or two. The big thing hanging up video telephones has been the bandwidth problem: How to get thirty TV images per second across? Recent approaches involve only sending information about the parts of the scene which have just changed. The cyberspace solution could also work well—instead of sending detailed photos of the room the speakers are in, each site builds up a VR model from agreed-upon algorithms and then proceeds to "delta" or "change the positions" of the actors in sync with the low bandwidth info about their motions.

ISDN is short for Integrated Services Digital Network. The ISDN standard specifies the conventions according to which users of high-bandwidth phone lines should send mixed messages that might include print, voice, video, and computer output.

crazy stupor is only possible because of this sense we have of being passive, with the world presented to us. There's this model that it's easier to watch television than to do something, because you're being passive. There's this equation of passivity with easiness. The idea of luxury revolves around being passive.

Which is a very strange concept if you think about it. I'm amazed at how the rich seem to lose the quality in their lives even quicker than the poor people.

In virtual reality, there's no question that your reality is created by you. You made it. Or somebody else did whom you know. There's no sense of it being handed to you on a platter. In virtual reality, even your body looks like you did it. It's undeniable. I think being in that mode of realizing how active every moment in life is will break through the stupor. It's just got to make people notice what's in their lives when they have that experience. That's what I'm hoping.

DEALING WITH THE DATACLOUD

The whole idea of information…I think the opposing idea is experience. Information is alienated experience.

Computers are great, but they require making life into information, since that's all a computer can hold.

The first problem is that it's information. The second problem is that it's linear information. And the third problem is that it's false information.

ALL IS ONE

In virtual reality, you don't have "you" exactly. You see, in virtual reality the whole world is your body—equally—and everybody shares the same body. Check it out. It's true.

You know how Alan Watts once formulated the universe as a creature that looks at itself in a million ways and each of the ways was a person? Virtual reality is a reality just like that.

THE VR SPONGE

My fantasy is that virtual reality will be a sponge that will absorb human energy. And it's asymmetrical. If virtual reality absorbs aggressive, evil, ugly energy, then all you

ALAN WATTS wrote dozens of great popularizing books about enlightenment and the Eastern religions.

MARK LANDMAN

get is fantasy concentration camps or whatever, which might not be good but has got to be better than real ones. Whereas if it absorbs beautiful, loving energy, what you get is wonderful art, wonderful experience.

So it denatures the bad, but the good is inherently natured when it's sucked up into virtual reality.

MAKE TIME RUN BACKWARDS

In virtual reality there are two kinds of time. The particular experiences that make up time can be decoupled from physical time. You can play back your old experiences, you can go through them backwards or forwards, fast or slow. And that's a pretty profound thing, because, as it happens, the way people experience time is very much based on the outside world and not on internal sense.

VR AND THE HUMAN SPIRIT

All the big introductions of media technology in this century have had huge effects on the culture. I think virtual reality will too.

All the others have limited people's ability to communicate with each other and to experience the world. Now that's not common wisdom. Common wisdom would say that television's brought us the world and created a Global Village. But actually it separates us from the actual experience of the world. Instead, it gives us a little denatured version, and one that we're not in control of...so we lose our activity. That's where we really lose the world, because activity is everything.

Virtual reality is the first medium to come along that doesn't narrow the human spirit. That's the most important thing about it.

MY FIRST TRIP IN CYBERSPACE

John Barlow: All that remains of the aging shambles which usually constitutes my corporeal self is a glowing, golden hand floating before me like Macbeth's dagger. I point my finger and drift down its length to the bookshelf on the office wall.

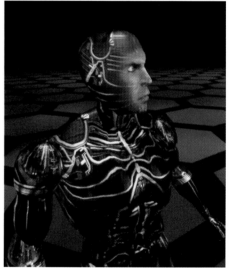

ANGEL STUDIO

I try to grab a book, but my hand passes through it.

"Make a fist inside the book and you'll have it," says my invisible guide.

I do, and when I move my hand again, the book remains embedded in it. I open my hand and withdraw it. The book remains suspended above the shelf.

I look up. Above me I can see the framework of red girders which support the walls of the office…above them the blue-blackness of space. The office has no ceiling, but it hardly needs one. There's never any weather here.

I point up and begin my ascent, passing right through one of the overhead beams on my way up. Several hundred feet above the office, I look down. It sits in the middle of a little island in space. I remember the home asteroid of *The Little Prince* with its one volcano, its one plant.

How very like the future this place might be: a tiny world just big enough to support the cubicle of one Knowledge Worker. I feel a wave of loneliness and head back down. But I'm going too fast. I plunge right on through the office floor and into the bottomless indigo below. Suddenly I can't remember how to stop and turn around. Do I point behind myself? Do I have to turn around before I can point? I flip into brain fugue.

"Just relax," says my guide in her cool, clinical voice. "Point straight up and open your hand when you get where you want to be."

Sure. But how can you get where you want to be when you're coming from nowhere at all?

At least I know where I left my body. It's in a room called Cyberia in a building called Autodesk in a town called Sausalito, California. Planet Earth. Milky Way. So on and so forth. My body is cradled in its usual cozy node of space-time coordinates.

But I…or "I"…am in cyberspace, a universe churned up from computer code by a Compaq 386 and a pair of Matrox graphics boards, then fed into my rods and cones by VPL Eyephones, a set of goggles through whose twin, parallax-corrected video

AUTODESK ⏏ is a computer software company which derives most of its income from sales of the computer-aided design program AutoCAD. A good part of Autodesk's corporate style is determined by John Walker, co-founder and Hacker King. In September of 1988, John Walker wrote an internal Autodesk white paper called "Through the Looking Glass: Beyond 'User Interfaces.'" In it he proposed an "Autodesk Cyberpunk Initiative" to produce within sixteen months a doorway into cyberspace…available to anyone with $15,000 and a 386 PC clone computer. The project's motto: "Reality Isn't Enough Anymore." Autodesk's Cyberia Project was running hard by Christmas 1988, staffed by William and Meredith Bricken, Eric Gullichsen, Pat Gelband, Eric Lyons, Gary Wells, Randy Walser, and John Lynch. Gullichsen had even registered William Gibson's term "cyberspace" as an Autodesk trademark, prompting an irate Gibson to apply for trademark registration of the term "Eric Gullichsen." By June 1989, they had an implementation which, though clearly the Kitty Hawk version of the technology, endowed people with an instantaneous vision of the Concorde level.

As of 1991 there has been a nearly complete turnover of the Cyberia staffing, with Randy Walser the only continuing member. The project is still going full-bore, however, although the most recent plans are shrouded in secrecy.

screens I see this new world.

When I move my head, the motion is tracked by a Polhemus  magnetic sensor, and the imaging engine of cyberspace is instructed to alter what I see accordingly. Thus, having made a controlled ascent back up through the floor of the "office," I turn to the left and I see a red chair with a desk behind it. I turn to the right and I see a door leading out onto the floating platform.

The configuration and position of my right hand is fed into the system by a VPL DataGlove, also with a Polhemus attached to it. The relationship between my hand and the Eyephones is precisely measured by the two trackers, so that my hand appears where I would expect it to. When I point or make a fist, the fiber optics sewn into the DataGlove convert kinesthetics into electronics. For a tenth of a second or so, my hand disappears and then reappears, glowing and toon-like, in the appropriate shape.

Standard equipment for the current Autodesk "deck" includes a 32-bit Compaq PC clone—these are the heaviest-duty PCs available. The Matrox graphics cards are from a company in Montreal. Once you download the geometry of a 3D scene onto a card like the Matrox, the hardware and chips of the card can very rapidly show how the 3D scene will look from any possible viewpoint. The Polhemus device is a so-called "six-dimensional sensor" which returns three position coordinates and three "attitude" coordinates, which specify the pitch, roll, and yaw of the device. The Polhemus is about the size of a plastic sugar cube, and you put one on the top of your Eyephones (for head tracking) and one on the back of your wrist (for hand tracking). Based on electromagnetic field lines, the Polhemus is made in, of all places, Virginia Beach, Virginia. There are a wide range of other 6D sensors coming out on the market: One of the most promising will be from Logitech, makers of the Logitech Mouse.

VPL

VPL, the other trading post on the VR frontier, isn't much fatter, although internal synergy seems to magnify output. Since its incorporation in 1985, it's had two *Scientific American* covers and produced the DataGlove, DataSuit, the PowerGlove, Swivel 3-D, and VPL Eyephones, the only commercially available head-mounted display. It's been in a couple of big lawsuits (one, just concluded to its satisfaction, with Stanford University) and creates, at a distance, the mirage of a fair-sized company going at it pretty hard.

But up close, one can get on a first-name basis with every VPL employee in the course of an afternoon. The company has yet to outgrow the third floor of its slightly tacky building at the Redwood City yacht harbor.

VPL is Jaron Lanier's company. VPL  originally stood for "Visual Programming Language." The VPL Eyephones are almost the only commercially available head-mounted displays in existence, just as the VPL DataGloves are almost the only available hand-position input devices. Lanier holds a number of fundamental patents, and VPL has been taking a very aggressive legal stance in discouraging competition. VPL enjoyed a recent big success in licensing its sensor-glove technology to Mattel games as the PowerGlove Nintendo game accessory. (See "Politics" for a description of Jaron.)

IVAN SUTHERLAND

John Barlow: Virtual reality, as a concept, first found form at the University of Utah over twenty years ago in the fecund cranium of Ivan E.

SUTHERLAND'S first head-mounted display showed a topographic map of the U.S. He has since gone on to build a company specializing in extremely high-end computer-graphics simulations; we're talking $3 million per machine. His best customer? The U.S. Air Force. The U.S. pilots who flew over Iraq went through

Sutherland, the godfather of computer graphics and the originator of about every Big Computer Idea not originated by Alan Kay or Doug Englebart. In 1968, he produced the first head-mounted display. This was the critical element in VR hardware, but it was so heavy that it had to be suspended from the ceiling...at some peril to its wearer. The Sword of Damocles was mentioned.

extensive virtual fly-throughs using Sutherland Graphics equipment. The demos are all but indistinguishable from actual films, even down to things like the fuel trucks driving around on the runways and the dust clouds kicked up by the jets' exhaust.

TOWARD CYBERCAD

There is a reason why Autodesk is involved in this enterprise besides some daydream of the Ultimate Hack. Whatever adventures it might entertain it affords by selling AutoCAD, the most popular drafting program for architecture. How many architects have dreamed of the ability to take their clients on a walk inside their drawings before their miscommunications were sealed in mortar?

Virtual reality has already been put to such use at the University of North Carolina. There Sitterman Hall, the new $10 million home of UNC's computer science department, was designed by virtual means.

Using a head-mounted display along with a handlebar-steerable treadmill, the building's future users "walked through" it, discovering, among other things, a discomforting misplacement of a major interior wall in the lobby. At the point of the discovery, moving the wall out was cheap. A retrofit following the first "real" walk-through would have cost more, by several orders of magnitude. Thus, one can imagine retrofit savings from other such examples, which could start to make DataSuits as common a form of architectural apparel as chinos and tweed.

Given the fact that AutoCAD is already generating about $170 million dollars a year even without such pricey appurtenances as cyberspace design tools, it isn't hard to imagine a scenario in which developing workstations for virtual architecture comes to look like very shrewd business.

DAMOCLES once talked too much about Dionysus's happiness and good fortune. To teach Damocles a lesson, Dionysus invited him to a feast, and put a hanging sword, suspended by a single hair, over Damocles's head. Like, "See, man, it's not always so easy staying high!" Another reason—besides the weight—that Sutherland's colleagues were made uneasy by his head-mounted display was that when you wore it, there was an electrical line carrying fifty thousand volts draped down your back

JERRY GARCIA IN CYBERSPACE

Knowing that Garcia is a sucker for anything

which might make a person question all he knows, I gave him a call not long after my first cyberspace demo. Hell yes, he was interested. When? If I'd told him 6 A.M., I think he'd have been there on time.

He adapted to it quicker than anyone I'd watched, other than my four-year-old daughter, Anna (who came home and told her sisters matter-of-factly that she'd been to a neat "place" that afternoon).

By the time he crossed back over to our side of reality Horizon, he was pretty kidlike himself. "Well," he finally said, "they outlawed LSD. It'll be interesting to see what they do with this."

CYBERDELIC!

The closest analogue to virtual reality that I know is the psychedelic experience, and, in fact, cyberspace is already crawling with delighted acidheads.

Another reason for relating this to acid is the overwhelming sense of its cultural scale. It carries with it a cosmic titillation I haven't experienced since 1966—always a telling sign that you are "time-tracking."

Timothy Leary is all excited again. He's a kind of zeitgeist chameleon. He spent the forties in the army. In the fifties, he was a tweedy young college professor, a Jules Feiffer cartoon. In the sixties, he was, well, Timothy Leary. In the seventies, he became, along with H. R. Haldeman, a political prisoner. He lived up the material eighties in Beverly Hills. Whatever America is about to do, Tim starts doing it first.

When I visited him recently, he was already as cyberpunk as he had been psychedelic when I last saw him at Millbrook twenty-two years ago. Still, his current persona seems reasonable, even seraphic. He calmly scored a long list of persuasive points, the most resonant of which is that most Americans have been living in virtual reality since the proliferation of television. All cyberspace will do is make the experience interactive instead of passive.

MICHAEL SWAINE

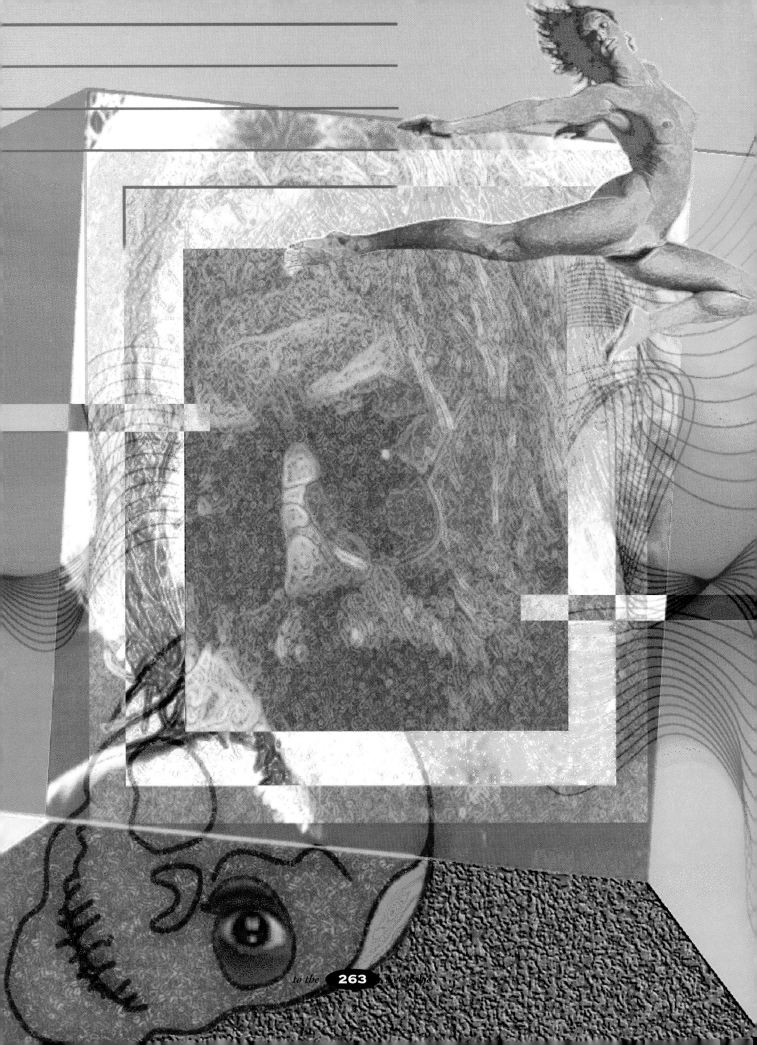

"Our brains are learning how to exhale as well as inhale in the data-sphere," he said.

The latest bus is pulling out of the station. As usual, Leary has been on it for a while, waiting impatiently for it to depart.

VIRTUAL REALITY IS NOT LIKE LSD

Jaron Lanier: Virtual reality affects the outside world and not the inside world. Virtual reality creates a new objective level of reality. You enter it in a waking state. There's a clear transition.

If you're ever confused about which reality you're in, you put your hand on your eyes and see if you're wearing Eyephones or not. That simple. You take them off and you're out. Drugs are such a powerful metaphor that it's easy to forget the differences. Let me tell you the thing that's the most vital: You go inside of virtual reality and there are other people there. Other people are the life of the party. That's the key. Sanity is made of other people. They're there in virtual reality. They're not really there in LSD.

CYBERSPACE EMBODIES

Cyberspace is a medium that gives people the feeling they have been transported, bodily, from the ordinary physical world to worlds purely of imagination. Although artists can use any medium to evoke imaginary worlds, cyberspace carries the worlds themselves.

No one can know what will happen from one moment to the next in a cyberspace, not even the spacemaker. Every moment gives every participant an opportunity to create the next event. Whereas film is used to show a reality to an audience, cyberspace is used to give a virtual body, and a role, to everyone in the audience. Print and radio tell. Stage and film show. Cyberspace embodies.

THE COMPLEAT CYBERSPACE DECK

A cyberspace deck has seven components:

1. A CYBERSPACE ENGINE to generate a simulated world and mediate the player's interaction with it.

CYBERSPACE EMBODIES: This is from a paper by Randy Walser, who has been with the Autodesk cyberspace project since its inception in 1988.

A CYBERSPACE DECK: The use of the word "deck" for an assemblage of cyberspace machinery is taken directly from William Gibson's novels. Close reading of these books leaves one's image of a Gibson deck quite vague. It does seem to have a plug which seems to connect to a socket in the user's head. Getting rid of the head-socket was the key move in making cyberspace into a near-term consumer product that people actually want to have.

2. A CONTROL SPACE—a box of physical space—where the player's movements are tracked.

3. SENSORS to monitor the player's actions and body functions.

4. EFFECTORS to produce certain physical effects and stimulate the player's senses.

5. PROPS to give the player solid analogues of virtual objects and vehicles.

6. A NETWORK INTERFACE to admit other players to the simulated world.

7. An ENCLOSURE (or some sort of physical framework) to hold all the components.

Many decks will have just one prop, like a stationary bicycle, a railing, or a chair, and some decks will have no props at all.

The sole purpose of cyberspace technology is to trick the human senses and sensibilities, to help people buy into and sustain an illusion. Head-mounted visual displays are important because they flood the human sense of sight with illusory images, making it much easier for most people to suspend their disbelief. Nonetheless, head-mounted displays are merely one means among many, including out-the-window visual displays, three-dimensional audio displays, motion platforms, force-feedback devices, credible-simulation worlds, dramatic tension, high stakes, engaging stories, and social reinforcement. The upshot is that there is no surefire way to put people into cyberspace; ultimately the job is an artistic one.

STATIONARY BICYCLE: At the 1990 Cyberthon—an all-day festival organized by the Point Foundation (closely associated with *Whole Earth Review*)—in San Francisco, Autodesk showed a cyberspace based on a stationary bicycle. You put on the helmet and got on the bicycle, and the faster you pedaled, the faster you would move around a virtual race course. There were some other (artificial) riders and a blimp overhead as well. If you liked, you could switch your viewpoint to the blimp.

An "OUT-THE-WINDOW" visual display is a system with a large computer screen that acts like a window you are looking through. This is done by mounting a Polhemus sensor on your head so that the computer knows which direction you are looking at it from. The effect of an out-the-window display is that if, say, there is something you can't quite make out at the left edge of the screen, you can lean to the right and be able to see more of what is to the left.

A SALUTE TO MORTON L. HEILIG

Eric Gullichsen: Mr. Heilig is the holder of U.S. Patent 3,050,870, filed in 1961 for a device known as the "Sensorama Simulator." The

Sensorama apparatus is intended to realistically present simulated experiences by "stimulating the nervous system with a wide variety of sensory stimuli in forms that are natural to it, i.e., color, visual movement, complete peripheral vision, 3D, binaural sound, breezes, odor, and tactile sensations."

Some thirty years ago, Mr. Heilig was able to assemble this mechanical device incorporating film loops, odor canisters triggered electromagnetically from information on a film track, and vibrating knobs and seat. Considerations were even given to hygiene, with a built-in UV light sterilizing the brow rests between uses.

Heilig's intent was to provide a "natural" rather than a synthetic environment simulator, for purposes of training people in realistic situations without the cost or dangers associated with the real thing.

Only today are virtual reality researchers beginning to rediscover the potential utility of video in virtual environments. And none of the existing VR implementations today employ as wide a range of sensory stimuli as did Sensorama. One of the early Sensorama demonstrations involved a simulated motorcycle ride through Manhattan, complete with potholes and wafting smells of pizza!

THE PHOSPHOTRON

The Virtual Light instrumentation I have developed proves that it is possible to produce optical sensations directly in the eye without the use of photons. This means that we can foresee virtual reality devices which do not require television display technologies. Rather, we can access a much higher bandwidth sensation information channel DIRECTLY to the brain. Best of all, we can accomplish this noninvasively—without resorting to surgical implants.

One of my inventions, the Phosphotron, embodies certain specific components of Virtual Light to cause a viewer wearing the goggles to see specific, repeatable optical phenomena of

THE PHOSPHOTRON: This is from Stephen Beck, Chief Scientist at Lapis Technology, which makes display cards & solutions for the Macintosh. Beck is also an inventor, and he's the creator of some amazing acid-graphical videos. The Phosphotron "goggles" are a glasses-shaped piece of metal connected to a source of weak electrical currents. These currents produce a changing electrical field around the Phosphotron, and the electrical field penetrates into the user's eye tissues, retina, and optic nerve. The idea is that the electrical fields can trigger the tissue to release stray electrons that cascade into nerve impulses, producing visual imagery. The images seen are similar to the phospenes that you see if you press on your eyes or if you flash lights on your closed eyes.

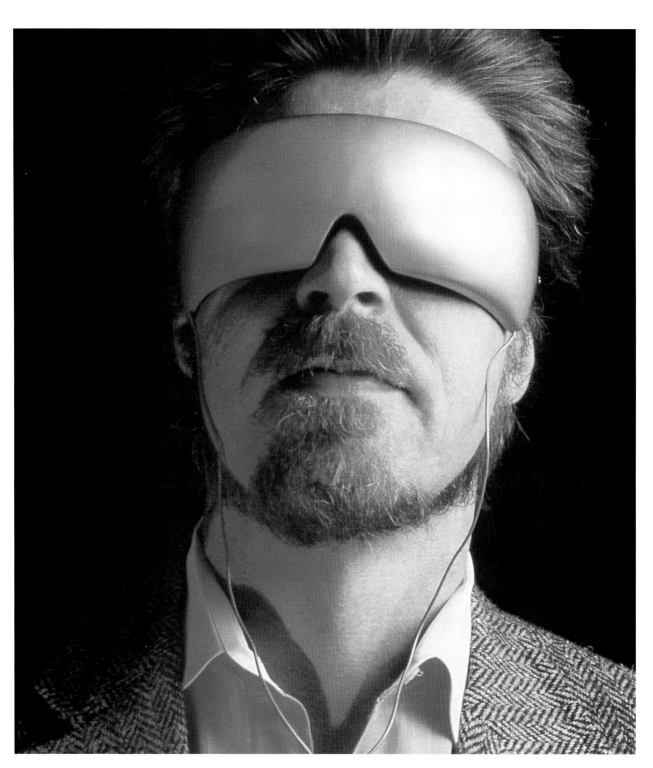

lights, flashing patterns, and micro-
textures.

The Phosphotron causes sensations
of light by direct use of electrons, either
by conduction or induction. Neural signals
into the optic nerve are triggered, which the
brain interprets as light. This light—which I call
Virtual Light—has directionality, temporality,
color, form, and shape.

Virtual Light can be modulated with information.

A LEXICON OF CYBERSPEAK

Actor: An OTHERWORLD traveler who is able to
effect changes in the OTHERWORLD.

Artificial Reality: The oxymoron on the
table. Stereoscopic, interactive, data
base-based worlds displayed with such
a wide field of view that the actor is on
the inside looking out, as opposed to
being on the outside looking in, as
with conventional monitors, no matter
how large the screen.

Binaural: Like stereo sound, but recorded
with two microphones in the ear canals of a
dummy head with pinnae qv, and listened to only
with headphones. Eerie effect of being there.

Corneal Field: Coined by us to denote regions of the
visual field that are "behind the edge" of the entrance pupil
of an HMD lens system but which can be perceived if the
eye axis is aligned with the optical axis of the lens
system. Refraction at the cornea surface provides a
vantage point about a half inch closer to the eye
lens than the center of the eyeball, hence a
wider cone of view.

Cybernetics: Coined by Professor
Norbert Weiner for his book of that

A LEXICON OF CYBERSPEAK: These definitions of
terms used in virtual reality work were supplied as part
of an advertisement by Eric Howlett of LEEP Systems.
LEEP Systems/POP-OPTIX LABS, 241 Crescent St., Waltham,
MA, 02154.

title in 1948. From the Greek for steersman, he defined it in a subtitle as "control and communication in the animal and the machine." He would have become dyspeptic at some of the uses of his word in the last forty years, but not, we think, with Cyberspace. He would note, however, that the loop has to be closed, that it isn't cyber-anything if the actor can't interact with the space.

Field of View (FOV): A complexity. Of the eye itself, we speak of the direct field (the solid cone swept out by the axis of the eye as it rotates in its socket, usually about 90 degrees except where the nose and the brows interfere) and of the peripheral field—everything beyond, perceivable because of refraction at the cornea, usually about 270 degrees laterally for healthy eyes. (For the limitation of the field by optical systems, see corneal field and peering field.)

HMD: Acronym for head-mounted display. A viewing system that mounts on, and turns with, the head. Should provide an image filling at least the direct field of view, an image that changes according to the head movement of the wearer so the surroundings appear stationary.

Knothole Effect: In which you can see more if you don't look directly.

LEEP: The acronym for Large Expanse Extra Perspective.

Otherworlds: Comprising remote real-object spaces as well as computer-generated environments and combinations thereof. Our coinage. We needed it because we serve them all.

Peering Field: Another term we needed—this time to describe the region directly

visible only if you move your eyeball centers significantly off the viewer optical axis, an action normally not possible in the head-mounts, but common with tabletop viewing systems.

Pinna: pl. pinnae. The external part of the ear; auricle.

Puppet: The dummy head with microphone ears and video eyes that represents the actor in any real otherworld.

Real Images: These will show up on a screen, if there is a screen where they are.

Reality, Virtual or Artificial: Real reality will be left as an exercise for the student.

Resolutions: Something the eyes are very good at in the middle, but dismal elsewhere. At the current state of the art, wide-angle head-mounted displays are dismal everywhere.

Stereoscopic: From the Greek for "solid." Viewed from two slightly separated points, so that the objects can be seen to be solid and separated in depth. There can be spectacular results from an exquisite dynamic sense in some higher animals. *V*

VIRTUAL SEX

A HOT NIGHT

Picture yourself a couple of decades hence, getting dressed for a hot night in the virtual village. Before you climb into a suitably padded changer and put on your head-mounted display, you slip into a lightweight—eventually, one would hope, a diaphanous—bodysuit. It would be something like a body stocking, but with all the intimate snugness of a condom. Embedded in the inner surface of the suit, using a technology that does not yet exist, is an array of intelligent effectors. These effectors are ultra-tiny vibrators of varying degrees of hardness, hundreds of them per square inch, that can receive and transmit a realistic sense of tactile presence in the same way the visual and audio displays transmit a realistic sense of visual and auditory presence. You can reach out your virtual hand, pick up a virtual block, and by running your fingers over the object, feel the surfaces and edges, by means of the effectors that exert counterforces against your skin. The counterforces correspond to the kinds of forces you would encounter when handling a nonvirtual object of the specified shape, weight, and texture. You can run your cheek over virtual satin and feel the difference when you encounter virtual human flesh. Or you can gently squeeze something soft and pliable and feel it stiffen and rigidify under your touch.

Now, imagine plugging your whole sound-sight-touch telepresence system into the telephone network. You see a lifelike but totally artificial visual representation of your own body and of your partner's. Depending on where you go and where you are allowed and what you are willing to pay (or trade or do), you can find one partner, a dozen, a thousand, in various cyberspaces that are no further away than a telephone number.

A HOT NIGHT: This badinage comes from Howard Rheingold, a Bay Area-based cultural observer. He will never live down usurping Ted Nelson's term "teledildonics" to describe sex via virtual reality technology. He is editor of *Whole Earth Review* and recently authored the fascinating book *Virtual Reality*.

INTELLIGENT EFFECTORS: Cyberspace theorists often use the words sensors and effectors to mean what hackers used to call computer-input and computer-output devices. The sensors provide a way for the user to send signals to the cyberspace (and the other users in it), and the effectors are the channel by which the cyberspace sends information back to the user. The DataGlove is a sensor, while the Eyephones are an effector. There are several current approaches to the problem of how to create a glove which is an effector as well as a sensor—a glove which "pushes back." One approach is to run a flow of compressed air through channels in the glove and sphincter the air's outlet closed on a finger that is supposed to be touching something. That finger's air channel swells up and pushes on the finger. Another approach is to use titanium-nickel alloy, or "memory metal." You can warm up a wire of this stuff, put a bend in it, and then straighten it out after it cools. Every time it gets reheated, the bend will reappear. You could thus pass a slight current through a wire to make it bend and push on your finger.

Opposite: Angel Studio's virtual sex scene from the movie *The Lawnmower Man*

LET'S SHAKE!

If you can map your hands to your puppet's legs, and let your fingers do the walking through cyberspace, there is no reason to believe you won't be able to map your genital effectors to your manual sensors and have direct genital contact by shaking hands.

POLYGONAL LOVE DOLLS?

John Barlow: I have been through eight or ten Q & A sessions on virtual reality, and I don't remember one where sex didn't come up. As though the best thing about all this will be the infinite abundance of shaded polygonal party dolls. As though we are devising here some fabulously expensive form of Accu-jac.

This is strange. I don't know what to make of it, since, as things stand right now, nothing could be more disembodied or insensate than the experience of cyberspace. It's like having had your everything amputated. You're left mighty underendowed, and any partner would be so insubstantial you could walk right through her without either of you feeling a thing.

And I did overhear the word "DataCondom" at one point…Maybe the nerds who always ask this question will get a chance to make it with their computers at long last.

MACPLAYMATE

Most games are performance tests—violent performance tests. Most look as if they've been programmed by sadistic nerds—this is largely because they were.

I wanted to create a nonviolent interactive simulation that a user could enjoy simply for the experience. I needed some form of redundant animation that could fit on a single floppy, that had high entertainment value—something a user wouldn't get bored with immediately.

Redundant yet somehow engaging—like sex, that rutting aspect of sex. This was MacPlaymate, and the rest is cybersex history. Underground comics were a big influence, of course. Woody Allen's Orgasmatron in *Sleeper*. Tijuana bibles. I was fascinated by the novelty ads in comic books. X-Ray Specs—the Buddy Holly from Hell with a foot-long tongue, goggling at a prom queen's panties—you know the one.

CYBERPIMPING

We rented a booth at MacWorld to sell the program. The response was overwhelming—I realized I was onto something. The second day the

PUPPET: What do you call the body-icon that you use to stand for yourself in cyberspace? Rheingold uses the word "puppet," and others have used the word "avatar." Or how about "tuxedo"?

MACPLAYMATE: This is from Mike Saenz, a hairy, evil-smelling genius computer artist. He authored some of the first computer-drawn comic books, and then hit on the idea of creating a pornographic computer game. This was MacPlaymate for the Mac. A regular computer disk can't really hold very many images, but the new CD-ROMs can hold many screens of images. CD-ROM stands for "Compact Disc Read-Only Memory," with "Read Only" meaning that you can't easily WRITE data to the discs. Saenz's next move was to create a pornographic CD-ROM game for the Mac: Virtual Valerie. Saenz founded his own company, Reactor, Inc., to distribute Virtual Valerie and has recently started shipping a more evolved (and nonpornographic) CD-ROM game called Spaceship Warlock.

Vice Squad came by and gave us a firm hand-slap and said: "We can run you in, we can confiscate all your hardware because this is a violation of certain uh, penile codes." Finally, all they had us do was turn the Macs away from the audience. We were allowed, however, to invite them into the booth to interact with it.

Wink, nudge. And I didn't know how to deal with the guys who thought I was some kind of sex fanatic. The image of my Mac as a hooker with me in the role of cyberpimp got in the way of the fun I was having. I didn't follow MacPlaymate with anything sexual until years later.

VIRTUAL VALERIE

Virtual Valerie…she's your cybernetic fantasy! When CD-ROM came I dove into it—I founded Reactor, Inc., and put out Virtual Valerie in six weeks, working 72 hours a day.

She's a full-color MacPlaymate with virtual reality aspects, 90-degree turns, navigating through the 3D space of rooms, etc…but the sex bits could be better.

Valerie's world is so detailed that it became this huge project, and by the time I got to the sex, I was, you might say, fucked out. We've had complaints that people are getting carpal tunnel syndrome from trying to please Valerie.

CYBERNETIC FANTASY: If you eventually get to Virtual Valerie's bedroom, she gets on all fours on the bed and two penis/dildos appear at the bottom of the screen. You click your mouse on one of them and slide it into Valerie's vagina. She turns her head back and forth and says, "Harder, harder, faster, faster, harder, harder, faster, faster…" as you the user jiggle the mouse back and forth.

VIRTUAL SEX

This is our chance to create a whole new form of erotic art. And very practically, porno is what made the VCR market what it is today, and I think virtual sex will do the same for VR. Virtual sex is also easy to understand. When I explain virtual reality to the uninitiated, they just don't get it. But they warm immediately to the idea of virtual sex.

Actually, VR has no interest for everyday people unless it deals with telepresence in a practical way—so users can actually affect the real world—or presents a superior stimulus. A good sex simulation would be much more fun—and more thought-provoking—than a flight simulation.

X-RATED FUTURE

I have a silly idea for a product called Strip Teacher. She goes, "Tell me the name of the thirteenth president of the United States and I'll show you my tits."

I think lust motivates technology. The first personal robots, let's face it, are not going to be bought to bring people drinks.

INTERACTIVE MADONNA

I'd like to do an Interactive Madonna. It would be a blockbuster. Madonna, if you're reading this, give me a call. Let's do this thing.

NO REPROACH

I see a lot of people practicing self-censorship, which is hateful. People have assumed, incorrectly, that I've been under attack for MacPlaymate and Virtual Valerie. In fact I hear absolutely nothing—no contact from irate groups, moral fascists…Software is probably still in the window of no reproach.

THE PLEASURE-DOME PROJECT

Nick Herbert: The pleasure-dome project is partly inspired by Ilone Staller, a former porn star elected by popular acclaim to the Italian Senate, who calls for the replacement of atomic weapons with "anatomic weapons," the renunciation of warfare in favor of face-to-face sensual contact between peoples of the world. To those who complain that a scientific study of pleasure is frivolous in light of more pressing social needs, I point out that the word "defense lab" is only a thin cover for the scientific search for more ingenious ways of delivering pain and death. Let's turn that ingenuity around!

As a prototype of the pleasure-dome principle I propose converting the Lawrence Livermore Laboratory in Northern California—currently the nation's largest nuclear weapons research lab—into the D. H. Lawrence Livingmore Laboratory—the world's largest scientific center dedicated solely to the pursuit of happiness.

In the D. H. Lawrence domes, work will proceed to develop new sensory and motor prostheses, including the power of "telesensation": taking on (via radio or laser links) the body image of a robot spatially separated from your physical body. Intellectually you may know that you are suspended in a Lilly Tank in Livermore, but experientially you are sounding the Ramapo Deep with sonar senses and a dozen tentacles, alert for the scent of predatory sperm whale. Or you may prefer to fly, flapping and soaring on light wings. Now that the body's load can be shed, mankind lifts free of gravity in a second Kitty Hawk. Disguised as bear, hawk, mole, mouse, salmon, men and women reenter the animal kingdom, living the lives of numerous species, sharing animal emotions, celebrations, and migrations, not as outsiders but inside the very skin of the beast. Closing the wound symbolized by Adam's Fall, mankind will scatter itself in a thousand proxies throughout the Great Chain of Being. ∎

A LILLY TANK is a darkened pool of saltwater in which one floats in complete sensory deprivation. Its use was pioneered by John Lilly.

A computer VIRUS is a piece of computer code which can be attached to a legitimate piece of software. Once a virus gets into your computer's memory, it is likely to attach copies of itself to every program you run. If you then give a program to someone else, the virus can get on his or her machine. Aside from copying itself, a virus may also take certain undesirable actions. The most typical bad thing that it does is to keep your machine from running, and the worst thing it is likely to do is to erase all your files. If you have a modem, it's even possible (remotely) that a virus might dial out for a pizza and print a message on your screen asking you to slip the pizza into your disk-drive's slot.

THE H-BOMB OF THE INFORMATION AGE

Michael Synergy: Welcome to the H-Bomb of the Information Age. The ultimate lever action: remote, numerous, targetable, anonymous.

I've just worked out a hard-core worm. A nice feature of current networks is that there are networks hanging *off* of networks. This worm breaks into a computer and seeds itself into all the component systems. Once seeded, the worms mutate into a specific configuration and grab any new resources available on each machine. Then the worms bounce back out into the main network. The growth rate with mutations would allow for a few hundred new worms, minimum, on the network per hour. Considering that the Internet worm crippled so many machines for so long without trying, a few thousand distinct worms would shut the whole system down. Good-bye banks, good-bye telephones, good-bye welfare checks. How much money do you carry in your wallet? It might be all you have left.

THE H-BOMB OF THE INFORMATION AGE: As we reported in the "Crackers" section, the Internet worm shutdown an estimated 6,600 computers tied to Internet and caused an estimated loss of forty to ninety million dollars. And that was poorly written and not intended for destructive activity. What Synergy is pointing out here is that if a creative hacker released a virus with the intention of doing maximum damage to the nation's vital systems, the electronic destruction would be phenomenal. In this sense, computer viruses could be a weapon for a foreign enemy in a war. Or it could be seen as the *only* way to strike a blow against an increasingly fascist empire in the digital age.

A WORM is a computer virus that replicates itself across a network.

GOOD COMPUTER VIRUSES

Viruses can clean up your computer, and they can be used as a hacking tool. They provide a good way of investigating closed systems. You can send viruses to all parts of the operating system to look for patterns as it is running. Kind of a logic analyzer, if you like. Viruses can act like a logic analyzer.

As the virus goes through the operating system, it stops at certain checkpoints, doing its rounds in a given amount of time. This checkpoint will report back what the condition is. Should a condition not be right, it will attempt to correct that situation. It will find the part that went bad, for example, and replace it. Essentially the virus will serve as a means of creating a self-repairing system. The customer buys an infected system, infected with viruses designed for self-repair. They will also defend against invading viruses. If an alien virus tries to replicate in the system, it will alert one or more of the checkpoints. At that point it will be removed by the system viruses. If viruses are going to attack my program, I'm going to write viruses that attack viruses. The goal is a self-repairing, crash-resistant system, similar to the way our bodies repair themselves. Biologically we are the product of thousands of microorganisms cooperating together. We can apply that kind of thinking in the computer world. We are modifying the concept of a virus to serve us.

LANGUAGE IS A VIRUS

William S. Burroughs: Language acts like a virus. A virus repeats copies of itself. So does a word. A word is alive by its nature and function.

We're always talking about the difference between humans and other animals. Well, no other animal is right- or left-handed. Now that, to me, is one of the really striking differences, to have two brain hemispheres—a dominant verbal hemisphere and a nondominant hemisphere which is spatial, innovative, etc. So there you have a split. Possibly a fusing of those two hemispheres, or at least a functioning smoothly together, would be a tremendous forward step. **V**

GOOD COMPUTER VIRUSES: This from Bill Me Tuesday, a hacker to be found in the Santa Cruz Mountains. Like other virus workers, he is unwilling to reveal his name.

LANGUAGE IS A VIRUS: A biological virus is little more than a piece of DNA with some claws attached to it. A virus reproduces by attaching itself to a cell wall and pushing its DNA into the cell. The viral DNA takes over the cell's processes and makes the cell fill itself with replicas of the original virus. The cell then bursts and the process continues. Burroughs has often said that language is a virus, meaning that the words and ideas we use are in some way using us in order to spread themselves. An evangelist might be thought of as the Bible's way of replicating itself. The singer/performer Laurie Anderson had a Burroughs-based song called "Language Is a Virus" on her *Home of the Brave* album. The notion of ideas using people to reproduce themselves can also be found in the writings of the biologist Richard Dawkins, who speaks of self-reproducing ideas as "memes." One of the best essays on this theme is Douglas Hofstader's "On Viral Structures and Self-Replicating Structures," which appears in his anthology, *Metamagical Themas*.

ERIC WHITE

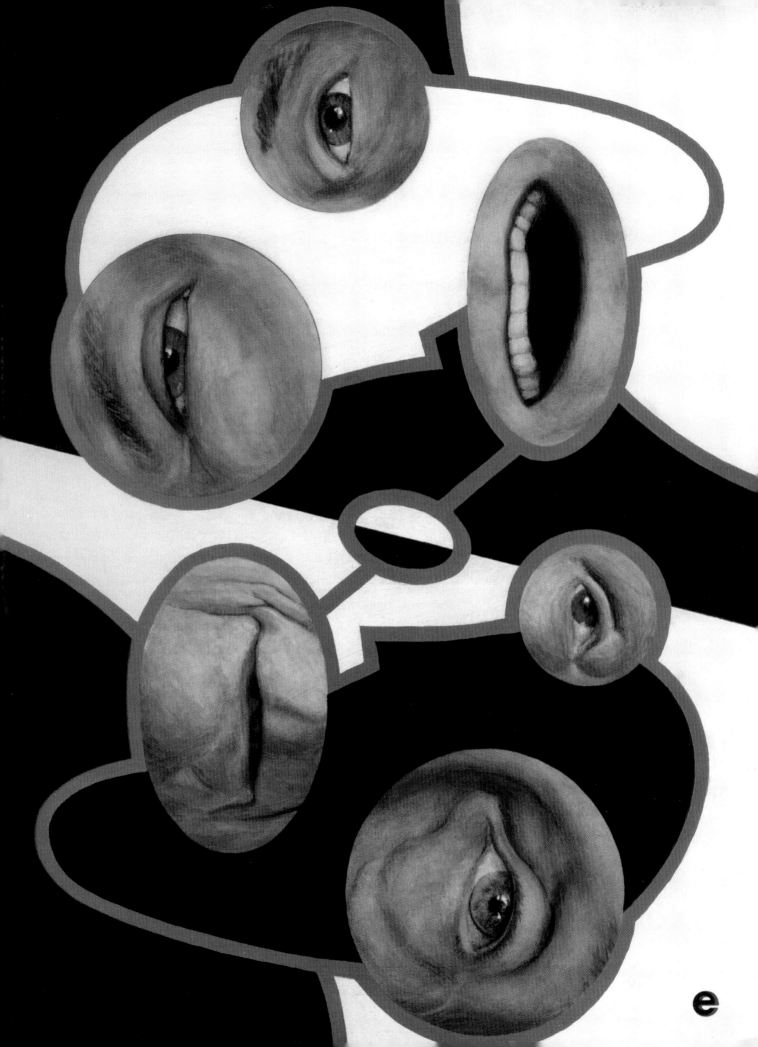

WETWARE

WHAT IT IS

Suppose you think of an organism as being like a computer graphic that is generated from some program. Or think of an oak tree as being the output of a program that was contained inside the acorn. The genetic program is in the DNA molecule. Instead of calling it software like a computer program, we call it wetware because it's in a biological cell where everything is wet. Your software is the abstract information pattern behind your genetic code, but your actual wetware is the physical DNA in a cell. A sperm cell is wetware with a tail, but it's no good without an ovum's wetware. A fertilized seed is self-contained wetware. A plant cutting is wetware—plants can reproduce as clones.

HAWAII

The islands of Hawaii are at the very north of the great Polynesian triangle that runs from New Zealand to Easter Island at the bottom. The first Polynesians to get as far as Hawaii came there by accident, and then they had to fight their way back. They couldn't stay because they hadn't brought the right wetware. They didn't have the taro-cuttings and yams and women that they needed to stay and grow their world. So they went back and got the wetware and came again.

INSULIN

There are parts of the DNA you can change that don't matter very much to the cell. Take insulin. Ordinarily, insulin would be an enzyme, something grown by

WETWARE:

These comments are taken from an interview with Max Yukawa, a Hawaiian-born bioengineer now active in Silicon Valley.

an animal cell. But it's hard to keep a big culture of animal cells alive. Instead we use a kind of bacteria called Escherichia coli— these are the guys who live in our large intestines. Shit germs. They're the darling of the bioengineers. What we're able to do is to splice the DNA that makes insulin into the DNA of the E. coli. So this particular germ has insulin inside it, and all its children do too. You breed up a vat of them, then blenderize it and extract the insulin. That's how most of the insulin sold to diabetics is now made. We did insulin first because it's a relatively simple molecule. But some of the really complex mood-changing hormones could be next.

GENETIC ENGINEERING

There's this dream of being able to manipulate DNA to the point where you can like grow a perfectly formed six-inch elephant, or a man with ten-foot-long legs. It's never going to be that simple. The organic environment is a full-blown chaotic system— everything in it depends on everything else. When you change something here, it changes something else over there. Getting rid of obvious disease-causing genes is certainly in the cards, and then prospective parents will start being tempted to have someone sift through their sperm and egg cells to find the best ones. Or maybe you could mix and match, get a few chromosomes here and a few over there. **W**

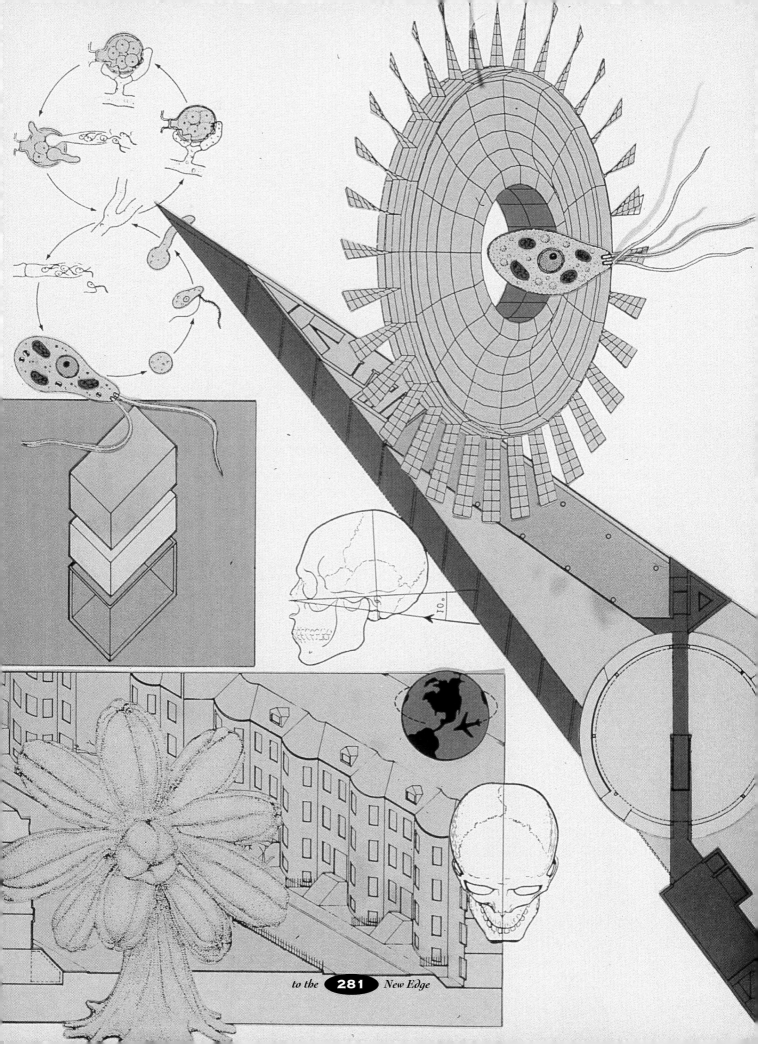

Zines

R. U. Sirius: Zines are small, free-form, low-circulation magazines or newsletters. There are now thousands of them as the result of desktop publishing technology and generations of kids hooked on media. Here are the best ones out there:

2600 ($18/yr from P.O. Box 752, Middle Island, NY 11953-0752): The premier zine for the explorers and outlaws working at the frontier where silicon meets wetware. Hacking, phreaking, social engineering, circuit diagrams, cautionary tales, and fervent defense of the First Amendment all show up here.

BOING BOING ($14/ 4 issues from 11288 Ventura Blvd. #818, Studio City, CA 91604): "I've had it up to here with this entropy business," its subscription blank reads. Inside you'll find all sorts of things to massage your brain into new modes of thought. So far this zine has interviewed Robert Anton Wilson and Rudy Rucker, played with fractals and brain machines, and printed comics and fiction that live up to the promise of "guerrilla reality engineering."

ZINES: This list is from Mike Gunderloy, former publisher and editor of the amazing guide to alternative communications products (zines, cassettes, etc.), *Factsheet Five*. *Factsheet Five* is now under new management.

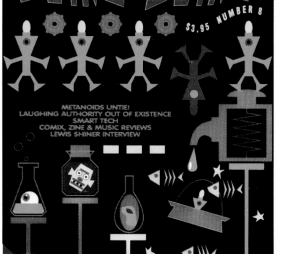

CRYONICS ($2 from ALCOR, 12327 Doherty St., Riverside, CA 92503): News from the most organized bunch of cryonicists around. If you're giving any thought to launching your frozen body on a journey into the future, you need this. It can update you on the technology, sign you on (in toto or just your brain), and keep you up to date on the wild happenings when our legal system is forced to confront the possibility of conquering death.

EXTROPY ($2 from Max O'Connor, c/o Mudd Hall of Philosophy, USC, Los Angeles, CA 90089-0451): Extropians are folks who oppose entropy, through a variety of technological and philosophical means. They're into life extension, memes, anarchy, nanotechnology, groovy drugs, and ultimate freedom. Wild and woolly.

GENDER EXPRESSIONS ($30/yr from Bisley Enterprises, c/o Lifestyle Books, 7580 W. 16th Ave., #201, Lakewood, CO 80215): Gender bending is one of the waves of the future, and this zine of transsexual/transvestite liberation will give you some hints of the coming turmoil. These folks are laying down the legal and medical footwork for a future where gender and sex are conscious decisions rather than accidents of biology.

GOING GAGA (No longer publishing, but back issues and complete sets are available from Gareth Branwyn, 2630 Robert Walker Pl., Arlington, VA 22207): Gareth is a linker, someone who spreads information like the fertilizer it is. He goes back into the communities movement and forward into the cyberfrontier, linking it all up with the zine crowd. Virtual realities, wild artwork, cyberpunk, dangerous drug experiences, crazy surreal art experiences, and more fill these pages to the bursting.

HIGH-TECH NOMADNESS ($3 from Nomadic Research Labs, P.O. Box 2390, Santa Cruz, CA 95063): Steve Roberts has one of the ultimate fun tech jobs. He rides around the country on a recumbent bicycle, loaded with computers, radio, satellite dishes, solar power, and regenerative braking that has the side effect of keeping the beer cool. And now he's trying to organize a whole community of technological nomads. This is the way to get in touch.

LIZZENGREAZY ($2 from c/o Fletcher, Shuhoso #8B, Umegaoka 1-56-4, Setegaya-Ku, Tokyo 154, JAPAN): If there's a MONDO country in the world, it must be Japan. This zine comes from a bunch of American expatriates, and pulls together key issues on Japanese culture as seen by outsiders. Shoplifting tips, Japanese romance novels, Japan's fascination with baseball, koi, and the Tokyo subway system are among the themes thus far explored. They also review an international cast of books, music, and zines.

OFFSHORE MEDICAL THERAPIES ($19/yr from P.O. Box 833, Farmingdale, NY 11737): This serious newsletter tracks interesting and useful drugs that aren't yet available in the U.S. Longevity and unusual cures are the emphasis, and medical literature references are given for everything cited. If you've got the urge to be your own guinea pig, you can never have too much information.

SCIENCE FICTION EYE ($10/3 issues from P.O. Box 18539, Asheville, NC 28814): A slick zine of science fiction and beyond with cyberpunk/postcyberpunk leanings. In a recent issue, Misha and Tad Kepley take dual looks at the *RE/SEARCH* line of publications, while Pat Murphy, Lisa Goldstein, and Karen Joy Fowler talk about the links between feminism and SF.

TRAJECTORIES ($6 from the Permanent Press, P.O. Box 700305, San Jose, CA 95170): This is Robert Anton Wilson's showcase, a place for this modern performer to show off his wit and wisdom and make some connections for people. Whether it's picking on the war on drugs, looking at Damned Things, or arguing for global energy networks, virtual reality and nanotechnology, Wilson is sure to enrage—and inspire.

GUIDE TO HACKER ZINES

Gareth Branwyn: Hacker zines are small, often funky little publications that cater to the subculture of hackers, crackers, and others who populate the lawless frontiers of cyberspace. The debate over frontier justice, the need for new ethics, and the nature of digital good and evil fill the pages of these zines. You can also expect to find technical information on hacking and phreaking (phone tinkering), plus lots of gossip, shouting, and name-calling in the letters columns. While this can get rather juvenile at times, some very bright, energetic, and unruly people call these publications home.

TAP ($2 from P.O. Box 20264, Louisville, KY 40250): *TAP*, which currently stands for Technological Advancement Party, is alive again after a long hiatus. This digest-sized magazine grew out of the yippie movement, with its penchant for monkey wrenching the state and big corporations. The original focus on phreaking has now expanded to include hacking, high-tech electronics, scams and rip-offs, anarchist tactics, and generally "forbidden" information. *TAP* also operates a bulletin board containing similar material and a library of all the major electronic hacker zines (see below). *TAP* On-line can be reached at 502-499-8933.

IRON FEATHER JOURNAL ($2 from P.O. Box 1905, Boulder, CO 80306): *IFJ* is a dense assault of anarchism and "techno-phun." Its pages are crammed with articles, newspaper headlines, graphics, and cultural litter. It too is branching out from being specifically about hacking to containing broader news and information of interest to the hacker/anarchist subculture. Funky and fun.

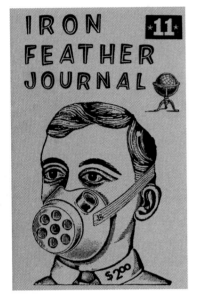

INTERTEK: The Cyberpunk Journal #1 ($2.50 from Steve Steinberg, 325 Ellwood Beach, #3, Goleta, CA 93117): This is the first issue of *Intertek*, a reincarnation of the old *W.O.R.M.* magazine. It is professionally produced with a clean design and excellent graphics. It contains everything from system-specific technical information to essays and interviews with such cyberspace luminaries as John Barlow and Dorothy Denning. Designer drugs, cryonics, and nanotechnology are also covered. Keep an eye on this one.

CYBERTEK ($10/yr from OCL/Magnitude, P.O. Box 64, Brewster, NY 10509): Another cyberpunk/hacker's zine covering all facets of computer technology, culture, and security.

ZINES ON-LINE

There are a number of electronic hacker's journals available via Internet and on various hacker BBSs such as *TAP* On-line (see above). These include *Phrack Classic* (not to be confused with Neidorf's *Phrack*), *A.T.I.*, *Phantasy Magazine*, and the *Syndicate Report*.

The *Computer Underground Digest* is an on-line forum dedicated to sharing information among computerists on hacker arrests, legal cases, ethics, and other timely telecommunication issues.

The Electronic Frontier Foundation offers its *EFF News* to those wanting to keep abreast of that organization's activities. If you have an Internet address you can get on the *EFF News* mailing list by sending email to: effnews-request@eff.org.

Issues of *Hack-Tic* are available for $2.30 U.S. from pb 22953, 1100 DL Amsterdam, The Netherlands, or on UUCP: ropg@ooc.uva.nl

THE
SHOPPING
MALL

A Directory

of Source Materials

for the Gourmand of Experience

Listed and Annotated by Jas. Morgan

APHRODISIACS

BOOKS

Camphausen, Rufus C. *The Encyclopedia of Erotic Wisdom: A Reference Guide to the Symbolism, Techniques, Rituals, Sacred Texts, Psychology, Anatomy and History of Sexuality* (Inner Traditions International, 1991).

Dean, Ward and Morgenthaler, John. *Smart Drugs & Nutrients: How to Improve Your Memory and Increase Your Intelligence Using the Latest Discoveries in Neuroscience* (B & J Publications, 1991). $12.95 + $3 shipping (California residents add $.94 tax) from B & J Publications, P.O. Box 48313, Santa Cruz, CA 95061.

Douglas, Nik and Slinger, Penny. *Sexual Secrets: The Alchemy of Ecstasy* (Destiny Books, 1979).

Gottlieb, Adam. *Sex, Drugs and Aphrodisiacs* (Loompanics, 1974).

Gracie & Zarkov. *Notes From Underground: A "Gracie and Zarkov" Reader* (privately printed preliminary edition available at cost; published version expected mid 1992). For information about this title write to: Gracie and Zarkov, c/o *MONDO 2000*, P.O. Box 10171, Berkeley, CA 94709. Can also be obtained through Flashback Books or Rosetta (See out of print books, recordings, & ephemera).

Martinetz, Dieter and Lohs, Karlheinz. *Poison: Sorcery and Science—Friend and Foe* (Edition Leipzig, 1987).

Pearson, Durk and Shaw, Sandy. *Life Extension: A Practical Scientific Approach* (Warner Books, 1982).

Pearson, Durk and Shaw, Sandy. *The Life Extension Companion* (Warner Books, 1984).

Pelton, Ross with Pelton, Taffy Clarke. *Mind Food and Smart Pills* (Doubleday, 1989).

RECORDINGS

Digital Underground. *Sex Packets* (Tommy Boy, 1990).

SOURCES (DURK PEARSON & SANDY SHAW DESIGNER FOODS)

Life Services Supplements, Inc.
81 First Ave., Atlantic Highlands, NJ 07716
800-542-3230
908-872-8700 (phone)
908-872-8705 (fax)
800-345-9105 (Canada)

Smart Products
870 Market Street, Suite 1262
San Francisco, CA 94102
800-858-6520
415-989-2500

SOURCES (SMART DRUGS)

InHome Health Services
P.O. Box 3112, CH-2800
Delemont, Switzerland

Interlab
BCM Box 5890
London, WC1N 3XX, England

Interlab is an excellent source for non-FDA approved "smart" products, including:

Deaner (Deanol) 50 x 100mg tablets $19.00
Deaner (Deanol) 200 x 100mg tablets $69.00
Deprenyl (Jumex) 50 x 5mg tablets $55.00
Deprenyl (Jumex) 150 x 5mg tablets $140.00
Hydergine (Generic) Sublingual 100 x 4.5mg tablets $32.00
Hydergine (Generic) Sublingual 400 x 4.5mg tablets $115.00
L. Dopa (Sinemet) 100 x 110mg tablets $29.00
Piracetam 60 x 800mg tablets $12.00
Piracetam 240 x 800mg tablets $64.00
Vasopressin Nasal Spray (Diapid) 12ml bottle $32.00
Vasopressin Nasal Spray (Diapid) 4 x 12ml bottles $112.00

Air Mail Post: add $10.00 (Accelerated Air Mail Post: add $15.00.) Request order form, as price, availability and legal status are subject to change.

As of this writing (03-18-92) the FDA policy regarding "smart drugs" is quietly changing. While it is technically legal to obtain these compounds from overseas distributors, the FDA has issued instructions to U.S. Customs and the U.S. Postal Service to confiscate shipments without a doctor's prescription or in amounts deemed "too large" for personal use. Get a doctor's prescription showing his license number and include it in your order.

APPROPRIATION

BOOKS

Acker, Kathy. *The Adult Life of Toulouse-Lautrec* (TVRT Press, 1978).

Acker, Kathy. *In Memoriam to Identity* (Grove Weidenfeld, 1990).

Burroughs, William S. *The Adding Machine* (Seaver Books, 1986).

Burroughs, William S. and Gysin, Brion. *The Third Mind* (Viking Press, 1978).

Breton, Andre. *Manifestos of Surrealism* [Translated from the French by Richard Seaver and Helen R. Lane] (Univ. of Michigan Press, 1969).

[Duchamp, Marcel] Schwarz, Arturo, ed. *The Complete Works of Marcel Duchamp.* With a catalog raisonne, over 750 illustrations including 75 color plates (Abrams, 1969). [Of particular interest: "LHOOQ" and "Nude Descending a Staircase"].

Gysin, Brion and Wilson, Terry. *Here to Go: Planet 101* (Quartet Books, 1985).

Lippard, Lucy R. Overlay. *Contemporary Art and the Art of Prehistory* (Pantheon Books, 1983).

Tzara, Tristan. *Seven Dada Manifestos and Lampisteries.* Translated by Barbara Wright; ill. by Francis Picabia (Calder, 1977).

Warhol, Andy. *The Philosophy of Andy Warhol: From A to B and Back Again* (Harcourt Brace Jovanovich, 1975).

Warhol, Andy and Hackett, Pat. *POPism: The Warhol '60s* (Harcourt Brace Jovanovich, 1980).

[Warhol, Andy] Hackett, Pat, ed. *The Andy Warhol Diaries* (Warner Books, 1989).

RECORDINGS

Cabaret Voltaire (Restless/Mute).

Negativland. *Helter Stupid* (SST). *U2* (SST). Recalled. For a high quality, real-time cassette sens $7 (Cash only) to: COPYRIGHT VIOLATION SQUAD, 2103 Harrison N.W., Suite #2101, Seattle, WA 98502-2607

Oswald, John. *Plunderphonics.* Controversial private mailing for this title. A sampling extravaganza (The CD opens with the final chord of the Beatles' "A Day in the Life"). Your best chance of finding this is at used CD stores or—far more likely—record conventions. Worth the trouble. Good luck!

Psychic TV (Temple/Wax Trax!).

Psychic TV *Ultrahouse: The L.A. Connection* (Wax Trax! 1991).

The Shamen (Epic).

Throbbing Gristle (Rough Trade).

Varèse, Edgard. *The Varèse Album* (Columbia MG 31078).

Various Artists (Psychic TV). *Jack the Tab/Tekno Acid Beat* (Wax Trax! 1990).

Vincent, Rickey . The Funk Feast. KALX radio, Berkeley, CA.

Xenakis, Iannis. *Electro-Acoustic Music* (Nonesuch H71246).

ARTIFICIAL LIFE

BOOKS

Churchland, Patricia Smith. *Neurophilosophy: Toward a Unified Science of the Mind/Brain* (MIT Press, 1986).

Gould, Stephen Jay. *Wonderful Life: The Burgess Shale and Nature of History* (W. W. Norton, 1989).

Kelly, Kevin, ed. *SIGNAL: Communication Tools for the Information Age—A Whole Earth Catalog* (Harmony Books, 1988).

Langton, Christopher G., ed. *Artificial Life I: The Proceedings of an Interdisciplinary Workshop on the Synthesis and Simulation of Living Systems* (Addison-Wesley, 1989).

Langton, Christopher G., ed. *Artificial Life II: The Proceedings of an Interdisciplinary Workshop on the Synthesis and Simulation of Living Systems* (Addison-Wesley, 1992).

Prusinkiewicz, Przemyslaw and Lindenmayer, Aristid. *The Algorithmic Beauty of Plants* (Springer-Verlag, 1990).

Rucker, Rudy. *Mind Tools: The Five Levels of Mathematical Reality* (Houghton Mifflin, 1987).

Rucker, Rudy. *The Fourth Dimension: A Guided Tour of the Higher Universes* (Houghton Mifflin, 1984).

Rucker, Rudy. *Software* (Avon Books, 1983).

Rucker, Rudy. *Wetware* (Avon Books, 1988).

Wolfram, Stephen. *Mathematica: A System for Doing Mathematics by Computer*, 2nd ed. (Addison-Wesley, 1991).

JOURNALS

The Journal of Complex Systems. Stephen Wolfram, ed. $50 (student), $85 (individual), $275 (institution)/year (6 issues) from: Complex Systems Publications, Inc., P.O. Box 6149, Champaign, IL 61826. This is an excellent scientific journal featuring the very latest in Cellular Automata-related research.

SOFTWARE

Rudy Rucker's CA Laboratory [IBM] $59.95 + $8 S&H from: Autodesk, Inc., Science Series Dept., 2320 Marinship Way, Sausalito, CA 94965. For information or ordering call toll free, 800-228-3601. International orders may use Fax# 415-289-4718.

Gleick, James. James Gleick's Chaos: The Software [IBM] $59.95 + $8 S&H from: Autodesk, Inc., Science Series Dept., 2320 Marinship Way, Sausalito, CA 94965. For information or ordering call toll free, 800-228-3601. International orders may use Fax # 415-289-4718.

Wolfram, Stephen. Mathematica 2.0: A System for Doing Mathematics by Computer [Versions for Macintosh, IBM, Sun, Silicon Graphics, etc.]. Contact: Wolfram Research, Inc., P.O. Box 6059, Champaign, IL 61826-6059. 217-398-0700. 217-398-0747 (fax).

BIO/CYBERNETICS

Bateson, Gregory. *Steps to An Ecology of Mind* (Ballantine, 1972).

Bateson, Gregory. *Mind and Nature: A Necessary Unity* (Dutton, 1979).

Wiener, Norbert. *Cybernetics: Control and Communication in the Animal and the Machine* (J. Wiley, 1948).

Wiener, Norbert. *The Human Use of Human Beings: Cybernetics and Society* (Houghton and Mifflin, 1954).

BRAIN IMPLANTS

BOOKS

Burroughs, William S. *Naked Lunch* (Grove, 1959).

Effinger, George Alec. *When Gravity Fails* (Bantam, 1987).

Delgado, José M. R. *Physical Control of the Mind: Toward a Psychocivilized Society* (Harper & Row/World Perspectives Series, Vol. 41, 1969).

Dick, Philip K. *Do Androids Dream of Electric Sheep?* [aka *Blade Runner*] (Ballantine, 1968).

Gibson, William. *Neuromancer* (Ace, 1984).

Gibson, William. *Count Zero* (Ace, 1986).

Gibson, William. *Mona Lisa Overdrive* (Bantam, 1988).

Robinson, Spider. *Mindkiller: A Novel of the Near Future* (Holt, Rinehart and Winston, 1982).

2030, F.M. [F.M. Esfandiary]. *Upwingers* (Popular Library/CBS, 1977).

2030, F.M. *Are You A Transhuman?* (Warner Books, 1989).

FILM

Blade Runner (Director: Ridley Scott, 1982).

BURROUGHS, WILLIAM S.

BIOGRAPHY

Morgan, Ted. *Literary Outlaw: The Life and Times of William S. Burroughs* (Henry Holt & Co.,1988).

BOOKS

Burroughs, William S. *Junky* [Originally published as *Junkie* under the pen name William Lee, 1953] (1st complete and unexpurgated ed., Penguin Books, 1977).

Burroughs, William S. *Naked Lunch* (Grove Press, 1959).

Burroughs, William S., and Ginsberg, Allen. *The Yage Letters* (City Lights, 1963).

Burroughs, William S. *The Soft Machine* (Grove Press, 1966).

Burroughs, William S. *The Ticket that Exploded* (Grove Press, 1967).

Burroughs, Wiliam S. *Nova Express* (Grove Press, 1964).

Burroughs, Wiliam S. *The Last Words of Dutch Schultz* (London: Cape Goliard Press., 1970).

Burroughs, William S. *Cities of the Red Night* (Holt, Rinehart and Winston, 1981).

Burroughs, William S. *The Western Lands* (Viking, 1987).

Burroughs, William S. *The Adding Machine: Selected Essays* (Seaver Books, 1986).

BOOKS OF RELATED INTEREST

Maynard, Joe and Miles, Barry. *William S. Burroughs: A Bibliography 1953-1973.* (Univ. of Virginia Press, 1978).

Odier, Daniel. *The Job: Interviews with William S. Burroughs—revised and enlarged* (Grove Press/An Evergreen Book, 1974).

Porush, David. *The Soft Machine: Cybernetic Fiction* (Methuen, 1985).

DREAMACHINE

Dreamachine Plans: Created by Brion Gysin (OV Press, 1986). For ordering information on this title write: OV Press, P.O. Box 18223, Denver, CO 80218.

FILM

Burroughs: The Movie (Director: Howard Brookner, 1983).

Drugstore Cowboy (Director: Gus Van Sant, 1989).

Naked Lunch (Director: David Cronenberg, 1992).

RECORDINGS (COMPACT DISC)

Uncommon Quotes (Caravan of Dreams Productions, 1988).

Dead City Radio (Island Records, 1990).

VIDEO

Towers Open Fire (with William S. Burroughs). Four films by Anthony Balch. 35 min. $29.95 + $4 S&H and $1 each additional tape (NY residents add 8.25% sales tax) from: Mystic Fire Video, P.O. Box 9323, Dept. C5, S. Burlington, VT 05407. Call toll free 800-727-8433.

CHAOS

BOOKS

Abraham, Frederick David with Abraham, Ralph and Shaw, Christopher D. *A Visual Introduction to Dynamical Systems Theory for Psychology* (Aerial Press, 1991).

Abraham, Ralph H. and Shaw, Christopher D.
The Visual Mathematics Library:
Vol. 0: *Manifolds and Mappings*
Vol. 1: *Dynamics—The Geometry of Behavior Part 1: Periodic Behavior*
Vol. 2: *Dynamics—The Geometry of Behavior Part 2: Chaotic Behavior*
Vol. 3: *Dynamics—The Geometry of Behavior Part 3: Global Behavior*
Vol. 4: *Dynamics—The Geometry of Behavior Part 4: Bifurcation Behavior* (Aerial Press).

Bass, Thomas A. *The Eudaemonic Pie* (Vintage Books/Random House, 1985).

Myers, Norman (General ed.). *Gaia: An Atlas of Planet Management* (Anchor/Doubleday, 1984).

Gleick, James. *Chaos: Making a New Science* (Viking, 1987).

Lovelock, James E. *Gaia: A New Look at Life on Earth* (Oxford Univ. Press, 1979).

Mandelbrot, Benoit B. *The Fractal Geometry of Nature* [updated and augmented] (W.H. Freeman, 1983).

Peitgen, Heinz-Otto and Richter, Peter H. *The Beauty of Fractals: Images of Complex Dynamical Systems* (Springer-Verlag, 1986).

Ruelle, David. *Chance and Chaos* (Princeton Univ. Press, 1992). David Ruelle published the first scientific paper to define chaos. This title is excellent, short and fun to read.

Thom, René. *Semiophysics: A Sketch* [Aristotelian Physics and Catastrophe Theory] (Addison-Wesley, 1990).

SOFTWARE

Gleick, James. James Gleick's Chaos: The Software [IBM] $59.95 + $8 S&H from: Autodesk, Inc., 2320 Marinship Way, Sausalito, CA 94965. For information or ordering call toll free, 800-688-2344. International orders may use Fax # 415-289-4718.

Jurgens, Hartmut. The Beauty of Fractals Lab: Graphics Software for the Macintosh (Springer-Verlag, 1990).

VIDEO

Chaos, Eros, Gaia: A Post-Savage Oracle (with Ralph Abraham). An alchemical computer assemblage of thought, sound, and image. 30 min., VHS. $30 from Rose * X, P.O. Box 728, Petaluma, CA 94953. 707-763-4233. Other titles from Rose * X include *Experiment at Petaluma*, with Terence McKenna ($30), and *Strange Attractor* (forthcoming).

COMPUTER GRAPHICS

BOOKS (ART AND TECHNICAL)

Bernstein, Saul and McGarry. *Making Art on Your Computer: A Comprehensive Course in Drawing and Painting for the Personal Computer User* (Watson-Guptill, 1986).

Deken, Joseph. *Computer Images: State of the Art* (Thames and Hudson, 1983).

Em, David. *The Art of David Em: 100 Computer Paintings* (Abrams, 1988).

Foley, James D., van Dam, Andries, Feiner, Steven K., Hughes, John F. *Computer Graphics: Principles and Practice*, 2nd ed. (Addison-Wesley, 1990).

Goodman, Cynthia. *Digital Visions: Computers and Art* (Abrams, 1987).

Kawaguchi, Yoichiro. *Growth Morphogenesis: A Journey to the Origins of Form* (JICC Publishing, 1985). A difficult-to-find art book of images from the greatest computer graphics artist/animator in the world. Excellent! Try special order from Japanese book specialists: Kinokunia Bookstores of America Co., Ltd., 1581 Webster Street, San Francisco, CA 94115. 415-567-7625. [Some of Dr. Kawaguchi's animations are available from *SIGGRAPH Video Review*; see below].

Latham, Roy. *The Dictionary of Computer Graphics Technology and Applications* (Springer-Verlag, 1991).

Lewell, John. *Computer Graphics: A Survey of Current Techniques and Applications* (Van Nostrand Reinhold, 1985).

Prusinkiewicz, Przemyslaw and Lindenmayer, Aristid. *The Algorithmic Beauty of Plants* (Springer-Verlag, 1990).

Rivlin, Robert. *The Algorithmic Image: Graphic Images of the Computer Age* (Microsoft Press, 1986).

Smith, Thomas G. *Industrial Light & Magic: The Art of Special Effects* (Del Rey/Ballantine, 1986).

Todd, Stephen, and Latham, William. *Evolutionary Art and Computers* (Academic Press, 1992).

Upstill, Steve. *The RenderMan Companion: A Programmer's Guide to Realistic Computer Graphics* (Addison-Wesley, 1990).

FILMS OF MENTION

The Abyss (Director: James Cameron, 1989).

The Lawnmower Man (Director: Brett Leonard, 1992).

Star Trek II: The Wrath of Khan (Dir: Nicholas Meyer, 1982).

Terminator II (Director: James Cameron, 1991).

Tron (Director: Steven Lisberger, 1982).

MAGAZINES & JOURNALS

Cinefex...The Journal of Cinematic Illusions. Each issue offers an inside look at personalities, technologies and techniques involved in the creation of special effects for three major motion pictures. $20/year (4 issues) from Cinefex, P.O. Box 20027, Riverside, CA 92516.

Computer Graphics World. $34/year (12 issues) from Computer Graphics World, P.O. Box 122, Tulsa, OK 74101. 800-331-4463, 918-832-9295 (fax). Excellent!

The Journal of Visualization and Computer Animation. A highly technical journal of research papers. Color illustrations. $161.25/year (4 issues-personal), $215/year (4 issues-institutional) from Journals Subscription Department, John Wiley & Sons Ltd., Baffins Lane, Chichester, West Sussex, PO19 1UD, England.

Leonardo: The Journal of the International Society for the Arts, Sciences, and Technology. Leonardo is a beautifully printed journal focusing on the application of technology to the visual arts and music. 2030 Addison Street #600, Berkeley, CA 94704. Bimonthly subscription ($60/year) includes ISAST membership, *Leonardo Music Journal* and Compact Disc).

NewMedia. A computer magazine which focuses on products and applications related to multimedia, desktop publishing, desktop video, computer animation and interactive technologies. $36/year (12 issues) from NewMedia, P.O. Box 1771, Riverton, NJ 08077-9771.

Pixel: The Magazine of Scientific Visualization. $21/year (6 issues) from Pixel, 245 Henry Street, H2G, Brooklyn, NY 11201-9889. 718-624-3386.

Pixel Vision: A glossy, oversize publication devoted entirely to the visuals of computer graphics. Also product reviews and calendar listings of upcoming conferences, workshops and educational events. $35/year—$45 outside of U.S.—(5 issues) from Pixel Vision, Box 1138, Madison Square Station, NY 10159.

Verbum: The Journal of Personal Computer Aesthetics. Focuses on electronic art & design, animation, interactive multimedia, scanned imagery, 3D graphics, digital color separation and prepress, etc. $24/year (4 issues) from Verbum, P.O. Box 12564, San Diego, CA 92112. 619-233-9977, 619-233-9976 (fax). (*Verbum* also publishes a series of technical books about desktop publishing, scanning and typography, as well as *Verbum Interactive 1.0*—a fully integrated magazine with music on CD-ROM—$49.95.)

ORGANIZATIONS

ACM SIGGRAPH [The Association for Computing Machinery's Special Interest Group on Computer Graphics and Interactive Techniques]

SIGGRAPH Conferences:
SIGGRAPH '92: 26–31 July, 1992, Chicago, IL
SIGGRAPH '93: 1–6 August, 1993, Anaheim, CA
SIGGRAPH '94: 24–29 July 1994, Orlando, FL
SIGGRAPH '95: dates TBA, Los Angeles, CA

For conference information, contact:
312-644-6610. 312-321-6976 (fax).

For SIGGRAPH membership, contact:
212-869-7440. 212-764-5537 (fax).

Kodak Center for Creative Imaging
An international art and learning center offering classes in electronic imaging taught by artists and industry experts with state-of-the-art technology. For course catalog call toll free 800-428-7400.

VIDEO

The Media Magic Catalog is a mail order resource for a wide range of books, videotapes, software and other media relating to computers in science & art. Catalog from: Media Magic, P.O. Box 507, Nicasio, CA 94946. 800-882-8284 (credit card orders), 415-662-2426 (customer service), 415-662-2225 (fax order line).

SIGGRAPH Video Review. The world's most widely circulated video-based technical publication. The *SIGGRAPH Video Review* illustrates the latest concepts in computer graphics and interactive techniques. To order, contact First Priority, P.O. Box 576, Itasca, IL 60143-0576. 800-523-5503 (within U.S.), 708-250-0807 (outside U.S.), 708-250-0038 (fax).

The Whole Toon Catalog is a rich resource of books, videotapes, laserdiscs and just about anything else related to animation from the late 1800s to the present. Catalog from Whole Toon Access, P.O. Box 369, Issaquah, WA 98027. 206-391-8747, 206-391-9064 (fax).

COMPUTER INDUSTRY

BOOKS

Burnham, David. *The Rise of the Computer State* (Random House, 1983).

Gilder, George F. *Microcosm: The Quantum Revolution in Economics and Technology* (Simon and Schuster, 1989).

Hayes, Dennis. *Behind the Silicon Curtain: The Seductions of Work in a Lonely Area* (South End Press, 1989).

Kawasaki, Guy. *The Macintosh Way* (Scott, Foresman & Co., 1989).

Osborne, Adam and Dvorak, John. *Hypergrowth: The Rise and Fall of Osborne Computer Corporation* (Idthekkethan Pub. Co., 1984).

Rifkin, Glenn and Harrar, George. *The Ultimate Entrepreneur: The Story of Ken Olsen and Digital Equipment Corporation* (Contemporary Books, 1988).

Rose, Frank. *West of Eden: The End of Innocence at Apple Computer* (Penguin, 1989).

Roszak, Theodore. *The Cult of Information: The Folklore of Computers and the True Art of Thinking* (Pantheon, 1986).

Rothschild, Michael L. *Bionomics: The Inevitability of Capitalism* (H. Holt, 1990).

Sculley, John with Byrne, John A. *Odyssey: Pepsi to Apple, A Journey of Adventure, Ideas and the Future* (Harper & Row, 1987).

Solomonides, Tony and Levidow, Les eds. *Compulsive Technology: Computers as Culture* (Free Association Books, London, 1985).

Young, Jeffrey S. *Steve Jobs: The Journey is the Reward* (Scott, Foresman & Co., 1988).

CRACKERS

BOOKS

[Anonymous]. *Computers: Crimes, Clues and Controls* (Paladin, 1987).

[Brand, Stewart]. *The Essential Whole Earth Catalog* (Doubleday, 1986).

Cornwall, Hugo. *The Hacker's Handbook: An Insider's Guide to Modems and Telecomputing* (Loompanics, 1985).

Hafner, Katie and Markoff, John. *Cyberpunk: Outlaws and Hackers on the Computer Frontier* (Simon and Schuster, 1991).

Harry, M. *The Computer Underground: Hacking, Piracy, Phreaking and Computer Crime* (Loompanics, 1985).

Levy, Steven. *Hackers: Heroes of the Computer Revolution* (Dell, 1984).

Kelly, Kevin, ed. *SIGNAL: Communication Tools for the Information Age—A Whole Earth Catalog* (Harmony Books, 1988).

Stoll, Clifford. *The Cuckoo's Egg: Tracking a Spy Through the Maze of Computer Espionage* (Doubleday, 1989).

Sterling, Bruce. *Hacker Crackdown* (forthcoming).

JOURNALS

Cybertek. $10.00/year from OCL/Magnitude, P.O. Box 64, Brewster, NY 10509.

Hack-Tic. Issues available for $2.30 from pb 22953, 1100 DL Amsterdam, The Netherlands.

TAP (Technological Advancement Party). $2.00 from P.O. Box 20264, Louisville, KY 40250. *TAP* Online can be reached at: 502-499-8933.

2600. P.O. Box 752, Middle Island, NY 11953-752.

LEGAL

Electronic Frontier Foundation (EFF). One Cambridge Center, Cambridge, MA 02142. 617-577-1385. email eff-request@eff.org

ONLINE

The WELL (Whole Earth 'Lectronic Link). The WELL, 27 Gate 5 Road, Sausalito, CA 94965; Voice 415-332-4335 for inquiries, Modem connections 415-332-6106. (email requests: info@well.sf.ca.us). Costs: $10/ month, $2/hr. Visa/Mastercard no processing fee. $25 processing fee for billed accounts. Access through CompuServe packet network from anywhere in contiguous 48 states: additional $4/hr. You need not be a CompuServe member to access the WELL through CPN.

CYBERPUNK

BOOKS

Hafner, Katie and Markoff, John. *Cyberpunk: Outlaws and Hackers on the Computer Frontier* (Simon and Schuster, 1991).

McCaffery, Larry, ed. *Storming the Reality Studio: A Casebook of Cyberpunk and Postmodern Fiction* (Duke Univ. Press, 1991).

Sterling, Bruce, ed. *Mirrorshades* (Warner Books, 1986).

GAMES, BOARD

GURPS Cyberpunk, Steve Jackson Games, $16.95 includes shipping. P.O. Box 18957 Austin, TX 78760.

SOFTWARE

Beyond Cyberpunk is a HyperCard stack (Macintosh) by Mark Frauenfelder, Gareth Branwyn, and Peter Sugarman that comes on four 800K floppy disks. It's packaged in a clear microcassette case with an intro booklet and a fun mini-comic. This massive stack has essays and hundreds of reviews on postmodern science fiction, critical theory, underground culture, street tech, and lots more (over 325 items). It provides a dense, high-contrast snapshot of the high technology underground as it looks in the first few hours of the 1990s. $29.95 from The Computer Lab, Route 4, Box 54C, Louisa, VA 23093.

VIDEO

Cyberpunk: The First Program of the Next Century. Directed by Marianne Trench, produced by Peter von Brandenburg. (Intercon Productions, 1990). Includes virtual reality, hacking & piracy, art & fashion, industrial music, mind machines & cyborgs, William Gibson, Timothy Leary, Scott Fisher, and Michael Synergy. $49.95 from ATA/Cyberpunk, P.O. Box 12, Massapequa Park, NY 11762.

CYBERPUNK SCIENCE FICTION

BOOKS

Blumlein, Michael. *The Movement of Mountains* (St. Martin's Press, 1987).

Brunner, John. *The Shockwave Rider* (Harper & Row, 1975).

Burroughs, William S. *Naked Lunch* (Grove, 1959).

[Delaney, Samuel R.] Chang, Glenn, Gotlieb, Phyllis and McGarry, Mark J., eds. *The Edge of Space: Three original Novellas of Science Fiction* (Elsevier/Nelson Books, 1979).

Gibson, William. *Neuromancer* (Ace, 1984).

Gibson, William. *Count Zero* (Ace, 1986).

Gibson, William. *Burning Chrome* (Ace, 1987).

Gibson, William. *Mona Lisa Overdrive* (Bantam, 1988).

Gibson, William and Sterling, Bruce. *The Difference Engine* (Bantam, 1991).

Kadrey, Richard. *Metrophage* (Ace, 1988).

Laidlaw, Marc. *Dad's Nuke* (D.I. Fine, 1985).

Laidlaw, Marc. *Neon Lotus* (Bantam, 1988).

McCaffery, Larry, ed. *Storming the Reality Studio: A Casebook of Cyberpunk and Postmodern Fiction* (Duke Univ. Press, 1991).

Murphy, Pat. *The Falling Woman* (St. Martin's Press, 1986).

Pynchon, Thomas. *Gravity's Rainbow* (Viking, 1973/Penguin Books, 1987).

Shirley, John. *City Come a-Walkin'* (Dell, 1980).

Shirley, John. *Eclipse* (Warner Books, 1985).

Shirley, John. *Eclipse Penumbra* (Warner Books, 1987).

Shirley, John. *Eclipse Corona* (Warner Books, 1989).

Shirley, John. *A Splendid Chaos: An Interplanetary Fantasy* (F. Watts, 1988).

Sterling, Bruce. *Crystal Express* (Arkham House Publishers, 1989).

Sterling, Bruce. *Islands in the Net* (Morrow, 1988).

Sterling, Bruce, ed. *Mirrorshades* (Warner Books, 1986).

Sterling, Bruce. *Schismatrix* (Arbor House, 1985).

Vinge, Vernor. *True Names* (Bluejay Books/St. Martin's Press, 1984).

Vinge, Vernor. *True Names and Other Dangers* (Baen/Simon and Schuster, 1987).

BOOKS OF RELATED INTEREST

[Duchamp, Marcel] Schwarz, Arturo, ed. *The Complete Works of Marcel Duchamp*. With a catalog raisonne, over 750 illustrations including 75 color plates (Abrams, 1969). [Of particular interest: "LHOOQ" and "Nude Descending a Staircase"].

[Fredkin] Wright, Robert. *Three Scientists and Their Gods: Looking for Meaning in the Age of Information* (Times Books, 1988).

Leyner, Mark. *My Cousin, My Gastroenterologist* (Harmony Books, 1990).

Weisenburger, Steven. *A Gravity's Rainbow Companion: Sources and Contexts for Pynchon's Novel* (University of Georgia Press, 1988).

COMICS AND GRAPHIC NOVELS

De Haven, Tom and Jensen, Bruce. *Neuromancer: The Graphic Novel*, Vols. 1-3 (Epic Comics, 1989).

Moore, Alan and Gibbons, Dave. *Watchmen* (Bud Plant Comic Art, 1987).

FILMS

Blade Runner. (Director: Ridley Scott, 1982).

Brazil. (Director: Terry Gilliam, 1985).

Naked Lunch. (Director: David Cronenberg, 1991).

Road Warrior/Mad Max 2. (Director: George Miller, 1981).

Robocop. (Director: Paul Verhoeven, 1987).

Terminator. (Director: James Cameron, 1984).

Terminator II. (Director: James Cameron, 1991).

Total Recall. (Director: Paul Verhoeven, 1990).

Videodrome. (Director: David Cronenberg, 1983).

MAGAZINES AND JOURNALS

Mississippi Review 47/48 (Volume 16, Numbers 2 & 3, 1988). Single issue of literary journal which explored various aspects of Cyberpunk SF. Back issue prices on request from Mississippi Review, Southern Station, Box 5144, Hattiesburg, MS 39406-5144.

TELEVISION

Max Headroom. Cinemax (1 August 1986–19 December 1986; 23 July 1987–9 October 1987).

Max Headroom. ABC (31 March 1987–5 May 1987; 14 August 1987–16 October 1987).

(*Max Headroom* is now available on video).

COSMOLOGY

BOOKS

Barrow, John D. and Tipler, Frank J. *The Anthropic Cosmological Principle* (Oxford Univ. Press, 1986).

Crick, Francis. *Life Itself: Its Origin and Nature* (Simon and Schuster, 1981).

Davies, Paul C. W. *The Accidental Universe* (Cambridge Univ. Press, 1982).

Goldsmith, Donald, ed. *The Quest For Extraterrestrial Intelligence* (University Science Books, 1980).

Hawking, Stephen W. *A Brief History of Time: From the Big Bang to Black Holes* (Bantam, 1988).

Hoyle, Fred and Wickramasinghe, Chandra. *Living Comets* (Univ. College Cardiff Press, 1985).

Ponnamperuma, Cyril and Cameron, A.G.W., eds. *Interstellar Communication: Scientific Perspectives* (Houghton Mifflin, 1974).

DECONSTRUCTION

BOOKS

Derrida, Jacques. *Of Grammatology* (Johns Hopkins University Press, 1976).

Derrida, Jacques. *Speech and Phenomena* (Northwestern Univ. Press, 1973).

Derrida, Jacques. *Writing and Difference* (University of Chicago Press, 1978).

Lacan, Jacques. *Television* [Translated by Denis Hollier, Rosalind Krauss, and Annette Michelson; *A Challenge to the Psychoanalytic Establishment;* Translated by Jeffrey Mehlman; edited by Joan Copjec] (Norton, 1990).

Ronell, Avital. *The Telephone Book: Technology, Schizophrenia and Electric Speech* (University of Nebraska Press, 1989).

RECORDINGS

[See Hip-Hop, House Music, Industrial/Post-Industrial Music and Art.]

DNA MUSIC

RECORDINGS

McLaughlin, Riley. *DNA Music.*

McLaughlin, Riley and Deamer, Dr. David. *DNA Suite.*

(Both cassette tapes available for $11.99 from: Science and the Arts, 144 Mayhew Way, Walnut Creek, CA 94596.)

SCIENTIFIC PAPERS

Ohno, Susumu. "Evolution By Gene Duplication" (Springer-Verlag, 1970).

Ohno, Susumu. "Major Sex Determining Genes" (Springer-Verlag, 1979).

Ohno, Susumu. "Protochordata, Cyclostomata, and Pisces" (Gebruder Borntrager, 1974).

Ohno, Susumu. "Sex Chromosomes and Sex-Linked Genes" (Springer-Verlag, 1967).

Bored of the old microscopes, Dr. Ohno conducts scientific visualization in the acoustic medium. He "listens" to the genetic code.

DRUGS

BOOKS

Brecher, Edward M. and eds. *Licit & Illicit Drugs: The Consumers Union Report on Narcotics, Stimulants, Depressants, Inhalants, Hallucinogens and Marijuana—including Caffeine, Nicotine and Alcohol* (Little Brown, 1972). Way ahead of its time conceptually and still a great compendium. The first book to state that psychoactive drugs' harmfulness and legality are not correlated.

[Consumer Reports]. *Complete Drug Reference* (Consumer Reports, 1990).

Griffith, H. Winter. *Complete Guide to Prescription & Non-Prescription Drugs* (Putnam, 1990).

Hoffman, Abbie with Silvers, Jonathan. *Steal This Urine Test: Fighting Drug Hysteria in America* (Penguin, 1987).

Palmer, Cynthia and Horowitz, Michael. *Shaman Woman, Mainline Lady: Women's Writing on the Drug Experience* (Putnam, 1982). Available for $15 ppd. from: Flashback Books, 906 Samuel Drive, Petaluma, CA 94952.

Lee, Marty A. and Shalin, Bruce. *Acid Dreams: The CIA, LSD and the Sixties Rebellion* (Grove Press, 1985).

Long, James W. *The Essential Guide to Prescription Drugs* (Perennial/Harper & Row, 1991).

McKenna, Terence. *Food of the Gods* (Bantam, 1992).

Ronell, Avital. *Crack Wars: Literature, Addiction, Mania* (University of Nebraska Press, 1992).

Shulgin, Alexander T. *The Controlled Substance Act: A Resource Manual of the Current Status of the Federal Drug Laws* (Ronin, 1988).

Szasz, Thomas. *Ceremonial Chemistry: The Ritual Persecution of Drugs, Addicts, and Pushers* (Learning Publications, 1974/1985 rev. ed.).

Weil, Andrew and Rosen, Winifred. *Chocolate to Morphine: Understanding Mind-Active Drugs* (Houghton Mifflin, 1983).

Weil, Andrew. *The Natural Mind: A New Way of Looking at Drugs and the Higher Consciousness* (Houghton Mifflin, 1972).

ELECTRONIC FREEDOM

ONLINE INFORMATION

The WELL (Whole Earth 'Lectronic Link) see page 296.

ORGANIZATIONS

Electronic Frontier Foundation (EFF). One Cambridge Center, Cambridge, MA 02142. 617-577-1385. email eff-request@eff.org

VIDEO

(Of the First Conference On) *Computers, Freedom & Privacy: Pursuing Policies to Safeguard American Freedoms in the Information Age*—Video Library Series. A variety of speakers on video tape from the first conference. Titles include: "The Constitution in the Information Age," "Trends in Computers & Networks," "Personal Information & Privacy," and "Law Enforcement Practices & Problems." Request information from Sweet Pea Productions, P.O. Box 912, 1673 Happy Trail, Topanga, CA 90290. Credit cards or info: 800-235-4922, 213-455-3915.

ELECTRONIC MUSIC

BOOKS

[Boulez, Pierre] Peyser, Joan. *Boulez: Composer, Conductor, Enigma* (Schirmer Books, 1976).

Darter, Tom and Armbruster, Greg. *The Art of Electronic Music* (Quill/William Morrow, 1983).

[Eno, Brian] Tamm, Eric. *Brian Eno: His Music and the Vertical Color of Sound* (Faber and Faber, 1989).

[Fripp, Robert] Tamm, Eric. *Robert Fripp: From King Crimson to Crafty Master* (Faber and Faber, 1990).

Holmes, Thomas B. *Electronic and Experimental Music* (Scribners, 1985).

Randel, Don Michael, ed. *The New Harvard Dictionary of Music* (Belknap-Harvard, 1986).

Schafer, R. Murray. *The Tuning of the World* (University of Pennsylvania Press, 1977).

JOURNALS AND MAGAZINES

Computer Music Journal, Stephen Travis Pope, ed. $33 (individual), $68 (institution), $28 (student/retired)—Outside U.S. and Canada add $12 (surface mail), $18 (airmail)—/year (4 issues) from MIT Press Journals, 55 Hayward Street, Cambridge, MA 02142-9949.

Experimental Musical Instruments: For the Design, Construction and Enjoyment of Unusual Sound Sources. Bart Hopkin, ed. $20/year—$27 overseas—(6 issues) from Experimental Musical Instruments, P.O. Box 784, Nicasio, CA 94946.

Leonardo Music Journal (LMJ). Journal of the International Society for the Arts, Sciences and Technology. Published in one issue with CD. $35/year (personal), $70/year (institutional), from Pergamon Press, 395 Saw Mill River Road, Elmsford, NY 10523. *LMJ* is an international journal for contemporary composers and sound and multimedia artists.

Keyboard. Dominic Milano, ed. $27.95/year (12 issues) Keyboard, P.O. Box 50404, Boulder, CO 80321-0404.

Option. Scott Becker, pub. Countless reviews of small label cassettes, experimental and weird musics. $12/year (6 issues) from: Sonic Options Network, P.O. Box 491034, Los Angeles, CA 90049.

Sound Choice. David Ciaffardini, ed. Reviews of independently produced recordings and cassettes, punk, electronic, avant garde, etc. $12/year (6 issues) from: Audio Evolution Network, P.O. Box 1251, Ojai, CA 93023.

RECORDINGS

Cage, John and Hiller, Lejaren. *HPSCHD,* for harpsichords & computer generated sound tapes (Nonesuch, 1969).

D'Cückoo. *3DCD:* $15 (compact disc also available at Tower Records). Tapes: Vol. 1: All the up and dancing marimba tunes, Vol. 2: Seven lush and orchestrated epic songs, Vol. 3: Pre-release mixes of CD. 3-color T-Shirts on white or black background, available in S, M, L, or XL. Specify size and color. T-Shirts are $12 each and cassette tapes are $7 each. Make checks payable to: Aisle of Women, 6114 LaSalle Ave., Ste #414, Oakland, CA 94611.

Deee-Lite. *World Clique* (Elektra, 1990).

Deee-Lite. *Infinity Withun* (Elektra, 1992).

Eno, Brian. *Before and After Science* (EG/Caroline).

Eno, Brian. *Here Come the Warm Jets* (EG/Caroline).

Machover, Tod. *FLORA* (Bridge Records, 1991).

Machover, Tod. *VALIS* (Bridge Records, 1989).

Stockhausen, Karlheinz. *Studie I—II* (Deutsche Grammophon Gesellschaft, 1959).

Sun Ra. *Live At Montreux* (Inner City, 1976).

Terenzi, Dr. Fiorella. *Music From the Galaxies* (Island Records, 1990).

Varèse, Edgard. *The Varèse Album* (Columbia MG 31078).

Xenakis, Iannis. *Electro-Acoustic Music* (Nonesuch H71246).

PAPERS

[Biomuse] Lusted, Hugh and Knapp, R. Benjamin. "A Bioelectric Controller for Computer Music Applications" (*Computer Music Journal,* Vol. 14, No. 1, Spring 1990, Massachussetts Institute of Technology). Single copy of back issue $17 from: M.I.T. Press Journals, 55 Hayward St., Cambridge, MA 02142-9949.

SOFTWARE OF MENTION

Dr. T's Music Software. Call or write for location of local dealers: 100 Crescent Rd., Suite 1-B, Needham, MA 02194. 617-455-1454, 617-455-1460 (fax). Demonstration disks for applications listed are available for $10 each.

M. M is an interactive composing and performing environment for the Macintosh. Unlike a sequencer, M's musical controls allow you to shape or change aspects of a composition while hearing it.

Jam Factory. Intuitive Macintosh application for composing, editing and MIDI improvisation.

UpBeat 2.0. A Rhythm sequencer for the Macintosh. The original MIDI software to offer device lists, automatic variation and instantaneous feedback—allowing the user to monitor rhythms as created.

The Computers & Music Report is a mail order catalog/sourcebook for a large selection of music software for Atari, IBM and Macintosh platforms. Also some related hardware, technical manuals, and books. Each issue includes articles of interest, reports on the current state of the technology, and recommended system configurations. Request catalog from: Computers & Music, 647 Mission Street, San Francisco, CA 94105. 800-767-6161, 415-541-5350, 415-543-6792 (fax).

EVOLUTIONARY MUTATIONS

BOOKS

Bowles, Paul. *Let it Come Down* (Random House, 1952).

Burroughs, William S. *The Ticket that Exploded* (Grove Press, 1967).

Drexler, K. Eric. *The Engines of Creation: Challenges and Choices of the Last Technological Revolution* (Anchor Press/Doubleday, 1986).

Minsky, Marvin. *The Society of Mind* (Simon and Schuster, 1986).

Moravec, Hans. *Mind Children: The Future of Robot and Human Intelligence* (Harvard Univ. Press, 1988).

Radnitzky, Garard and Bartley III, W. W. *Evolutionary Epistemology, Rationality and the Sociology of Knowledge* (Open Court, 1987).

Regis, Ed. *Great Mambo Chicken & the Transhuman Condition* (Addison-Wesley, 1990).

2030, F.M. *Upwingers* (Popular Library, 1977).

2030, F.M. *Are You a Transhuman?* (Warner Books, 1989).

Vinge, Vernor. *True Names* (Bluejay Books/St Martin's Press, 1984).

Vinge, Vernor. *True Names and Other Dangers* (Baen/Simon and Schuster, 1987).

Wilson, Robert Anton. *Prometheus Rising* (Falcon Press, 1983).

FASHION

Ameba. 1732 Haight Street, San Francisco, CA 94117. 415-750-9368, 800-BYAMEBA.

Anarchic Adjustment. (Future streetware. Fatigues for the 21st century) Pajet Design Group, 1592 Alum Rock Ave., San Jose, CA 95116. 408-926-6888, 408-929-6888 (fax).

Behind the Post Office. 1504 Haight Street, San Francisco, CA 94117. 415-861-2507.

Berkeley Designs. High-Res computer graphic imagery on T-Shirts. Catalog: Berkeley Designs, 2615 Shasta Road, Berkeley, CA 94708. 510-549-0129.

Ellen Schippers Fashions. Catalog available for $15.00 from: Ellen Schippers Fashion, 1^e Jan Steenstraat 112 (3rd floor), 1072 NR Amsterdam, The Netherlands.

Housewares. 1322 Haight Street, San Francisco, CA 94117. 415-252-1440

Walking Man. Available from: Cronan Artefact, Eleven Zoe, San Francisco, CA 94107-1709. 415-543-5222, 415-543-4482 (fax).

X-BERLIN. Unisex CyberLeathers, "armor" jackets, "worm" suits, woven leather jackets. 415-826-5300.

MAGAZINES

FAD. Fashion•Art•Design $14.95/6 issues, $24.95/12 issues from FAD Magazine, P.O. Box 420•656, San Francisco CA 94142. Esp recent Cyber Issue.

FIBER OPTICS

NEWSLETTERS

Caruso, Denise, ed. *Digital Media: A Seybold Report.* Subscriptions $395.00 (U.S.) from Seybold Publications Inc., Box 644, Media, PA 19063, 215-565-2480, 215-565-4659 (fax).

FRINGE SCIENCE

BOOKS

Barr, Frank E. with Saloma, J. S. and Buchele, M. J. "Melanin: The Organizing Molecule" (in *Medical Hypotheses* 11: 1-140/Churchill Livingstone, 1983). Dr. Barr suggests that melanin is the major organizing molecule for living systems. This paper constitutes the entire issue of the journal and cites almost 800 technical references! Far-out and profound material.

For order information on this title and Dr. Barr's second paper, "Melanin and the Mind Brain Problem," send SASE to: Institute for the Study of Consciousness, 2924 Benvenue, Berkeley, CA 94705. Also cassette and video recordings from Sound Photosynthesis [See Sound Photosynthesis].

Brockman, John, ed. *Speculations: The Reality Club 1* (Prentice Hall, 1990).

Brockman, John, ed. *Doing Science: The Reality Club 2* (Prentice Hall, 1991).

Brockman, John, ed. *Ways of Knowing: The Reality Club 3* (Prentice Hall, 1991).

Casti, John and Karlqvist, Anders. *Beyond Belief: Randomness, Prediction and Explanation in Science.* $39.95/Outside U.S. $47.95 from CRC Press, Inc., 2000 Corporate Blvd., N.W., Boca Raton, FL 33431. Toll free orders: 800-272-7737.

Feynman, Richard P. *QED* [Quantum Electrodynamics]: *The Strange Theory of Light and Matter* (Princeton Univ. Press, 1985).

Herbert, Nick. *Quantum Reality: Beyond the New Physics* (Anchor Press/Doubleday, 1985).

Herbert, Nick. *Faster Than Light: Superluminal Loopholes in Physics* (New American Library, 1988).

Jahn, Robert G. and Dunne, Brenda J. *Margins of Reality: The Role of Consciousness in the Physical World* (Harcourt Brace Jovanovich, 1987).

Pagels, Heinz R. *The Cosmic Code: Quantum Physics As the Language of Nature* (Simon and Schuster, 1982).

[Sarfatti, Jack] Toben, Bob. *Space-Time and Beyond: Toward an Explanation of the Unexplainable* [Bob Toben in conversation with physicists Jack Sarfatti and Fred Wolf] (E.P. Dutton, 1975).

Sheldrake, Rupert. *A New Science of Life: The Hypothesis of Formative Causation* (J.P. Tarcher, 1981).

Sheldrake, Rupert. *The Presence of the Past: Morphic Resonance and the Habits of Nature* (Times Books, 1988).

Sheldrake, Rupert. *The Rebirth of Nature: The Greening of Science and God* (Bantam, 1991).

Schultz, Ted, ed. *The Fringes of Reason: A Whole Earth Catalog—A Field Guide to New Age Frontiers, Unusual Beliefs & Eccentric Sciences* (Harmony, 1989).

Thom, René. *Semiophysics: A Sketch* [Aristotelian physics and catastrophe theory] (Addison-Wesley, 1990).

MONOGRAPHS AND PAPERS

Sarfatti, Jack. "Design for a Superluminal Signaling Device," *Physics Essays*, Vol. 4, number 3, 1991.

Sirag, Saul-Paul. "Why There are Three Fermion Families," *Bulletin of the American Physics Society* 27. 1-31 (1982).

Sirag, Saul-Paul. "Physical Constants as Cosmological Constraints," *International Journal of Theoretical Physics*, Vol. 22 1067-1089. (1983).

Sirag, Saul-Paul. "A Discrete Approach to Unified Field Theory," *Proceedings of the first annual Western Regional ANPA Meeting*, Stanford University, Alternative Natural Philosophy Association (1985).

Sirag, Saul-Paul. "An E7 Unification Scheme Via the Octahedral Double Group," contributed paper at The XXIII International Conference on High Energy Physics, Berkeley, CA (1986).

Sirag, Saul-Paul. "A Finite Group Algebra Unification Scheme." *Bulletin of the American Physics Society* 34 (1989).

VIDEO

Thinking Allowed Video Collection (Hosted by Dr. Jeffrey Mishlove. Catalog available from: Thinking Allowed, 2560 Ninth Street, Suite 123-F, Berkeley, CA 94710. 510-548-4415. Many different takes on fringe science with the likes of John Lilly, Terence McKenna, Frank Barr, Ralph Abraham, and many others. Dr. Mishlove is the only person to hold a Ph.D in metaphysics (UC Berkeley)!

GEEK HUMOR

BOOKS

Cringely, Robert X. *Accidental Empires: How the Boys of Silicon Valley Make Their Millions, Battle Foreign Competition and Still Can't Get a Date* (Addison-Wesley, 1992).

Raymond, Eric. *The New Hacker's Dictionary* (MIT Press, 1991). An updated, re-edited version of the Jargon File.

Silicon, Saint (Jeffrey Armstrong). *The Binary Bible* (Any Key Press, Santa Cruz, 1987).

COMIX

Landman, Mark. *BUZZ* (Kitchen Sink Press: 2 Swamp Road, Princeton, WI 54968).

Welz, Larry. *Cherry (Poptart) Comix*. Issues #1–#12 available for $3.50 each ppd. or $35 for all twelve from: Last Gasp, P.O. Box 410067, San Francisco, CA 94141. All orders must be accompanied with an age statement and CA residents please add 7% sales tax. Cherry Poptart T-shirts (S, M, L, XL) may also be ordered from Last Gasp for $9.95 ea. + $1 S&H per order at the following address: Last Gasp, P.O Box 212, Berkeley, CA 94701.

RECORDINGS

Mau-Mau, Somerset. *Cosmic Healing Tape*. Discount House of Healing, (also available: assorted whacky New Age Novelties; our choice for ordering Minotaur semen and other exotica.) Request catalog from 1537 A Fourth St., #49, San Rafael, CA 94901. 415-459-6968.

HACKERS

BOOKS

Levy, Steven. *Hackers: Heroes of the Computer Revolution* (Dell, 1984).

Stallman, Richard. *GNU Emacs manual* (Free Software Foundation, 1986).

Steel, Jr., Guy L. [et al.]. *The Hacker's Dictionary: A Guide to the World of Computer Wizards* (Harper & Row, 1983).

HIP-HOP

BOOKS

Costello, Mark and Wallace, David Foster. *Signifying Rappers: Rap and Race in the Urban Present* (The Ecco Press, 1990).

Nelson, Havelock and Gonzales, Michael A. *Bring the Noise: A Guide to Rap Music and Hip-Hop Culture* (Harmony Books, 1991).

Toop, David. *Rap Attack 2: African Rap to Global Hip-Hop* (Consortium, 1992).

RECORDINGS

Roots:
  Miscellaneous Jazz
  Stax/Volt Soul
  James Brown and the J.B. All-Stars
  Parliament/Funkadelic

Hip-Hop Sampler:
  Afrika Bambaata, Beastie Boys, Big Daddy Kane, Biz Markie, Boogie Down Productions (KRS-ONE), Brand Nubian, Cypress Hill, De La Soul, Del Tha Funkee Homo Sapien, Digital Underground, Dream Warriors, Eric B. and Rakim, GangStarr, Geto Boys, Grandmaster Flash and the Furious Five, Ice Cube, Ice-T, Jungle Brothers, Kool Moe Dee, L.L. Cool J., M.C. Lyte, N.W.A., Paris, Poor Righteous Teachers, Public Enemy, Queen Latifah, Stetsasonic, Too Short, 3rd Bass, Tribe Called Quest, X-Clan.

HOUSE MUSIC

MAGAZINES

Evolution. Quarterly magazine devoted to the history and present cultural forms of psychedelic experience and lifestyle, designed in the tradition of the San Francisco Oracle. Interesting music-related material. This group is also producing a series of singles with figures like Timothy Leary and Allen Ginsberg speaking over house tracks. Subscriptions £15/year (4 issues) *Evolution*, Box 833 London NW 6.

Freakbeat Magazine. Ultra-psychedelic in design and content, with an emphasis on music, from 60s acid rock to the current post-acid house sounds. Uses 3D color effects and usually contains a hot flexi-disc. P.O. Box 1288, Gerrard's Cross, Bucks, SL9 0AN. £4.5 (airmail) per issue.

Spin. Widely distributed (in U.S.) music magazine which also covers political and social issues—such as investigative reports on AIDS research—and popular culture. Subscriptions: $11.95/year (12 issues) plus new music tape. Overseas orders $50 (U.S.), Canada $30 (U.S.). Basic annual subscription rate is $18. Check out a newsstand copy first to choose from the selection of tapes and to confirm continuing availability of tape deal.

Q: The Modern Guide to Music and More. Superb London music monthly. Features, interviews, reviews of recordings and Hi-Fi gear. All put together with intelligence, style and great English humor. Also interesting classified ad section with useful contacts for ordering hard-to-find recordings and music-related items from the U.K. These are the folks who produced the 100-page tour programme for the last McCartney World tour. Subscriptions: U.S. Direct, £70 (that's about $125.75 U.S.)/year (12 issues), *Q* Subscriptions, P.O. Box 500, Leicester, LE99 0AA. Credit Card orders: 0858 410888. Try finding this one at newsstands that carry a selection of international magazines, where copies of *Q* sell for around $7 each.

SAN FRANCISCO/BAY AREA RAVES

Anarchic Adjustment. Pajet Design Group, 1592 Alum Rock Ave., San Jose, CA 95116. 408-926-6888, 408-929-6888 (fax).

Mr. Floppy's Flophouse, 415-541-5042.

ToonTown, 171 South Park #1, San Francisco, CA 94107. Information Line: 415-512-8666.

Hyperdelic/TransMedia Foundation: Great rave and psychedelic video, 415-956-9776.

Rave Bulletin Board: sfraves@soda.berkeley.edu

Rave information available at Ameba, Housewares and Behind the Post Office (see fashion section)

HYPERTEXT/HYPERMEDIA

BOOKS

Delany, Paul and Landow, George P. eds. *Hypermedia and Literary Studies* (MIT Press, 1991).

Nelson, Theodor Holm. *Computer Lib/Dream Machines.*

Nelson, Theodor Holm. *Literary Machines* (Mindful Press). Available for $25 in U.S., $40 elsewhere, $5 for purchase order from Mindful Press, 3020 Bridgeway, Sausalito, CA 94965. 415-331-4422. General information about Xanadu Repository Publishing, a new form of electronic delivery that promises world-wide impact in the mid-90s.

Nielsen, Jakob. *Hypertext & Hypermedia* (Academic Press, 1990).

HYPERCARD STACKS

Branwyn, Gareth, Frauenfelder, Mark, and Sugarman, Peter. *Beyond Cyberpunk.* $29.95 from The Computer Lab, Rt. 4, Box 54c, Louisa, VA 23093.

PUBLIC ACCESS

Public Access Xanadu (PAX). To get on the mailing list for PAX developments, write to Public Access Xanadu, 3020 Bridgeway #295, Sausalito, CA 94965.

SOFTWARE DEVELOPERS INFORMATION

For information on Xanadu software and how to connect to it, contact Xanadu Operating Company, 550 California Avenue, Palo Alto, CA 94306. 415-856-4112, 415-856-2251 (fax).

VIDEO

Technical Overview of the Xanadu Hypertext System. VHS videotape. Available for $50 in U.S., $65 elsewhere, $5 for purchase order from: Mindful Press, 3020 Bridgeway, Sausalito, CA 94965. 415-331-4422.

HYPERREALITY

BOOKS

Baudrillard, Jean. *America* (Verso, 1988).

Baudrillard, Jean. *Simulations* (Semiotext(e), 1983).

Baudrillard, Jean. *In the Shadow of the Silent Majorities* (Semiotext(e), 1983).

Baudrillard, Jean. *Seduction* (St. Martin's Press, 1990).

Baudrillard, Jean. *Cool Memories* (Verso, 1990).

Eco, Umberto. *Foucault's Pendulum* (Harcourt Brace Jovanovich, 1989).

Eco, Umberto. *Travels in Hyper Reality: Essays* (Harcourt Brace Jovanovich, 1986).

INDUSTRIAL/POST-INDUSTRIAL MUSIC & ART

BOOKS

Industrial Culture Handbook (*RE/SEARCH* #6/7, 1983).

[Survival Research Labs (SRL), Mark Pauline] *Pranks!* (*RE/SEARCH* #11, 1987).

VIDEO

[Survival Research Labs] *A Scenic Harvest From the Kingdom of Pain* (Loompanics, Inc.).

[Survival Research Labs] *Virtues of Negative Fascination* (Loompanics, Inc.).

[Survival Research Labs] *Menacing Machine Mayhem* (*RE/SEARCH* Video).

RECORDINGS

Babyland. *Babyland* (Flipside).

Cabaret Voltaire (Restless/Mute).

Clock DVA. *Buried Dreams* (Wax Trax!).

Consolidated. *Friendly Fascism* (Nettwerk/IRS).

Eno, Brian. (EG/Caroline/Opal).

Front 242. *Tyranny for You* (Epic).

Hafler Trio. *Kill the King* (Silent Records).

Ministry. (Sire/Warner).

Muslimgauze. *United States of Islam* (Silent Records).

Nine Inch Nails. *Pretty Hate Machine* (TVT).

Pelican Daughters. *Fishbones and Wishbones* (CCP).

Skinny Puppy (Nettwerk/Capitol).

Sound Traffic Control

SPK (Side Effects).

Throbbing Gristle (Rough Trade).

Yeht Mae. *1000 Veins*.

Young Gods. *L'Eau Rouge* (Play it again Sam, USA).

Zoviet France. *Shadow, Thief of the Sun* (DOVe).

SOURCES

Silent Records. Carries their own releases, imports, and hard-to-find titles as well as industrial and experimental music zines. A free copy of their catalog is available from: 540 Alabama Street, Suite 315, San Francisco, CA 94110.

Technology Works is an industrial music zine. Each issue is filled with reviews and band interviews. Sample copies are $1.50 from Paul Moore, P.O. Box 477, Placentia, CA 92670-0407.

Wax Trax! Records, 1659 North Damen Ave, Chicago, IL 60647, 312-252-1000. 312-252-1007 (fax).

FILMS

Videodrome (Director: David Cronenberg, 1983).

LEARY, TIMOTHY

BIBLIOGRAPHY

Horowitz, Michael, Walls, Karen and Smith, Billy. *Timothy Leary: An Annotated Bibliography*. 305 pp., illustrated, clothbound, containing over 1,200 entries. (Shoe String Press, 1988). Available for $40 ppd., from The Shoe String Press, P.O. Box 4327, Hamden, CT 06514.

Out of print titles by Timothy Leary—such as *High Priest*—can be ordered at reasonable collectors prices from Flashback Books [See Out of Print Books, Recordings, and Ephemera].

BOOKS IN PRINT

Leary, Timothy. *The Psychedelic Experience.*

Leary, Timothy. *Changing My Mind, Among Others: Lifetime.* Writings selected and introduced by the author (1982).

Leary, Timothy. *Flashbacks* (J.P. Tarcher, 1983/enlarged 1990).

Leary, Timothy. *Info-Psychology: A Manual On the Use Of the Human Nervous System According To the Instructions*

Leary, Timothy. *What Does WoMan Want?* (Falcon Press, 1988).

Leary, Timothy. *Neuropolitique* (Falcon Press, 1988).

Leary, Timothy. *The Politics of Ecstasy* (Ronin).

Leary, Timothy. *Greatest Hits Vol. 1, 1980-1990* (1990). This title, books, software and other interesting items by Tim are available from KnoWare, 11288 Ventura Blvd. #702, Studio City, CA 91604. Write for catalog.

RECORDINGS (COMPACT DISC)

Turn On, Tune in, Drop Out: The Original Motion Picture Soundtrack (Performance Records, 1988/1967)

You Can Be Anyone This Time Around (RYKODISC, 1992/1970)

SOFTWARE

Mind Mirror (Electronic Arts, 1986). Only available from Mindware for $29.95 (IBM) Call 800-447-0477 for software specifics and ordering information. The author's first "Headware." The Mindware catalog offers many other software titles of similar interest.

LONGEVITY

ACCESS

ALCOR, publisher of *Cryonics Magazine*. $10/12 issues, 12327 Doherty Street, Riverside, CA 92503. 800-367-2228.

Cryonics Institute. 24041 Stratford, Oak Park, MI 48237. 313-967-3104. Offers biopreservation services.

The Immortalist Society publishes *The Immortalist*. Subscriptions are $25, 24443 Roanoke, Oak Park, MI 48237.

Lifequest is a magazine that publishes fiction dealing with Cryonics and looks at what might be in store for twentieth century people who return to life decades or centuries after dying. $3/issue, P.O. Box 18690, South Lake Tahoe, CA 95706.

TransTime, Inc. 10208 Pearmine Street, Oakland, CA 94603. 510-639-1955. Offers biopreservation services.

BOOKS

Dean, Ward. *Biological Aging Measurement: Clinical Applications* (The Center for Bio-Gerontology, 1988).

Harrington, Alan. *The Immortalist* (Celestial Arts, 1977).

Rosenfeld, Albert. *Prolongevity II* (Knopf, 1985).

Pearson, Durk and Shaw, Sandy. *Life Extension: A Practical Scientific Approach* (Warner Books, 1982).

Segall, Paul and Kahn, Carol. *Living Longer, Growing Younger: Remarkable Breakthroughs in Life Extension* (Times Books, New York, 1989).

Silverberg, Robert. *Immortality.*

Walford, Roy L. *Maximum Life Span* (Norton, 1983).

Wowk, Brian and Darwin, Michael. *ALCOR: Threshold to Tomorrow.*

SOURCES: DURK PEARSON & SANDY SHAW DESIGNER FOODS

Life Services Supplements, Inc.
81 First Ave.,
Atlantic Highlands, NJ 07716
800-542-3230, 908-872-8700 (phone),
908-872-8705 (fax) 800-345-9105 (Canada).

Smart Products,
870 Market Street, Suite 1262
San Francisco, CA 94102
800-858-6520
415-989-2500

SOURCES: SMART DRUGS

InHome Health Services
P.O. Box 3112
CH-2800 Delemont, Switzerland

Interlab
BCM Box 5890
London, WC1N 3XX, England

McKENNA, TERENCE

Terence McKenna is a cunning linguist, psycho-activist and altered statesman. His focus is on the role of tryptamine psychedelics and their relationship to human evolution and language in a prehistorical and posthistorical sense. While it is fascinating to read McKenna, his natural gift for storytelling comes through most brilliantly on his many collected lecture and workshop tapes. These are available from Sound Photosynthesis [See Sound Photosynthesis]. Highly recommended.

BOOKS

McKenna, Terence and McKenna, Dennis J. *The Invisible Landscape* (Seabury Press, 1975).

[McKenna, Terence and McKenna, Dennis J.] Oss, O.T. and Oeric, O.N. *Psilocybin Mushroom Grower's Guide* (Ronin-And/Or, 1976). Available from Books-by-Phone. Call: 800-858-2665.

McKenna, Terence. *Food of the Gods* (Bantam, 1992).

RECORDINGS

McKenna, Terence. *True Hallucinations: A Talking Book* (Sound Photosynthesis, 1984). An eight tape set recounting the author/adventurer's explorations in the Himalayas and the jungles of the Amazon in the context of the psychedelic experience.

McKenna, Terence and McKenna, Kathleen Harrison. *Victorian Tales of Cannabis: An Audially Illuminated Manuscript* (Sound Photosynthesis, 1990). Readings from *The Lands of the Saracen* (Bayard Taylor), *Perilous Play* (Louisa May Alcott), *A Thousand and One Nights* (trans. Sir Richard Burton), and *The Hashish Eater* (Fitzhugh Ludlow).

McKenna, Terence. *History Ends In Green: Gaia, Psychedelics, and the Archaic Revival* (Mystic Fire Audio, 1992). Six tape set $49.95 + $4 S&H from: Mystic Fire Audio, P.O. Box 9323, Dept. c5, S. Burlington, VT 05407. Call toll free 800-727-8433.

SOFTWARE

Timewave (IBM). Available from Sound Photosysnthesis. Fascinating software that illustrates McKenna's theories regarding the "fractal nature of time."

VIDEO

The Experiment in Petaluma.

Various Lectures (available from Sound Photosynthesis)

McLUHAN, MARSHALL

BIOGRAPHIES & COLLECTIONS

Marchand, Philip. *Marshall McLuhan: The Medium and the Messenger* (Ticknor & Fields, 1989).

Sanderson, George and Macdonald, Frank, eds. *Marshall McLuhan: The Man and His Message* (Fulcrum, 1989). With an introduction by John Cage. A very accessible introduction for the general reader.

Molinaro, Mattie, McLuhan, Corinne and Toy, William, eds. *The Letters of Marshall McLuhan* (Oxford Univ. Press, 1987).

BOOKS

The Mechanical Bride: Folklore of Industrial Man (Vanguard Press, 1951).

The Gutenberg Galaxy (Univ. of Toronto Press, 1962).

Understanding Media (McGraw-Hill, 1964).

McLuhan, Marshall [with additional contributions]. *Verbi-Voco-Visual Explorations* (Something Else Press, 1967).

McLuhan, Marshall and Fiore, Quentin. *The Medium is the Massage: An Inventory of Effects* (Random House, 1967/Simon and Schuster, 1989).

McLuhan, Marshall and Fiore, Quentin. *War and Peace in the Global Village* (McGraw Hill, 1968/Simon and Schuster, 1989).

McLuhan, Marshall and Parker, Harley. *Through the Vanishing Point: Space in Poetry and Painting* (Harper and Row: World Perspectives Series Vol. 37, 1968).

McLuhan, Marshall with Watson, Wilfred. *From Cliche to Archetype* (Viking, 1970).

McLuhan, Marshall. *Culture is Our Business* (McGraw Hill, 1970).

McLuhan, Marshall and Nevitt, Barrington. *Take Today: The Executive as Drop Out* (Harcourt Brace Jovanovich, 1972).

McLuhan, Marshall, Hutchon, Kathryn and McLuhan, Eric. *The City as Classroom: Understanding Language and Media* (Book Society of Canada, Ltd., 1977).

McLuhan, Marshall and McLuhan, Eric. *Laws of Media: The New Science* (Univ. of Toronto Press, 1988).

McLuhan, Marshall and Powers, Bruce R. *The Global Village: Transformations in World Life and Media in the 21st Century* (Oxford Univ. Press, 1989).

BOOKS OF RELATED INTEREST

Joyce, James. *Finnegan's Wake* (Viking Press, 1939/ Penguin pbk., 1976). McLuhan made frequent reference to Joyce's work to illustrate and illuminate his own theories and ideas. An understanding of Joyce and his multileveled quantum linguistic style is helpful.

Schwartz, Tony. *The Responsive Chord: How Radio and TV Manipulate You…Who You Vote For…What You Buy…And How You Think* (Anchor/Doubleday, 1973).

TAPES OF RELATED INTEREST—AUDIO

McKenna, Terence *Speaking Metaphorically.* Discusses the impact of language on our worldview and our self-image. McKenna makes fascinating references to McLuhan's ideas in the context of his own psychedelic scenario. Recorded Oct. 1983, Berkeley, CA. 80 min. Available from Sound Photosynthesis [See Sound Photosynthesis].

MEAT

BOOKS

Bataille, Georges. *Story of the Eye* (Urizen Books, 1977).

Juno, Andrea and Vale, V. *Modern Primitives: An Investigation of Contemporary Adornment & Ritual* (RE/SEARCH #12, 1989).

Kroker, Arthur and Marilouise. *Body Invaders* (St. Martin's Press, 1987).

Tattootime. Ed Hardy, ed. Issues 1&2 $12, Issues 3&4 $17, Issue 5 $20 from: *RE/SEARCH* Publications, 20 Romolo, #B, San Francisco, CA 94133. 415-362-1465.

Tattoo Advocate. Shotsie Gorman, ed. $15/year (2 issues; overseas $18.50) from: Tattoo Advocate, P.O. Box 8390, Haledon, NJ 07538-0390.

NEWSLETTERS

Body Art. Issues 2-4 $16.50, 5-11 $19.45, 12-13 $21.45 (ppd.) from: Last Gasp Distributors, P.O. Box 410067,

San Francisco, CA 94141. 415-824-6636.

PFIQ (Piercing Fans International Quarterly). Jim Ward, ed. $40/year (4 issues) from: PFIQ, 8720 Santa Monica Blvd., Los Angeles, CA 90069. 213-657-6677.

MEDIA PRANKS

BOOKS

Dawkins, Richard. *The Selfish Gene* (Oxford Univ. Press, 1976/1989).

Hoffman, Abbie. *Revolution For The Hell Of It* (Dial Press, 1968).

[Hoffman, Anita] Fettamen, Ann. *Trashing* (Straight Arrow Books, 1970).

Juno, Andrea and Vale, V., eds., *Pranks!* (RE/SEARCH #11, 1987). For information on *Pranks!* and other titles in this series, contact: *RE/SEARCH* Publications, 20 Romolo #B, San Francisco, CA 94133. 415-362-1465.

Rubin, Jerry. *Do It!: Scenarios of the Revolution* (Simon and Schuster/Ballantine, 1970).

Wolfe, Tom. *The Electric Kool-Aid Acid Test* (Farrar, Straus & Giroux, 1968/Bantam 1969).

RECORDINGS

Negativland. *Helter Stupid* (SST, 1988).

Negativland. *U2* (SST) recalled.

MONDO 2000

Subscriptions are $24.00 (U.S. and Canada) and $50.00 (Overseas) for five quarterly issues. *MONDO 2000* #3, #4 and #5 are available as back issues only for $7.00 ea. Order from: *MONDO 2000*, P.O. Box 10171, Berkeley, CA 94709.

MONDO 2000 T-Shirts are available for $18.50 in two exciting styles. (1) Classic CyberBaby with the Rudy Ruckerism "How fast are you, How Dense?" (2) Pirate CyberBaby with eye patch and the caption "We're a Pirate Mind Station." Both styles feature white graphics on high-quality black cotton.

PUBLISHING HISTORY

MONDO 2000 #1 (September, 1988)

MONDO 2000 #2 (June, 1990)

MONDO 2000 #3 (January, 1991)

MONDO 2000 #4 (July, 1991)

MONDO 2000 #5 (December, 1991)

MONDO 2000 #6 (April, 1992)

MONDO 2000 #7 (July, 1992)

MULTIMEDIA

BOOKS

Ambron, Sueann and Hooper, Kristina eds. *Learning with Interactive Multimedia.* (Microsoft Press 1990).

[See also Computer Graphics and Electronic Music].

JOURNALS AND MAGAZINES

[See Computer Graphics].

MPC World: Learning, Playing and Working with Multimedia PCs. [By PC World Communications] $14.95/year (6 issues) from: MPC World, Subscription Department, P.O. Box 54665, Boulder, CO 80323-4665. Add $10/year for Mexico and Canada.

Multimedia Review: The Journal of Multimedia Computing. A scholarly selection of papers by the experts and visionaries in the field(s). Excellent. $47/year (4 issues, business address), $ 39/year (4 issues, personal address), add $15 outside U.S., from: Multimedia Review, Meckler, 11 Ferry Lane West, Westport, CT 06880-9760. 800-635-5537; in CT 203-226-6967.

SOURCES OF EQUIPMENT

Voyager Co. Software and Interactive Laserdisc Catalog. Publishers of fine Interactive New Media. This catalog features expanded electronic books, CD-ROM with full-motion video, CD companions to musical masterpieces, Macintosh HyperCard stacks and hardware. Also request the Criterion Collection Catalog of Hollywood film and classic television laserdiscs. Request catalogs from: The Voyager Company, 1351 Pacific Coast Hwy., Santa Monica, CA 90401. 310-451-1383.

NANOTECHNOLOGY

BOOKS

Drexler, K. Eric. *The Engines of Creation* (Anchor Press/Doubleday, 1986).

Drexler, K. Eric and Peterson, Chris and Pergamit, Gayle. *Unbounding the Future: The Nanotechnology Revolution* (Morrow, 1991).

Hameroff, Stuart R. *Ultimate Computing: Biomolecular Consciousness and Nanotechnology* (Elsevier Science Pub., 1987).

Whitehouse, D. J. and Kawata, K., eds. *Nanotechnology: Proceedings of the Joint Forum/ERATO Symposium held at Warwick University, 21-22 August 1990* (Adam Hilger, 1991).

NETS

BOOKS

Vallee, Jacques. *The Network Revolution: Confessions of a Computer Scientist* (And/Or Press, 1982).

NOMADNESS

BOOKS

Bey, Hakim. *T.A.Z.: The Temporary Autonomous Zone, Ontological Anarchism, Poetic Terrorism* (1991). Contact: Autonomedia, P.O. Box 568, Williamsburgh Station, Brooklyn, NY 11211.

Roberts, Steven K. *Computing Across America: The Bicycle Odyssey of a High-Tech Nomad* (Learned Information, Inc., 1988).

HARDWARE

PC Private Eye [See Virtual Reality].

SOURCES

Roberts, Steve, Nomadic Research Labs, P.O. Box 2185 El Segundo, CA 90245

OUT-OF-PRINT BOOKS, RECORDINGS & EPHEMERA

SOURCES

Flashback Books. Rare, out-of-print, and really cool books, magazines, and artifacts of psychedelic arts & science, literature and lifestyle. Catalog $5 from: Flashback Books, 906 Samuel Drive, Petaluma, CA 94952. 707-762-4714.

... of the jungle. Exotic Botanicals: Unusual entheogenic, medicinal and ethnobotanical plants and tropical products. Send $2 for catalog. Box 1801 Sebastopol, CA 95473.

Red House Books. The Beats and 60s counterculture. Send $2 for catalog to: P.O. Box 460267, San Francisco, CA 94146

Rosetta. Ethnobotanical books and articles, original and re-printed. Send SASE to: P.O. Box 4611, Berkeley, CA 94704.

Skyline Books. Counterculture, beat and modern literature. Catalogs issued. P.O. Box T, Forest Knolls, CA 94933.

PERSONAL COMPUTING

BOOKS (GENERAL)

Pickover, Clifford A. *Computers and the Imagination: Visual Adventures Beyond the Edge* (St. Martin's Press, 1991).

MAGAZINES AND JOURNALS

Boardwatch Magazine. Interesting monthly magazine of bulletin board systems, telecommunications and the online world. $28/year (12 issues) from: Boardwatch Magazine, 5970 South Vivian Street, Littleton, CO 80127. 303-973-6038, 303-973-3731 (fax).

MacUser. General interest Macintosh publication. Features, reviews, etc. Excellent testing labs. $27/year from: MacUser, P.O. Box 56986, Boulder, CO 80321-6986. 303-447-9330, 303-378-5675 (fax).

Macworld. $30/year (12 issues) from: PCW Communications, Subscriber Services Dept., P.O. Box 54529, Boulder, CO 80322-4529. 303-447-9330, 303-525-0643 (fax).

MacWeek. This is the one to have. Top notch weekly reporting on the Macintosh Universe. Free to qualified subscribers or $99/year (54 issues) from: MacWeek, Customer Service Dept., P.O. Box 5821, Cherry Hill, NJ 08034. 609-428-5000.

MicroTimes. Mostly a PC magazine, but also offers good coverage of Macintosh, NeXT and Silicon Graphics Platforms. Tabloid format, approx. 230 pages per issue. Free if living in distribution area or $24/year (12 issues, 3rd class), $50/year (12 issues, 1st class), $160/year (12 issues, airmail overseas) from: BAM Publications, 3470 Buskirk, Pleasant Hill, CA 94523. 510-652-3810.

NeXTWorld. $23.95/ year (6 issues) from: NeXTWorld Magazine, Subscription Department, P.O. Box 56429, Boulder, CO 80323-6429.

Silicon Graphics World: A News & Information Journal Devoted to the SGI Community. $45/year U.S. (6 issues), $90/year airmail overseas and Canada from: Silicon Graphics World, P.O. Box 399, Cedar Park, TX 78613-9987. 512-250-9023, 512-331-3900 (fax).

SELECTED HARDWARE AND SOFTWARE COMPANIES

Lapis Technologies. 1-800-43-LAPIS (Full line of Apple-compatible, fixed and programmable, display cards; high quality monitors).

Diaquest, Inc., 1440 San Pablo Ave., Berkeley CA 94702. 415-526-7167, 415-526-7073 (fax).

Logitech. 800-231-7717, ext. 700. (MouseMan right-handed, left-handed and cordless mice for IBM and Macintosh systems.)

Berkeley Systems, 2095 Rose Street, Berkeley CA 94709. 510-540-5535. (Makers of the finest Macintosh screen saver, After Dark).

Silicon Graphics, Inc. (SGI). Makers of world-class 3D animation workstations, including the new IRIS Indigo series which starts at under $10,000. For information about the Indigo line call "SGI Express" at 800-800-SGI1 (7441).

USER'S GROUPS

BMUG (The Berkeley Macintosh User's Group). The oldest and largest Mac user group in the United States. $40/year membership includes two enormous newsletters (around 400 pages!), software, helpline access, and more. Contact: 510-849-9114. If you own a Mac, you can't afford not to be a member.

POLITICS/POST-POLITICS

BOOKS

Writers and Readers Documentary Comic Books: The "For Beginners Series." Absolutely amazing "Graphic Novel" style books written and drawn with intelligence and humor. Useful bibliographies suggest sources for the interested reader. Titles include: Anarchy, Architecture, Black, Brain, Capitalism, Computers, Cuba, Darwin, Das Kapital, DNA, Ecology, Economists, Einstein, Feminism, Food, French Revolution, Freud, Ireland, Lenin, Mao, Marx, Medicine, Newton, Nuclear Power, Orwell, Peace, Reagan, Reich, Sex, Socialism, Trotsky.

Deleuze, Gilles and Guattari, Felix. *Anti-Oedipus: Capitalism and Schizophrenia* (1977).

Hoffman, Abbie. *Steal This Urine Test: Fighting Drug Hysteria in America* (Penguin, 1987).

Hoffman, Abbie. *The Best of Abbie Hoffman* (Four Walls Eight Windows, 1989).

Thompson, Hunter S. *Fear and Loathing on the Campaign Trail '72* (Straight Arrow Books, 1973).

Thompson, Hunter S. *The Great Shark Hunt: Strange Tales From a Strange Time [Gonzo Papers, Vol. 1]* (Summit Books, 1979).

Thompson, Hunter S. *Generation of Swine: Tales of Shame and Degradation in the '80s [Gonzo Papers, Vol. 2]* (Summit Books, 1988).

Thompson, Hunter S. *Songs of the Doomed: More Notes on the Death of the American Dream [Gonzo Papers, Vol. 3]* (Summit Books, 1990).

OTHER

Amok Fourth Dispatch. "A thorough directory of the extremes of information in print…books offering [among other things] unflinching looks at mayhem, virus, and decay; dissections of today's global power structure; sexual impulses spinning out of control…" Catalog $4 from Amok, P.O. Box 861867 Terminal Annex, Los Angeles, CA 90086-1867.

The Directory of Libertarian Periodicals. (A listing of approximately 150 libertarian magazines and newsletters). $3 from Jim Stumm, Box 29, Hiler Branch, Buffalo, NY 14223.

Eclipse Books Trading Cards. Hysterically funny and very informative "baseball-style" trading cards with beautiful artwork and insightful explanations of topics on reverse. Titles include: Iran-Contra Scandal; Rotten to the Core: New York City Political Scandal; Friendly Dictators; Bush League; Coup D'Etat: The Assassination of JFK; Drug Wars: The Straight Dope on America's Dirtiest Deals; and Savings & Loan Scandal. Sets of trading cards are $8.95 ea. plus $1 S&H from: Eclipse Books, P.O. Box 1099, Forestville, CA 95436. Also available in better comic book stores.

Laissez-Faire Books. Their catalog contains long, thoughtful reviews as well as a large selection of libertarian books. Catalog: 942 Howard Street, San Francisco, CA 94103. 415-541-9780.

Loompanics Catalog. The finest resource for exotic, controversial, and suppressed printed information. Titles range from Fast Driving (Without Tickets) to Build Your Own Laser, Phaser, Ion Gun & Other Working Space-Age Projects. Many books listed in the *MONDO 2000* Shopping Mall are available from Loompanics. Catalog $5 from: Loompanics Unlimited, P.O. Box 1197, Port Townsend, WA 98368.

PSYCHEDELIC DRUGS

BOOKS

Eisner, Bruce. *Ecstasy: The MDMA Story* (Ronin, 1989).

Gracie & Zarkov. *Notes from Underground: A "Gracie and Zarkov" Reader* (privately printed preliminary edition available at cost; published version expected mid 1992). For information about this title write to: Gracie and Zarkov, c/o *MONDO 2000*, P.O. Box 10171, Berkeley, CA 94709. Can also be obtained through Flashback Books or Rosetta (See Out of Print Books, Recordings and Ephemera).

Grinspoon, Lester and Bakalar, James B. *Psychedelic Drugs Reconsidered* (Basic Books, 1979).

Hofmann, Albert. *LSD: My Problem Child* (J.P. Tarcher, 1983).

Huxley, Aldous. *The Doors of Perception/Heaven and Hell*. (Harper & Row, 1963/Perennial pbk.,1990).

[Huxley, Aldous] Horowitz, Michael and Palmer, Cynthia, eds. *Moksha: Writings on Psychedelics and the Visionary Experience* (1977; Tarcher 1982 pbk.). Forthcoming from City Lights Books, 1993.

Leary, Timothy [See Timothy Leary].

Lee, Martin A.,and Shlain, Bruce. *Acid Dreams: The CIA, LSD and the Sixties Rebellion* (Grove Press, 1985).

Lilly, John C., M.D., *Programming and Metaprogramming in the Human Biocomputer* (Julian Press, 1967, 1987 ed.).

Lilly, John C., M.D. *The Center of the Cyclone: An Autobiography of Inner Space* (Julian Press, 1972, 1985 ed.).

Lilly, John C., M.D. *Simulations of God: The Science of Belief* (Simon and Schuster, 1975).

Lilly, John C., M.D. and Lilly, Antonietta. *The Dyadic Cyclone: The Autobiography of a Couple* (Simon and Schuster, 1976).

Lilly, John C., M.D. *The Deep Self: Profound Relaxation and the Tank Isolation Technique* (Warner Books, 1977).

Lilly, John C., M.D. *The Scientist: A Metaphysical Autobiography* (Ronin, 1988).

Lilly, John C. M.D. and Jeffrey, Francis. *John Lilly, So Far...* (Tarcher, 1990).

McKenna, Terence [See Terence McKenna].

Palmer, Cynthia and Horowitz, Michael. *Shaman Woman, Mainline Lady: Women's Writing on the Drug Experience* (Putnam, 1982). Available for $15 ppd. from: Flashback Books, 906 Samuel Drive, Petaluma, CA 94952.

Shulgin, Alexander and Shulgin, Ann. *PIHKAL: A Chemical Love Story.* Available for $18.95 (+ $4.00 S&H, California residents add $1.38 tax) from Transform Press, Box 13675, Berkeley, CA 94701.

Stafford, Peter. *Psychedelics Encyclopedia* (Ronin, 1992).

Stevens, Jay. *Storming Heaven: LSD and the American Dream* (Atlantic Monthly Press,1987).

[Wasson, Robert Gordon] Riedlinger, Thomas, ed. *The Sacred Mushroom Seeker: Essays for R. Gordon Wasson.* $41 ppd. from Dioscorides/Timber Press, 9999 SW Wilshire, Portland, OR 97225

Wilson, Robert Anton [See Robert Anton Wilson].

JOURNALS

Albert Hofmann Foundation Newsletter. Edited by Phoenix Research Foundation. $30/year (4 issues) from The Albert Hofmann Foundation, 1341 Ocean Ave., Ste. 300, Santa Monica, CA 90401. 231-281-8110.

Island Views [Newsletter]. $25/year (4 issues) and

general membership in the Island Group organization: Island Group, 1803 Mission St., Ste. 175, Santa Cruz, CA 95060.

Psychedelic Monographs and Essays. Annual scholarly publication in the tradition of the *Psychedelic Review.* PME Publishing Group, P.O. Box 4465, Boynton Beach, FL 33424. Write for information.

(Many titles and resources related to Psychedelics and other topics of interest can be ordered from Books-by-Phone: Controversial & Underground Books. Catalog available for $2.00 from: Books-by-Phone, Box 522, Berkeley, CA 94701. 800-858-2665 orders, 510-548-2124 information. 9AM-5PM Mon.-Thurs.).

POSTER

Xochi Speaks. Beautiful full-color educational poster featuring the Aztec god of Flowers, 3-D molecular models of and information about contemporary neuro-specifics. Accompanied by a 16-page booklet, *Guide to the Psychedelics.* A *must* for rave venues. $25 ppd. from Lord Nose!, P.O. Box 170473MB San Francisco, CA 94117-0473.

RANTS

BOOKS

Dobbs, J.R. "Bob." *The Book of the SubGenius* (Simon and Schuster, 1983).

Lennon, John, *Lost Prophetic Writings.*

Parfrey, Adam, ed. *Apocalypse Culture* (Feral House, 1990 revised ed.).

Parfrey, Adam and Black, Bob, eds. *Rants and Incendiary Tracts: Voices of Desperate Illumination 1558 to Present* (Amok Press and Loompanics, Inc., 1989).

Stang, Ivan, ed. *Three Fisted Tales of "Bob"* (Fireside, 1990).

VIDEO

Arise: The SubGenius Video, Arise Video, c/o Ivan Stang, P.O. Box 140306, Dallas, TX 75214-0306.

ROBOTS

BOOKS

Asimov, Isaac. *The Robot Novels* (Ballantine Books, 1988).

Asimov, Isaac and Frenkel, Karen A. *Robots: Machines in Man's Image* (Harmony Books, 1985).

Holland, John M. *Basic Robotic Concepts* (Howard W. Sams & Co., 1983).

Jeter, K.W. *Dr. Adder* (NAL-Dutton, 1989).

Minsky, Marvin, ed. *Robotics* (Doubleday, 1985).

Schodt, Frederik L. *Inside the Robot Kingdom: Japan, Mechatronics and the Coming Robotopia* (Harper & Row, 1988).

FILMS OF MENTION

Metropolis (Director: Fritz Lang, 1926; German).

NEWSLETTERS

Robot Experimenter. Raymond Cote, ed. $24/year (12 issues) from Robot Experimenter, P.O. Box 458, Peterborough, NH 03458-0458.

SOURCES

Edmund Scientific. Catalog $5.00 from: Edmund Scientific Company, 101 East Gloucester Pike, Barrington, NJ 08007. 609-573-6250.

Heathkit. Catalog free from Heath Company, P.O. Box 1288, Benton Harbor, MI 49022. 800-253-0570.

Herbach & Rademan. Catalog free from H & R Corporation, 401 East Erie Ave., Philadelphia, PA 19134. 215-426-1708.

World of Robots. Catalog $6.25 from: World of Robots, 55 Earle Street, Milford, CT 06460. 203-877-4400.

SMART DRUGS

ARTICLES

Sirius, R. U. "May You Never Sleep: Cognition Enhancing Drugs" (*Whole Earth Review, Signal #57*, Winter 1987).

BOOKS

Dean, Ward and Morgenthaler, John. *Smart Drugs & Nutrients: How to Improve Your Memory and Increase Your Intelligence Using the Latest Discoveries in Neuroscience* (B & J Publications, 1991). $12.95 + $3 S&H (California residents add $.94 tax) from B & J Publications, P.O. Box 48313, Santa Cruz, CA 95061.

Pearson, Durk and Shaw, Sandy. *Life Extension: A Practical Scientific Approach* (Warner Books, 1982).

Pearson, Durk and Shaw, Sandy. *The Life Extension Companion* (Warner Books, 1984).

Pelton, Ross with Pelton, Taffy Clarke. *Mind Food and Smart Pills* (Doubleday, 1989).

SOURCES: DURK PEARSON & SANDY SHAW DESIGNER FOODS

Life Services Supplements, Inc.
81 First Ave.
Atlantic Highlands, NJ 07716
800-542-3230
908-872-8700 (phone)
908-872-8705 (fax)
800-345-9105 (Canada)

Smart Products
870 Market St., Ste. 1262
San Francisco, CA 94102
415-989-2500
800-858-6520

SOURCES: SMART DRUGS

InHome Health Services
P.O. Box 3112
CH-2800 Delemont, Switzerland

Interlab
BCM Box 5890
London, WC1N 3XX, England

SOUND PHOTOSYNTHESIS

Sound Photosynthesis Catalog. The tireless duo, Faustin Bray and Brian Wallace collect and distribute an enormous "new ideas" library of audio and video tapes. Hear the visionaries speak! Sound Photosynthesis is one of the most important resources of contemporary information. Of particular interest to New Edge people:

Ralph Abraham, Frank Barr, Frank Barron, Robert Bly, William S. Burroughs, Joseph Campbell, Fritjof Capra, Walter B. Clark, John Clauser, His Holiness The Dalai Lama Of Tibet, Ram Dass, Peter Dawkins, Umberto Eco, Bruce Eisner, Richard Feynman, Marija Gimbutas, Allen Ginsberg, James Gleick, Stan Grof, Eric Gullichsen, Gyuto Multiphonic Choir, Michael Harner, Ruth-Inge Heinze, Nick Herbert, Albert Hofman, Michael Hutchison, Aldous Huxley, Laura Huxley, Alison Kennedy, Ali Akbar Khan, Taras Kiceniuk, Paul Krassner, Stanley Krippner, J. Krishnamurti, Claudio Naranjo, Jaron Lanier, Timothy Leary, John Lilly, Luis Eduardo Luna, Lisa Lyon Lilly, William Lyon, Dennis McKenna, Kathleen McKenna & Nicole Maxwell, Terence McKenna, Ralph Metzner, Jeffrey Mishlove, Claudio Naranjo, Ted Nelson, Yoko Ono, Humphry Osmond, P. D. Ouspensky, Karl Pribram, Bhagwan Shree Rajneesh, Tom Robbins, Beverly Rubik, Carl Ruck, Rudy Rucker, Paul Segall, Rupert Sheldrake, Alexander Shulgin, Saint Silicon, Saul-Paul Sirag, Norman Spinrad, Gloria Steinem, Jay Stevens, Whitley Strieber, Luisah Teish, Roy Tuckman, Jacques Vallee, John Vincent & Susan Wyshyski, Andrew Weil, Colin Wilson, Robert Anton Wilson, and Arthur Young, to name but a few...

Catalog available for $2 from Sound Photosynthesis, P.O. Box 2111, Mill Valley, CA 94942.

SYNAESTHESIA

BOOKS

Cytowic, Richard E. *Synesthesia: A Union of the Senses* (Springer-Verlag, 1989).

Huysmans, Joris-Karl. *Against The Grain* [*Á Rebours*]. With an introduction by Havelock Ellis (Three Sirens Press, 1931/Dover, 1969).

Huysmans, Joris-Karl. *Against Nature* [*Á Rebours*]. [New translation by Robert Baldick] (Penguin Books, 1959/1986).

Luria, A.R. *The Mind of a Mnemonist: A Little Book About a Vast Memory* (Basic Books, 1968).

Suskind, Patrick. *Perfume: The Story of a Murderer* [Translated from the German by John E. Woods] (A.A. Knopf,1986).

SYNÆSTHETIC MEDIA

Synæsthetic Media. P.O. Box 12771 Berkeley, CA 94709. 510-549-3677. Synæasthetic Media is a hybrid team of technicians and researchers working with international holographic artist Stãrã to produce her interactive multimedia project, the Vulvic Ring Cycle. Available for sensorial viewing are Dancetrax, Video, and DVI.

TRANSREALISM

BOOKS

Rucker, Rudy. *Transreal!* (WCS, 1991).

VIRTUAL REALITY

BOOKS

Aukstakalnis, Steve and Blatner, David. *Silicon Mirage: The Art and Science of Virtual Reality* (Peachpit Press 1992).

Benedikt, Michael, ed. *Cyberspace: First Steps* (MIT Press, 1991).

Hamit, Francis. *Virtual Reality* (Miller Freeman, 1991).

Helsel, Sandra K. and Roth, Judith Paris, eds. *Virtual Reality: Theory, Practice and Promise* (Meckler, 1991).

Krueger, Myron W. *Artificial Reality II* (Addison-Wesley, 1991).

Laurel, Brenda. *The Art of Human-Computer Interface Design* (Addison-Wesley, 1990).

Laurel, Brenda. *Computers as Theatre* (Addison-Wesley, 1991).

COMPANIES—ACCESS TO HARDWARE, SOFTWARE AND SYSTEMS

Advanced Gravis Computer Technology Ltd. 7400 MacPherson Ave. #111, Burnaby, B.C. V5J 5B6 Canada. 604-434-7274. MouseStick (optical joystick for AT bus card).

Ascension Technology Corporation. P.O. Box 527, Burlington, VT 05402. 802-655-7879. Ascension Bird (6D magnetic tracker)

Autodesk, Inc. 2320 Marinship Way, Sausalito, CA 94965. Cyberspace Project.

CAE Electronics Ltd. C.P. 1800 Saint-Laurent, Quebec, H4L 4X4 Canada. 514-341-6780. Head-mount displays.

CiS. 285 Littleton Rd., Ste. 3, Westford, MA 01886. 603-894-5999, 508-692-2600 (fax). Geometry Ball Jr. (6D joystick).

Crystal River Engineering. 12350 Wards Ferry Rd., Groveland, CA 95321. 209-962-6382. Convolvotron (4 channel 3D audio card for PC).

Division Ltd. Quarry Rd., Chipping Sodbury, Bristol BS17 6AX England. 44-0454-324527. Specialized transputers used for VR applications.

Exos 8. Blanchard Road, Burlington, MA 01803. 617-229-2075. Hand-worn interface devices.

Fake Space Labs. 935 Hamilton Ave., Menlo Park, CA 94025. 415-688-1940. BOOM (stereo viewer on articulated arm).

Focal Point Audio 1402 Pine Ave. Suite 127, Niagara Falls, NY 14301. 415-963-9188. Focal Point (3D audio boards for Mac and PC).

Gyration, Inc. 12930 Saratoga Ave., Bldg. C, Saratoga, CA 95070. 408-255-3016. GyroPoint (optically sensed gyroscopic sensors).

Myron Krueger/Artificial Reality. 55 Edith, Vernon, CT 06066. 203-871-1375. Custom-designed virtual world environments.

Logitech Inc. 6505 Kaiser Drive, Fremont, CA 94555. 415-795-8500. Red Baron (6D mouse and head tracker).

Metaware, Inc. 2161 Delaware Ave., Santa Cruz, CA 95060-5706. 408-429-6382. HighC 386 compiler, Version 1.72.

Phar Lap Software Inc. 60 Aberdeen Ave., Cambridge, MA 02138. 617-661-1510. 386 DOS-Extender, Version 4.0.

Polhemus, Inc. 1 Hercules Drive, P.O. Box 560, Colchester, VT 05446. 802-655-3159. Polhemus (3Space 6D magnetic tracker).

Pop-Optix Labs. 241 Crescent Street, Waltham, MA 02154. 617-647-1395. Specialized optics for head-mount displays.

Sense8 Corporation. 1001 Bridgeway, P.O. Box 477, Sausalito CA 94965. 415-331-6318, 415-331-9148 (fax). VR software and systems (for PC, Sun & Silicon Graphics).

SimGraphics Engineering Corp. 1137 Huntington Drive, South Pasadena, CA 91030. 213-255-0900. Systems configuration house/OEM VR equipment supplier.

Spaceball Technologies, Inc. 2063 Landings, Sunnyvale, CA 94043. 408-745-0330. Spaceball (6D joystick).

StereoGraphics. 2171-H East Francisco Blvd., San Rafael, CA 94901. 415-459-4500. Stereoscopic displays.

Straylight. 150 Mount Bethel Road, Warren, NJ 07050. 908-580-0086. VR authoring systems.

Subjective Technologies. 1106 Second Street, Suite 103, Encinitas, CA 92024. 619-942-0928. Tools for controlling virtual environments.

TiNi Alloy Co. 1144 65th Street, Unit A, Oakland, CA 94608. 510-658-3172. Tactile feedback systems.

Virtual Research 1313 Socorro Ave., Sunnyvale, CA 94089. 408-739-7114. Flight Helmet (head mounted display).

Virtual Technologies. P.O. Box 5984, Stanford, CA 94309. 415-599-2331. Instrumented gloves and clothing.

The Vivid Group. 317 Adelaide Street, W., Suite 302, Toronto, Ontario, M5V IP9 Canada. 416-340-9290. 416-348-9809 (fax). Mandala (VR authoring systems).

VPL Research. 950 Tower Lane, 14th Floor, Foster City, CA 94404. 415-312-0200. Eyephones and DataGlove (head-mounted display and glove).

VREAM. 2568 N. Clark Street, #250, Chicago, IL 60614. 312-477-0425. VR authoring systems.

Xtensory Inc. 140 Sunridge Drive, Scolls Valley, CA 95066. 408-439-0600. Tactile feedback systems.

FILMS

Brainstorm (Director: Douglas Trumbull, 1983).

The Lawnmower Man (Director: Brett Leonard, 1992).

FILMS

Brainstorm (Director: Douglas Trumbull, 1983).

The Lawnmower Man (Director: Brett Leonard, 1992).

SCIENTIFIC JOURNALS

CyberEdge Journal. $129/year 6 issues, student rate (with I.D.) $75/year from 928 Greenhill Rd. Mill Valley, CA 94941-3406. 415-383-2458, 415-389-0251 (fax).

Presence: Teleoperators and Virtual Environments. $50/year (individuals) $120/year (institution). 4 issues, 100 pp. per issue from MIT Press Journals, 55 Hayward St. Cambridge, MA 02142. Call: 617-253-2889, 617-258-6779 (fax) for credit card orders (24 hours).

VIRTUAL SEX

BOOKS

Rheingold, Howard. *Virtual Reality* (Summit Books, 1991).

GAMES (ON CD-ROM)

Virtual Valerie $79.95 + S&H (Reactor, Inc., 1990).

Spaceship Warlock $69.95 + S&H (Reactor, Inc., 1991). Direct mail order from Educorp 1-800-843-9497.

VIRUS

BOOKS

Burger, Ralf. *Computer Viruses: A High Tech Disease* (Loompanics, 1988).

McAfee, John and Haynes, Colin. *Computer Viruses, Worms, Data Diddlers, Killer Programs and Other Threats to Your System* (St. Martin's Press/Cash Sales, 1989).

Lundell, Allan. *Virus!: The Secret World of Computer Invaders That Breed and Destroy* (Contemporary Books, 1989).

Roberts, Ralph. *Computes! Computer Viruses* (Loompanics, 1988).

SOFTWARE—VIRUS PROTECTION

SAM [Symantec AntiVirus for Macintosh]. Checks your disks after you insert them into your drive. Around $99.95 from Symantec, 135 South Rd., Bedford, MA 01730. 800-64THINK, 617-275-4800, 617-275-2124 (fax). Look for this title at your local Macintosh store.

Disinfectant 2.5.1 (Mac) by John Norstad, Northwestern University. The best virus fighting program available. Updated and distributed day after any new discovery. Available free from BMUG, Contact: 510-849-9114.

WILSON, ROBERT ANTON

BOOKS [FICTION]

Shea, Robert and Wilson, Robert Anton. *The Illuminatus! Trilogy* (Dell, 1984).

Wilson, Robert Anton. *Schroedinger's Cat Trilogy* (Dell, 1988).

Wilson, Robert Anton. *The Earth Will Shake* (NAL-Dutton, 1988/1991).

Wilson, Robert Anton. *The Widow's Son* (NAL-Dutton, 1988/1991).

Wilson, Robert Anton. *Masks of the Illuminati* (Dell, 1990).

BOOKS [NON FICTION]

Wilson, Robert Anton. *Sex and Drugs: A Journey Beyond Limits* (Playboy Press, 1973).

Wilson, Robert Anton. *The Book of the Breast* (Playboy Press, 1974).

Wilson, Robert Anton. *Cosmic Trigger: The Final Secret of the Illuminati* (And/Or Press, 1977).

Wilson, Robert Anton. *The Illuminati Papers* (And/Or Press, 1980).

Wilson, Robert Anton. *Right Where You Are Sitting Now: Further Tales of the Illuminati* (And/Or Press, 1982).

Wilson, Robert Anton. *Prometheus Rising* (Falcon Press, 1983).

Wilson, Robert Anton. *Natural Law, Or Don't Put a Rubber on Your Willy* (Loompanics, 1986).

Wilson, Robert Anton. *Wilhelm Reich in Hell* (Falcon Press, 1987).

Wilson, Robert Anton. *Coincidance: A Head Test* (Falcon Press, 1988).

Wilson, Robert Anton. *The New Inquisition: Irrational Rationalism and the Citadel of Science* (Falcon Press, 1986).

NEWSLETTERS

Trajectories Newsletter: The Journal of Futurism and Heresy.
$20/year (4 issues), $35/two years (8 issues), $50/ three
years (12 issues) from The Permanent Press, P.O. Box
700305, San Jose, CA 95170. All Robert Anton Wilson
books available at discount through Trajectories.

ZINES

PRINT (MUSIC ZINES)

Technology Works is an industrial music zine. Each issue
is filled with reviews and band interviews. Sample
copies are $1.50 from Paul Moore, P.O. Box 477,
Placentia, CA 92670-0407.

PRINT (SEX ZINES)

Frighten the Horses: A Document of the Sexual Revolution.
$16/year (4 issues) from Heat Seeking Publishing, 41
Sutter Street, #1108, San Francisco, CA 94104.

Libido: The Journal of Sex and Sensibility. $26/year
(4 issues) or $7 for single issue from P.O. Box 146721,
Chicago Il 60614.

On Our Backs: Entertainment for the Adventurous Lesbian.
$34.95/year (6 issues) from 526 Castro Street, San
Francisco, CA 94114.

The Sandmutopia Guardian. A hardcore S&M zine with
DIY building projects for restraints, torture devices,
etc. $24/year (6 issues) $6.95 sample issue, from
Desmodus, Inc., P.O. Box 410390, San Francisco, CA
94141. 415-252-1195. Always trendy!

Taste of Latex. $20/year (4 issues) from P.O. Box 460122,
San Francisco, CA 94146-0122.

Sexuality Library. Catalog features books, video and
magazines on almost any area of sexual interest. $2
from 1210 Valencia Street, San Francisco, CA 94110.
415-550-7399.

Good Vibrations. Catalog features high quality sex toys,
safe sex paraphernalia and information. $2 from
Good Vibrations, 1210 Valencia Street, San Francisco,
CA 94110. 415-550-7399.

Yellow Silk: Journal of Erotic Arts. $30/year from Y.S.,
P.O. Box 6374, Albany, CA 94706.

ZONES OF TEMPORARY AUTONOMY

COMPUTER NETS AND BULLETIN BOARDS

The Cyberden: A system that features, yes, many cyber-
conferences (cyberspace, cyberpunk, cyberdelic art, etc.).
425-472-5527.

Demon Roach Underground: Entry: thrash, New User
Password: fear. "This BBS may contain explicit descrip-
tions of or may advocate one or more of the following:
nudity, satanism, suicide, sodomy, incest, bestiality, sado-
masochism, adultery, murder, morbid violence, bad gram-
mar, or any deviant sexual conduct in a violent context, or
the use of illegal drugs or alcohol." But then again, it may
not. Has dial-ups for other boards. 806-794-4362.

Illuminati: The Steve Jackson Games BBS, of course.
Gaming, science fiction, fantasy. 512-447-4449.

Mindvox: New beautifully-designed venue. The best
four-star accomodations in cyberspace. Loll around
with systems designers, writers, and other dangerous
types. 212-988-5030 or phantom.com.

Pure Nihilism: "Not much disk space, but lots of attitude!"
Soon to be moving to San Francisco, it continues to bring to
the Telecom Community intense discussions of underground music, books, films, and zines. 517-546-0585.

Swagland: Swagland's users are engaging, eccentric and
entertaining. 805-562-8205.

Temple of the Screaming Electron: Probably the largest
non-Internetworked repository of computer hacking,
subversive, conspiratorial information in the United
States. If you want information, and don't have access
to the Internet, this is your one-stop shopping convenience. 510-935-5845.

The Void Black Crawling Systems: Run by a sysop who
daily prepares for the end of civilization, The Void caters
to conspiracy theorists, SETI freaks, the occult, and
techno-survivalists. 617-482-6356.

The WELL: (Whole Earth 'Lectronic Link): A conferencing system with writers, techies, and alternative political
types, the WELL is an on-line salon. Sometimes erudite
and funny as hell. 415-332-6106.